Dedicated
to the men and the women
of
No.77 Squadron, R.A.F. Elvington,
Yorkshire

Remembering the Service and the Sacrifice of all
Air and Ground crew who operated the Halifax
bomber in the liberation of Europe
and the formation of the
Free French Squadrons
at RAF Elvington.

Preface

LOOE in the County of CORNWALL came into prominence only after the development of its harbour which enabled sailing vessels to discharge cargoes up to a maximum of some 250 tons. This caused the advancement of many other trades about its newly built quaysides at both East and West Looe which ministered to the well being of such trading ships and the men who worked them, that came and went on the tides during the second half of the 19th., and the first quarter of the 20th.centuries.

This development included the laying of a G.W.R line which extended down alongside the East Looe quayside thus securing a direct link from the fish market to Billingsgate Market. The deepening of the harbour, building of the breakwater, widening of the harbour entrance, providing the means for the graving of ships, and the building of substantial warehouses. Other trades amounted to the brick works, granite works, five blacksmiths' shops, ships chandlers and iron mongers, two sailmakers, three 'barking' houses, (used not only for the 'barking' of fishing nets, but also for 'barking' the sails and ropes used by the trading vessels), three or more pit saws, two or more rope walks, general stores, cordwainers, boat builders, shipwrights and carpenters, timber stores, insurance brokers, pilots, coopers, fish pits and palaces to cope with a substantial pilchard trade, beer houses galore, inns & taverns, lodging houses, several tobacconists, shipping and mining agents, the trade list seemed endless.

During that period over fifty master mariners lived in the twin townships of East and West Looe, and about the same number of sailing vessels came and went each week which, combined with the progress of the fishing industry, brought much prosperity to the town.

Situated on the southern coast of the county of Cornwall, and well away from the gales and harshness of the Atlantic Ocean, Looe offered a place of tranquility, warmth and well being : where one would expect people seeking a certain quality in life to select such a place as a fount for adventure, a life at sea, to pursue their occupation, or simply a place in which to retire and many did - (some of whom I have made a superficial, yet interesting and humorous character study).

In 1945 John Arthur Grimer detrained at Looe Station, the terminus of the Liskeard to Looe branch line on which the steam tank engine bustled to and fro pulling its corridor-less carriages; (three carriages off season, and five during the summer months). John being newly married, his very attractive Cornish wife was already teaching at Liskeard Grammar School, had previously come to Looe to live... and now, fifty seven years later, John, a widower, is still living in Looe.

Acknowledgements

The compiler wishes to acknowledge the help of the contributors listed below and apologises for any inadvertent omissions. Christopher Balston, for the Grimer pedigree, (plus supplying me with a copy of the book "*ERMINGTON DAYS*," by Elaine Chaytor, being the life of Miss Violet Pinwill). John Grimer, the main feature in the cast, English scholar, and proof reader. Peter Grimer, (John's brother), for his important contribution to the text, as well as providing many of the photographs. The photographs of Oedelem on pp.11-14 was taken from the book OEDELEM, *In oude prentkaarteu*, Drr Henri Zutterman, (MCMLXXIV). The inscriptions beneath those photographs was translated by Maria Grimer *née* Bochaert. Alec Loretto, for his contribution and photograph of his family, as well as his interesting exemplary talk to me regarding the woodwind instrument - the recorder. John Garvin, ex--pupil of John Grimer, professional script writer, who provided the Introduction. Joyce Southern, (my wife), who provided me with the lengthy transcript of Maria Grimer's life; (from tapes) a task she much enjoyed doing, as well as proof reading the completed compilation. Peter Warden, Canadian artist, who provided the French proper nouns used in the transcript of Maria Grimer's life. Joyce Hobgen for allowing me to use the narrative *Bk.4, Pt.3* from "WITH PREJUDICE AND PRIDE," written by her late husband Charles Hobgen, and the photograph of the painting of S-Sugar commissioned by Charles. Harry Shrinkfield who provided John Grimer with many photographs from the splendid RAF Elvington Museum in Yorkshire, where he is the curator. Molly Blatchford *née* Toms of Polperro who successfully added the names of the young pupils shown in the two photographs of John Grimer and his class at Polperro School; two days before we went to print! Sammy Hawes of "Bosco Books," Looe, for correcting many grammatical errors, as well as rewriting a difficult sentence I kept finding in my text. John Appleby for giving me many of his free evenings to install a suitable programme onto my computer and then place the completed book onto disc. The several references I have thankfully taken from the internet - but always with acknowledgement. Lastly, the photograph on the rear board is of John Grimer taken by the compiler during the year 2000 © J.Southern.

Forward
by John Garvin

John Grimer once scrawled a comment in the margin of a homework assignment he set for me that reads, "Less is more! Don't use seven words when one will suffice!" I'll try to keep to the spirit of his suggestion and keep this introduction brief.

Mr. Grimer was my English teacher during the mid 1980's when I attended Looe Comprehensive school. Apart from his fearsome reputation, we knew very little about him - he certainly never spoke to us about the extraordinary life he led before becoming a teacher. All I know for sure is that he made a real difference in my life.

Whenever I return to Looe, I always make a point of visiting "Mr. Grim" for a cup of tea and a chat. On my last visit, he was astounded to see that I'd brought along a copy of my old English homework book to show him. It's the only schoolbook I have ever kept.

You see - whenever Mr. Grimer set homework, he refused to give us boring assignments. Instead, he encouraged us to write about things we felt passionate about. Leafing through my old homework book, Mr. Grimer was delighted to find it filled with stories about scuba-diving, sharks, spaceships and alien beings from other worlds. And unlike my other homework assignments (where typically I'd write as little as I could get away with) - these stories always ran to several pages. For the first time ever, writing didn't feel like homework. It felt like fun.

Reading Mr. Grimer's scribbled comments, you get the impression that he actually enjoyed reading these stories - he clearly wasn't just paying them lip service. "Oh yes", he admits, grinning away to himself as he flips through the pages, "I always love a good yarn!"

Under his continued guidance and encouragement, it wasn't long before "A" grades started to appear in my homework book - which was a first for me and a real turning point. "The A's must have been for your imagination," he growls, passing the book back to me. "Because your spelling is atrocious!"

I now work as a professional screenwriter - and have even managed to sell scripts in Hollywood. I'm pleased to report that my spelling has improved.

Quite often, if I find myself struggling to finish a draft or to meet a deadline, I'll pull out my old English homework book and read Mr. Grimer's comments. They never fail to inspire me. They remind me that writing should always be fun.

I suspect that many people reading this book will have their own "Grim" story to tell. John Grimer is a remarkable man and a wonderful teacher. I know he has helped shape many more lives than my own.

As such, I am extremely grateful to John Southern for writing this deserving book.

I'd give it an "A+".

John Garvin - Sept 2008   (see also "At School.")

Introduction
No.2 in a Series "Looe at War"

When I began quarrying for the names of those many men and women associated with Looe who had a record relating to war service, I knew I would miss a number of names of them who probably had contributed a far more valued service, suffered more severe hardship, or wounds, or bore the more distinctive of medals : sadly this was bound to happen. I did make many enquires but I knew I should earn the feeling of failure through the disappoint- ment felt by those families of the few I did miss : it is the order in life which occurs even within a close knit society such as Looe was.

Then there are those who went to war, did valiant deeds and returned, yet refuse to talk about their experience ; I can only bear with their decision, so include them only by name.

Lastly, there may be those I have failed to note, either by lack of asking local people with long memory who may have given me a further name ; or of some one whose family had become extinct, moved away, or emigrated to a far off country.

I began with the seventy four men who died during the two World Wars whose names are inscribed on the Looe War Memorial whom each year we proudly commemorate. To these names I have tried to obtain a photograph, and to record their place within the family to each of which each one belonged. I then downloaded the information available from the Commonwealth War Graves Commission, and finished up, (after photographing the war graves within the bounds of the West Looe cemetery and St.Martin-by-Looe burial ground), by adding any story or anecdote I could learn by questioning those people within the town whom I believed have the knowledge I quested after.

This edition JOHN GRIMER, is the first of a *Series* : Looe at War to be published : although listed as No.1. (No.1 covers the life of our famed WW2 submariner Alfred Mallett. Alfred was born in Looe of a Looe family. He was awarded the **DSO with two bars** which made him the most decorated submariner.

In putting together this yarn I have been blighted with my endeavour to place the events in some sort of chronological order; but have failed to do so. Peter Grimer successfully put my mind at rest when he told me that one of the joys of the yarn was how the story darts about: "after all," he added, "the Holy Bible darts about all over the place." But, when all is said and done one cannot place all I have written in any form of chronology.

Several more editions of the Series *"Looe at War"* are very nearly complete which will form a uniform collection. *(see About the Compiler)*.

Regretfully, a further hundred of more Looe man and women who served in the wars should be included, but to do so would need a team of researchers: I have written all I was able to do over the years of my retirement. I attempted to put together a list of those who served, but even that proved to be an impossible task, because such a list would be lacking too many names.

About the compiler of this book

John Southern was born at the Dawn Nursing Home, Hannafore, West Looe in 1935 where most of the children of Looe were born. He was the eldest child of six being the issue of a local Cornish father (whose family has been traced back in St.Martin-by-Looe to c.1650), and a mother from Plymouth (whose family has been traced back to the 17th.cent. from the bordering parishes between Devon & Cornwall). They married at Morval Church when his mother was working in service at Morval House, after which the couple moved to Looe where they lived for two years at No.2 North View, Shutta.

While at that place she worked part-time for Lt.Col.W.V.Moul of Shutta House, and up until the time the Colonel died the compiler frequently visited that lonely old batchelor: subsequently the compiler has written a remarkable and well illustrated booklet on the life of the Colonel.

In 1938 the family, which by then had the addition of a daughter, moved to a two bedroomed house in Prince's Court, West Looe, where they remained for the next twelve or thirteen years; thus enabling the compiler to spend his entire childhood on and about the quayside, where abounded many old sheds, stores, net-lofts, warehouses, and carpenters shops. That period also included World War Two, which he can still recall with much interest.

Now well into retirement he spends his time writing about his native town and the people who once graced that place, (particularly those who served in two World Wars, as well as those 74 men we commemorate on Looe War Memorial). For recreation he enjoys walking alone with his stick, often for some six hours at a time, listening to classical music, and reading when not actually sleeping! Sadly, his wife Joyce can no longer walk with him as she formerly did due to the infirmities of age, so she spends much time on their two linked Apple-Mac computers as well as transcribing numerous tape-recordings, the voices of those who have now passed on, but have left for posterity much local history.

This book is No.2 in a Series "Looe at War" being a compilation of the life of JOHN GRIMER, a man who became a school teacher at Looe for over thirty years. Prior to that time during WW2 he saw active service in the RAF until the heavy Halifax bomber he was in was shot down over France, the crew baled out, but the pilot, Kenneth Bond, his 'chute burned, remained with his plane which hit the ground and burst into an inferno. Flight Officer J.A.Grimer survived his ordeal, became a POW, and has now related his story.

Further books regarding Looe and its people are still being written. At least over thirty are nigh complete and due to be published during the following two years, and several others are still being added to. Those nigh completed are :-

ALLAN PAPE, the life of a LOOE boat builder & designer, illustrated.
BOAT BUILDERS at LOOE : *N.Pearn & Sons, Jim Curah, Roy DARR, George Pengelly, Clifford Adams, & others*, with numerous photographic illustrations.
A LIFE IN WEST LOOE (1935 - 1953). A well illustrated story rich in the lore of West Looe.
LOOE : *Story of Looe, told in Words & Pictures.*
LINDSAY DENING SYMINGTON, *Artist & Naturalist*, lavishly illustrated.
Dr. JOHN CAMPBELL CB., (1813-1904) of Looe, photographer, *a paper illustrating his life and work at Looe.*
LT.COL.W.V.MOUL. *A paper illustrating his life*, illustrated.
"SMALL TALK IN LOOE" (regarding St.Martin-by-Looe parish & its people; particularly the Revd. Mr.Martin Picken, late rector), illustrated.
50 True Stories appertaining to LOOE, CORNWALL, illustrated, Vol. One.
50 True Stories appertaining to LOOE, CORNWALL, illustrated, Vol. Two.
IVOR RAWE, *A tribute & thanksgiving for his being*, illustrated.
JAMES MAYES, *A Life at War with the Polish Partisans*, illustrated. (Now on www:// CyberHeritage) a Plymouth web site.
O! FOR A SAILOR'S LIFE, *103 years in the life of BILL EASTON RN.*
THE ORGAN *of St.James's Church, Kilkhampton, Cornwall*, (1968).
SPRY : a paper on Charles Spry, gardener at St.Martin-by-Looe rectory, illustrated.
CROSSBERG, *Photographer to the famous, Alfred Crossberg (Kreutzberger, his life & the life of his wife Mary,* illustrated with many photographs..
EILEEN LEWIS "Parachute Knickers" life of a Looe maid, illustrated.
No.1 in a Series "Looe at War" ALFRED MALLETT RN., DSO & 2 bars.
No.3 in a Series "Looe at War" ALLAN HAMILTON RN.
No.4 in a Series "Looe at War" RAY RAMSEY RAF.
No.5 in a Series "Looe at War" CHARLES JENNINGS RAF.
No.6 in a Series "Looe at War" BILLY RICHARDSON RAF.
No.7 in a Series "Looe at War" LENNIE SWEETT RAF.
No.8 in a Series "Looe at War" KEN MITCHELL D.C.L.I & his wife GLADYS BOARDMAN, A.T.S.
No.9 in a Series "Looe at War" STAN MINNETTE, RN., Coastal Forces.
No.10 in a Series "Looe at War" ERIC BLAKE RAF.
No.11 in a Series "Looe at War" JOHN EDWARD DOVE RN., WW1 hard-hat diver.
No.12 in a Series "Looe at War" THELMA"S STORY, Her Story told by Thelma Beare *née* Soady
No.13 in a Series "Looe at War" REX BARNES RAF., a Looe boatman.
No.14 in a Series "Looe at War" JACK PENGELLY RN., known as "Jack Bumble".
No.15 in a Series "Looe at War" SAM & GERALD SOADY, WW2.
No.16 in a Series "Looe at War" BILL RICHARDS RN. Japanese POW. etc.

Poem
by John Grimer

(Written after WW2 - probably in Germany when working with the M.R.E.S - 1947)

VERY awkward to reach the perspex nose of the Halifax,
with sextant, maps and parachute,
And 'Mae West' grotesquely strapped by heavy harness,
The floor slopes steeply, oddly.

But when you get there you can relax
Compose your thoughts and watch the evening clouds.
Now you can show your maps and check your sights
Fidget with your harness - jerkily chew your gum.
You've come a long way - you've had a very costly training :
Only make sure to leave yourself behind
    In the lavatory,
    Behind the dispersal,
    Where you prayed to the God you didn't believe in,

It made you feel better to pray - for the women and children.
It gave you a chance to pray for your crew too - for yourself -
Ah - for yourself !

Peering vacantly into space stupidly waiting.
Not knowing their immense disgrace,
Their self betrayal.
No Glory - no vindictiveness.
Only cold and individual loneliness
On the flight out.

"There's the target - that glow to port.
That's Hamburg burning. Right - right - steady - steady."
"Bombs away skipper." Thank Christ, no fighters ready.

The glow a little brighter now sinks to stern.
Three days now the people have seen the fire burn.
Eating the heart out of their city.
"Must'nt let it go out boys - you can't miss it."

"Is there any water in the streets to help the firemen ?
Where are the firemen ?
Two lie crumpled on the hot pavement the air sucked out of their lungs.
To feed the inferno above the street.
Is there any water in the Elbe tunnel ?
    Only the thick black heavy water of the river
    And the bodies of eighteen hundred people.

Her body had been white and sweet until she had embraced
The eternity of the four thousand pound bomb.
She was buried beneath three different city blocks.
Three days later - her separate limbs were green and filthy.

Three weeks later - some SS men sprayed the rubble with lime and Liquid fire to purge the putrid stench.

You can hear the eight o'clock news on the flight back.
It'll tell you, that you've just bombed Hamburg.
You're nearly safe now.
You've done a good job helping to win the war.
It's a pity you don't think so.
But then, you're only thinking that you're cold
And want your breakfast.

P.S. *" Wasn't on Hamburg raids - but experiences with M.R.E.S*
probably sparked me to write this.
Hamburg raids were during August 43
I joined Squadron 97 in Sept. 43."

Contents

Preface by J.Southern
Forward by John Garvin
Introduction by J.Southern
Poem by John Grimer
Grimer pedigree   p.1
Civil Service Rifles   p.3
General Allenby   p.3
Peter Grimer's narrative   p.6
Peter Grimer's narrative continued   p.8
"The Last Boat to leave Ostend"   p.15
further info: on Maria's story   p.24
"Childhood & misspent youth,"   p.25
Summary of John's WW2 service   p.29
Wartime (1939 - 1945)   p.29
Crash of a Halifax   p.35
The "Red Tap"   p.38
Story of "The Coal Bunker"   p.39
the Hill's   p.40
the Loretto's   p.40
John & Jean's wedding   p.44
No.77 Sqdn., S-Sugar   p.55
Op's Log, P/O Bond   p.56
Further info: on S-Sugar   p.59
"With Prejudice & Pride"   p.62
Medals   p.73

Appendix One	- The LOG BOOK of F/O J.A.Grimer.	p.75
Appendix Two	- M.R.E.S. (Missing, Research & Enquiry Service). Squadron Leader P.E.Laughton-Bramley M.B.E., O.N.M., (Fr.)., G.C.M. (P)., F.R.G.S., R.A F., (Retd.).	p.83
Appendix Three	- Letters - Jean Grimer to John, etc. (POW).	p.95
Appendix Four	- Poems by John Grimer.	p.101
Appendix Five	- *"Je suis blesse - Aidez moi."*	p.105
Appendix Six	- Essay by Victor Clare.	p.107
Appendix Seven	- Essay by Charles Hobgen.	p.117
Appendix Eight	- Photographs of Civil Service Rifles.	p.141

John Grimer

Descendants of John Grimmer & Grace née Jones.

I have added only a few of the many which make up the long line of the Grimer family.

My list of the descendants from John & Grace is simply a sort of "Cook's Tour" of the family. Should one require the full pedigree then one should contact Mr.Christopher Balston. (see below).

John Grimmer (abt.1731 - 1810) of Chester. Master Armourer at Chester Castle who married Grace Jones (1731 - 1808). Had issue :- William Grimmer (1767 - abt.1850) of Chester married Elizabeth (1772 - 1856) of Chester. William worked as a shipwright, later his occupation was Sergeant of Militia. The issue of William and Elizabeth was :-

John Grimmer (1793 - 1846), who like his grandfather was (1) Master Armourer at Chester Castle, and (2) Master Armourer at the Tower of London. About 1818 he married Margaret Topham (who died abt.1845) in London. Legend records that William when living at No.4 Mint Street fell into the moat at the Tower of London, probably when drunk, and died in St.Bartholomew's Hospital from the effects of drink. But the guns of the tower bear John Grimmer's name. Their issue was three sons :-

Thomas Topham Grimer (1823 - 1872), born in Islington, whose occupation was a G.P.O. clerk. He married Mary Ann Walker (1820 - 1895) on 30th.April 1842 at St.Peter's Church, Stepney, and resided at 24 Stonefield Street, Islington. The other sons were John H. Grimer (1825 - 1871), occupation brushmaker. George Topham Grimer (1834 - 1840) who died in The Tower of London aged six years.

The name Topham entered the family line through Margaret Topham (she married John Grimmer). "The Topham family owned substantial tracts of land around Aintree and has been involved with the management of the Grand National Racecourse since Topham's who appointed ex-Gaiety Girl Mirabel Topham to manage it. Mrs.Topham built a new track within the established National Racecourse and named it after Lord Mildmay, a fine amateur jockey and lover of the Grand National." 1

The five issue of Thomas Topham Grimer and Mary Ann née Walker was :-

(1) Henry Grimer (1843 - 1935) of Stonehouse Street, Islington who married Louisa Ann Bound (born 1852) on 17th.September 1874 at St.Luke's Church, Kentish Town. Henry died abt. 1935 in Brighton, East Sussex. (2) Arthur Grimer (1845 - 1931) in Stonehouse Street who married Jane Mary Ingledew (1844 - 1915) abt. 1870. She died abt 1915, while Arthur died in 1931 in Dover, Kent. (3) Walter Grimer (1849 - 1914), born 8th. February in Islington, married Emma Judges (1848 - 1935) of Alcester, Gloucestershire, on 24th. September 1871 in Whitechapel. Walter spent some years working as a school teacher in Surrey. He died during July 1914 in Islington, and was buried at Manor Park. Emma Ann died 15th.April 1935. (4) Emily Grimer (born abt.1850), and (5) Florence Grimer (born abt.1850). The five issue of Arthur Grimer and Jane Mary née Ingledew was :-

(1) Frederick A.Grimer (1868 - 1913) in Islington, occupation insurance manager who married Elizabeth Thompson (1869 - 1949). (2) Thomas Ingledew Grimer (1871 - 1950) in Islington, occupation meat wholesaler, married Louise Mayo (1873 - 1961). (3) Alice Jane Grimer (1875 - 1948), born 9th. February at 16 Waterloo Terrace, Islington, married Harry Alfred Balston. (4) Charles Grimer (born abt. 1876). (5) Reginald Flower Grimer (1881 - 1974) of Islington, owner of Sheerness Bus Company. Married Ellen Edith Grace Renton (1882 - 1944). Reginald died at Sheerness, Kent. The issue of Thomas Ingledew Grimer and Louise née Mayo was :

(1) Arthur Thomas Grimer (1893 - 1974) who married Marie Bockaert (1894 - 200?), and had four issue. (2) Robert Grimer (1896 - 1958) who married Marguerite Pignon (1902 - 1973), and had two issue. The four issue of Arthur Thomas Grimer and Marie née Bockaert was:-

(1) Robert Walter Grimer (born 1920), occupation civil servant, married Marguerite Foakes (born 1923) and had five issue. (2) John Grimer (born 1925), married Jean Loretto (1920 - 2005) and had one daughter. (3) Peter Grimer (born 1928), dental surgeon, married Margaret Howick (died 1st. July 1995), had four issue. (4) Francis Grimer (born 1932), married Patricia Neal, had nine issue.

1. http://www.aintree-grand-national.net/grand-national-history.php
Family pedigree by Christopher Balston, North Cheam, Surrey.

A small note book bound in full leather with a hinged brass clasp, (bearing a plain book-plate with the name T. Ingledew) contains one and a half pages of family documentation relating to the Ingledew's, viz :-

Thomas Ingledew February 6, 1822 AE 73

Hutchinson Ingledew, born Feby 23. 1773, *obt.* Novr. 1. 1837.
Mary Ingledew, born Aug. 9 - 1779 - born in M/x St.Luke's St.
Elizabeth Ingledew, born March 2 - 1800. - born at
Mary Ingledew, born July 28, 1803.
Ann Ingledew, born Oct. 5 - 1805. born at
Frances Ingledew, born April 8 - 1808 - Died Feby 13. 1817.
Thomas Ingledew, born July 4 - 1811.
Margaret Ingledew, born June 12 - 1814. Died May 1815.

Francis Ingledew, born July 9. 1775. died -
George Ingledew, born Augt. 10. 1777 -

Thomas Ingledew, born Oct. 31. 1779.
Sophia Ingledew, born Feby 14.

John Ingledew, born Novr. 16. 1782. Died July 2. 1827 -
Mary Ingledew   Died June 1830 -
Ann Mary Ingledew, born March 19. 1823 -
Arabella Chava   Millard, born April 4. 1816.

Distaff Antecedents of John Grimer

<u>BOCKAERT</u> Oscar Francisus Eligius Born: 20th.February 1863 at Knesselare. (Died 17th. August 1909 at Oedelem). Married: 3rd.May 1892 at Oedelem to Alida Maria Julia van Damme who was born: 22nd.May 1871 at Oedelem (her father - August Ludovicus van Damme, her mother - Candide Julia Johanna Cornelia Raes? (Maes?). Had issue ten children, three of which died in infancy :-

<u>Maria Ida Alida</u> - born 21st.February 1893 at Oedelem, died in infancy 29th. April 1894 at Oedelem.

<u>Maria Ida Alida Julia</u> - born 27th.May 1894, married Arthur Grimer in 1919, died 8th. December 1996 aged 103 years.

<u>Joseph August Lodewijk</u> - born 5th. December 1895 at Oedelem, Franciscan monk, died 9th. March 1983 in Gwent.

<u>Clothilde Julia August</u> - born 8th February 1898, married with four children, died 29th August 1961. Clothilde is buried at Tirelemont, Belgium.

<u>Laurent</u> - born 1899, no records or memories of him except that he worked as an engineer, married and had issue four children all born at Oedelem.

<u>Timon August</u> - born 20th.January 1901 at Oedelem, practised as a doctor of medicine, married with four children, died from liver failure thro' alcoholism 8th.December 1946.

<u>Timon</u> - born 8th.June 1902, died in infancy 1st.November 1902

<u>Pia Aline</u> - born 24th.January 1904 at Oedelem. Nursed in a leper colony in the Philippines, also in the Belgium Congo, but later retired to Belgium to look after her mother until her mother died. Pia died there when aged in her seventies.

<u>Walter Camiel Heliodoor</u> - born 15th.May 1905 at Oedelem, killed from a shell splinter on 24th.May 1940 at Poperinge by enemy action while serving with the Army Medical Unit.

<u>Oscar Eugene Joseph</u> - born 20th.January 1907, died young from meningitis following a fall on a boot scrapper.

The Civil Service Rifles

The Grimer family home was at No.17 Bowrons Avenue, Wembley. His grandfather, Arthur Grimer (b.1868), was a West Countryman being born in Plymouth, and John Grimer can remember virtually nothing about him. Although on one occasion his grandfather recalled a march past of the Royal Marines band in Plymouth where the spectacle and splendour of the event left him rather in awe.

His father Arthur Thomas Grimer moved to London from Dover where he worked as a civil servant for the Ministry of Labour and because of the meritorious manner in which he undertook his duties he was awarded the M.B.E. At the time when he worked at the Kew office in London the department put on an annual production of Gilbert & Sullivan. His wife Maria preferred to play Mozart! During WW1 Arthur Thomas Grimer enlisted in the Army as a private soldier with the (P.O.W.) *Civil Service Rifles*. (see below for a history of his WW1 service).

"In 1914 the Board of Trade had a staff of 7,500, of which 4,800 were engaged on labour issues - chiefly staffing the new labour exchanges. During WW1, more than 2000 staff left the Board to join the forces. Of these, 305 were killed in action or died as a result of the conflict. After the war, on the initiative of the staff, the names were inscribed on a handsome Roll of Honour, which was unveiled on 19th.December 1923 in the Park or West Entrance of the Boards headquarters by the Prime Minister, Stanley Baldwin . . ."

http://www.dti.gov.uk/warmemorial/ww1

During WW1 it was found that due to the loss of so many subalterns replacements had to be drawn from the ranks, and because of the nature of those who served in the *Civil Service Rifles* the regiment proved to be a valuable source for such replacements : but at what cost? After the removal of such a large number of men it left the regiment too short of other ranks!

The end of his service saw him entering Jerusalem with General Allenby which resulted in the defeat of the Ottoman empire. But at the time when he was entering Jerusalem Maria was abed suffering with Spanish flu., from which she survived when over a million such victims died. (The letters written by Artie and Maria during that time survive.)

General Allenby (the thirty-fourth conqueror of Jerusalem) entering that city on the 11th.December 1917.

The Middle East during World War One,
by Professor David R.Woodward

"Murray's failure to capture Gaza led to his replacement by General Sir Edmund Allenby, a soldier of great vigour and imagination, who was able to create a personal bond with his troops. His government helped to achieve a concrete victory to boost morale at home, and give him the flexibility to advance on Jerusalem.

In October, when the weather was more favourable, Allenby made good use of his infantry and a large mounted force, which included many troopers from Australia and New Zealand, to break through the Gaza-Beersheba Front. And after a difficult advance across the Judaean hills, he walked through the Jaffa Gate on 11th.December 1917 as the 34th. conqueror of Jerusalem, the first Christian conqueror since the Crusades.

Many of Allenby's soldiers were deeply conscious that they were fighting on sacred soil, some viewed themselves as modern-day crusaders, but their leader was acutely aware that many of the soldiers and workers were Islamic, and he vigorously played down any notion of a crusade.

Convinced that neither side had the means to achieve victory in France in 1918, Prime Minister Lloyd George sought to make Allenby's theatre the focus of his country's military effort. Germany's massive offensive closer to home during the first half of 1918, however, forced the government to recall most of Allenby's British soldiers to France. Allenby, who retained his cavalry, received replacements for his infantry in Egypt from many sources, predominately from India but also from many other diverse nations rangeing from Burma to the West Indies.

Allenby returned to the offensive at the Battle of Megiddo, on 19th.September 1918. With a decided advantage in manpower, artillery, air power and morale, and assisted by Arab allies on his flank, he quickly destroyed the Ottoman / Turkish armies facing him.

Once the enemy front was broken, the E.E.F's calvary dominated the campaign. Damascus fell on 1st.October, Aleppo, the last city to fall in the campaign, on 26th.October. Five days later an armistice with the Ottoman Empire came into effect. Since 19th.September Allenby's forces had advanced hundreds of miles and netted over 75,000 prisoners. "

Taken in Jerusalem after the entry with Allenby's Army.
on the back is written "To my dear Mother & Dad, Artie,
31. 1. 1918, Jerusalem."

Artie & Maria

"To my dearest Mother, Dad. Sorry! The camel moved ! Artie   August 1917."

Arthur Grimer married Maria Bockaert, a Belgian woman, who came from Oedelem, a village near Bruges. She was the eldest child of a family of ten children. Being the eldest Maria had to leave school and remain at home to care for the family when her father was stricken with leukaemia.

Peter Grimer wrote the following few lines relating to his parents and their work with X-ray machines when I asked him whether or not they had any direct connection with Marie Currie :

"The only connection is that Oscar Bockaert, my mother's father, was a medical student at Gwent in the early part of the last century, and during that time he worked with X-rays. In those days they would test the machine by putting their hand in front of it. There is no doubt that he did get burnt, and in his forties he had leukaemia and that disease is associated with X-rays, with a twenty or thirty year time lapse. That was his only loose connection with Marie Curie."

John Grimer confirmed his brothers statement : -

"Because Marie Curie had been discovering X-rays around the time my mother's father was a medical student, I remember my mother saying her father used to be working with X-rays in his surgery."

Maria left Belgium on the last boat to leave Ostend as the German military might entered the town. The boat embarked at Dover, where she had to pass through the various stages of emergency immigration, that she met Arthur Grimer. (see Maria's story (below) for a description of that journey)

When in old age she recorded the early years of her long life onto tape, prompted by her son John. She died aged 103 years.

After the war Arthur was once asked how such a gentle man as he, who maintained the strict tenets of Roman Catholicism together with his own strong convictions of altruism, gentleness, and as a pacifist could deliberately aim and possibly shoot and kill one of the enemy. His shocked response was in keeping with his character : " But I always aimed to miss."

Maria loved to recall that which she regarded as probably the most amusing spectacle in her life - of seeing Mahathma Gandhi, that fascinating, small, yet charismatic Indian leader walking along a street in London wearing a long white flowing robe and sandals!

Peter Grimer tells us the story of his family

"My father was Arthur Thomas Grimer, (known to us children as "Artie" or "Pop"). He was born in 1893 at West Ham in London. Subsequently his family moved to Dover in 1906, and he was sent over to the Francis Xavier College in Bruges, Belgium, where he remained for two terms until Easter 1907 when he returned to Dover to continue his education at Dover County School. In 1908 he passed the OXFORD local examination as a junior candidate followed by the boy clerks examination and put down for service in Britain and Ireland."

"In March 1909 he was sent to Ireland where he remained for three months working at Waterford Custom House; during which time he became a Roman Catholic.

Civil Service Rifles, Machine Gun Section.

Pte.A.T.Grimer was a gunner with the Machine Gun Section. His officers & sergeants were Lieut.W.S.H. Smith, 2nd.Lieut's E.E.Andrews & K.A.Higgs, Sgt's 3056 K.P.Neall & 1698 W.S.Pitkin. The 4 Sections & Transport were as follows :-

No.1 Section - 2430 L/Cpl. Endacott, Pte's 2285 K.A.Seville, 2276 F.S.Lloyd, 3335 H.Simmons. 4358 G.W.Harper, 3343 F.W.Coxon, 3147 J.T.Gardiner, 3203 A.P.Steward, 1816 R.C.Pickering, 1905 I.Hyman, 3381 A.V.Baker, 1307 A.W.Lane, 3189 E.C.Essery.

No.2 Section - 1722 Cpl.Gurney, Pte's 2455 F.C.Henson, 2421 P.V.Harling, 2627 C.B.Hull, 2176 C.H.Hall, 3486 J.A.Rogers, 2815 H.A.White, 3464 H.S.Wood, 4375 J.B.Biggs, 2899 J.H.Nash, 1408 A.T.Grimer, 2629 F.F.Morgan.

No.3 Section - Pt's 3043 H.H.Chapman, 3428 A.E.Batchelor, 3276 P.R.N.Crabbe, 3345 D.C.Inskip, 1877 E.J.Cook, 3222 W.C.Bryer, 3337 J.R.Burtt, 3329 J.H.Bowyer, 1922 P.W.Kerr, 3515 T.H.Hines, 2703 J.G.Baillie.

No.4 Section - 2251 L/Cpl.J.M.Chatfield, Pte's W.Christie, 3398 H.J.Pentacost, 2164 W.R.Clark, 3416 H.L.Prideaux, 3432 F.R.Ramsey, 2826 J.L.Batstone, 2243 H.C.Bendle, 3272 J.C.Young, 2822 E.Bastow, 2868 C.H.Gibbs, 1937 W.J.Walder.

Transport Attached - Pte's 1974 F.L.Dyer, 3315 A.H.Sheldrake, 2183 B.A.N.Kesby, 3216 L.W.Gibbs, 3099 J.H.Manley.   (for further photographs of the Civil Service Rifles see Appendix Seven.)

Maria Ida Aleda Julia Grimer *née* Bockaert

"On the 2nd.August 1914 Pte.A.T.Grimer, No.1408 was serving at a camp on Salisbury Plain with the 2 / 15th.Batt. County of London Regiment (Prince of Wales Own) *Civil Service Rifles*. The following day, on the night of August 3rd., they travelled back to London where they detrained at Paddington and marched to Somerset House where (my father told me), as war had been declared they were locked inside for two weeks to prevent any from running away,"

"There followed months of training at Cassiobury Park at Watford, Saffron Walden, and Warminster. On 28th. April 1916 the Battalion was sent to Ireland subsequent to the Easter Uprising in Dublin. It seems they marched around as a show of strength - but they had no encounters with any rebels, and not a shot was fired in anger. Later he told me it was difficult for them because of sniper fire and the women used to hide guns in their babies prams."

> "The visit to Ireland soon appeared like a dream, so sudden and so short it had been. The value of the Irish "Stunt" as it was commonly called cannot be discounted even if actual warfare had not been encountered. The battalion had learned to entrain and detrain, embark and disembark; and to move its home day by day and in general to become a mobile unit. The experience was invaluable." 1

1 History of the Prince of Wales Own - *Civil Service Rifles,*

Peter Grimer's Story cont.

"On the 22nd.June 1916 the Battalion went to France and within seven days after leaving his homeland he was in the front line on the borders of the Battle of the Somme under intense artillery fire."

"A few years ago I retraced his steps - although he was on the borders of the Battle of the Somme he didn't actually go over the top, but he told me of some terrible experiences he witnessed when they were under heavy artillery fire. Their job the following day was having to remove all the bodies of the London Scottish men who were blown up and they had to bring them back."

"The Battalion remained on the western front until they left Marseilles on 17th. November for the fronts at Salonica in Turkey, Mesopotamia, and eventually he was under the command of General Allenby when they entered and captured Jerusalem. It was there he received a minor wound and spent three days on the back of a camel, having been hit by a ricochet bullet on his boot which damaged his little toe, which in itself seems little damage, but in the desert this was a serious blow and that was the end of his fighting."

"The interesting thing about this point, fighting, is very surprising. He never talked about the war until about ten years before he died and then one day I asked him. "Well, what was it like shooting Germans ?" He replied "My son I was very lucky, I never got near enough to anybody which would have resulted in a situation of him or me. When I had to shoot at them I never aimed at them, I always aimed to miss." I was horrified at all those wasted British bullets and asked him why? "Well," he replied "I wouldn't have liked them to shoot me and I certainly didn't want to shoot them." That poor man went through the whole war with that frame of mind and it was afterwards discovered that he wasn't the only one like that."

"In 1918 they returned to France via Italy."

"My mother came in to Dover with her little sister Clothilde because they had contact with the Harbour Master at Dover who was billeted at my fathers' house. During the war Arthur corresponded on postcards and by letter to his fiancee Maria Bockaert, many of which have " passed by field censor" stamped on them - but these I treasure."

"Arthur was demobbed early in 1919, and on the 3rd. March he was married to Maria Bockaert in St.Paul's Catholic Church, Dover. Their first born was a son Robert, born on the 26th.August 1920, and they purchased their first and only family home, No.17 Bowrons Avenue, Wembley, in October of that year. Arthur was employed as a staff officer in the period from 1920 to 1940 when he worked mainly at the Ministry of Labours' premises at Kew, London."

"In 1940 his office was evacuated to Southport (Lancs) and Arthur would occasionally come down to Wembley for weekends. One one occasion, in 1942 during an air raid on Wembley when Arthur was home with us, our house was near missed by a bomb which caused minor damage only : probably a German aircraft who was lost and wanting to get home ! We were all saved, but Arthur was visibly shaken. After the war he was a senior executive officer at Acton, in the office of the Ministry of Pensions & National Insurance. At about the time of his retirement he was awarded the M.B.E (Civil Division). "

"Both Arthur & Maria had happy and a reasonably mobile and healthy retirement. Arthur died on February 10th. 1974.

"During WW2 my mother's services were required as an interpreter, because after Dunkirk there was lots of soldiers returning back to England, and civilians also coming ashore. Her job was to sort out the spies from the others and to put families in the correct homes - a working class family would go in a working class home, and a Catholic family would go in with a middle class home. I'm sorry, but that was the way it was, very class conscious, and she also knew from their accent where they had come from, whether they were telling the truth and all the rest of it. She was interviewing all these people, and she would say "Oh ! that person is no good for that, you must send them there ; I don't believe they came from such and such a place, I believe they are putting on airs" : and she had that job as an interpreter and analyst, and in her job she managed to collect two people. One was Father Van de Graaff who was a Catholic priest who we put up with for quite a long time. He was a good friend during and after the war and used to come to dinner with us on Sundays. The other man was Abbé Tirie who was an Army chaplain, and he was not such a 'good kettle of fish' He was actually afraid that if he was captured by the Germans in uniform they would treat him badly. So he went into the toilet and changed into his sudan, you know a long cassock, but with no trousers beneath. He left his military trousers in the toilet and he came back to England and landed here without trousers. He came to our house and she gave him a pair of fathers trousers. The reason my mother thought he was "not such a good kettle of fish" was because as he had used up a place on the boat from Ostend to escape the Germans, he should not have wanted to go back to Belgium ! We all took a very dim view of his decision to return, but unfortunately the Abbé Tirie didn't want to stay in England; so he went back."

"Father Van de Graaff was a lovely man, a man of the real world and a great friend to us. As he used to be an electrical engineer he helped me with my electronics.

I then asked Peter if he could tell me something regarding the remainder of the family.

e.g. What did Clothilde do with her life? It was John who replied that "she married a sculptor and artist who had a shop beneath the belfry in Bruges."

"Uncle Joseph? (Yes, he was the man who smoked a pipe) he was a nice man, a good person. Uncle Laurent was a pharmacist, he was married, and he was killed at Popering where, I believe, Uncle Joseph gave him the last rites. He was killed by a shell." [see Maria's story *"The Last Boat from Ostend"*]

Joseph became a priest, and according to Maria's autobiographical transcript (below) Joseph was a linguist and scholar, but he also was a pipe smoker ! This short poem was written by him.

Ma Pipe !	a loose translation made by John Grimer reads :-
Que de fois, a l'encontre de la grippe,	How oft in depression I turn to the pipe,
j'ai cueilli le fruit mur de la pipe :	And savour its fruits, so mellow and ripe,
des batons de colere, on les brule :	My anger I'll banish
des filets de soucis on annulle.	My worries will vanish.

"Timon was a doctor, he was a very good doctor but he suffered with an unhappy marriage and became an alcoholic. His brother Joseph persuaded him to give up the drink, and after a short spell of abstinence he died from alcoholism at the early age of forty two or three years."

"Pia was for quite a long time a nun in the Philippines where she used to nurse the lepers. She eventually returned back to look after her aged mother until she died about the age of ninety two years. Pia eventually was the one child who came back to stay with her family and to nurse her mother until her mother died. She would go to mass every morning. Then one day after she returned from mass she felt a little tired and so she would go and lie down for a while; and she quietly died."

"I did meet her mother, my grandmother in 1947, just after the war. She was a bit mentally unstable because she had so many pregnancies that she developed an abhorrence towards men; you know, she went right off them. During WW1 she was in and out of a mental hospital and when the Germans came to occupy Bruges they took over their house and she attacked them with a broom. According to my mother they were going to shoot her, but other people said "Look this poor woman is not very well, everybody knows she's a little unstable ; but they spared her her life but still commandeered her house. After the war when they got the house back they found the garden full of empty shell cases. I still have two of them."

"After the war I had the privilege of going back to Belgium with my mother where I met her mother. Meeting her was a very valuable experience for me, because she went around the large house rather in the manner of a chatelaine locking everything up behind her. She would not talk to me. In the drawing room of this house was a lovely Napoleonic fireplace adorned with gilded naked cherubs. She employed a plasterer to mould trousers onto each of those figures to hide their male nudity. The house has since been demolished; and today, in its place, stands a supermarket.

"I feel very fortunate to have met my grandmother because it helped me to understand my own mother. It was not until I was a student that my mother told me about her own difficult relationship with her own mother. I then realised what my mother had had to suffer. She was the eldest of all those children. Her hair had been pulled out as a child when her mother was angry which left her with a life long fear of becoming bald because her mother took against her, and resented her very presence: yet later she was the one who nursed her father when he was dying from leukaemia. She used to drive the horse and cart when visiting his patients, do all the pharmacy work, and so I could understand so much when I could actually see where she came from. That taught me something that I have always valued. You have to know where people come from before you can draw judgement. Grandmother came from a family of brewers, Tollemache, I don't know if you know Tollemache beer? She also had a history which helps form our own personality, and so what you are doing by writing our "story tree" if you like is so valuable." I answered that I have often wished I had been blessed with the ability to achieve the literary acumen of a biographer. Sadly this wasn't to be. But I do take some comfort by knowing that my attempt in preserving that which I learned from my questing, coupled with a application of some basic logic, may hopefully be thought provoking.]

"She also warned me before our visit to Bruges in April 1949 that her mother would ignore me, which indeed she did!"

"My mother was the dominant parent in my childhood. My father was at work and during most of the war he was evacuated to Southport, Lancashire. He was scrupulously honest, quite painfully so, and I remember when he found me using his office (H.M.S.O) pencil he took it away and said it was government property."

"He got very upset whenever a door "banged," and complained about a "door on his chest." He never related it to the war - indeed he never talked about the war until a few years before he died. As a child I loved to bang a door and watch him jump, I thought it quite good fun and I often did it. Years later I understood why a door "banging" upset him when I visited the battlefields of the Somme, and retraced his steps."

At this point in Peter's excellent extempory storytelling, John Grimer added how he could remember the German doctor who saved his own leg when he was in a POW hospital : coming into the ward in a white fury and waving a scalpel because our bombers had killed six of his nurses. He was threatening to cut off all our arms and legs.

Joseph, with Robert carrying the censor, and his brother John Grimer (right), in Belgium.

Joseph and his pipe !

Arthur & Maria at No.17 Bowrons Ave. Wembley. Note the runner beans.

The only known photograph showing members of the van Damme family. Before 1904 the only passenger transport from Oedelem to Bruges was the horse drawn mail called "The Male." On the front seat one sees the last coachman of the post mail of Oedelem Joseph van Hoorickx who lived in the Commune House where he also kept an "Estaminet" (Inn). Standing beside the Mail is his son Leon, sitting inside Julien & Jordan van Damme.

Dr.Bockaert's house at Oedelem, a village near Bruges.

Knessellaresttraat in 1909. All along the left was the brewery of the van Damme family, dating back to the 16th.cent. All that was demolished between 1954 & 1963. In the foreground left, stands ?   This the house of the family of Dr.Vandenberghe.

The renowned "Brewery Vandamme" on the other side, looking out on a large garden. This photograph dates from 1920. It would seem that the house is reversed and does not face Knessellaresttraat. Uncle Joseph on horse back, Tante Camilla in white dress, Tante Alice in a black dress. In the 17th.cent. this property was a large farm, and called the "property of the Holy Grail,' & before that "Saint Barbara."

The singers of the Congregation of the parish of St.Lambertus, dated 1908. (Your mother, aged 14, was the youngest singer). I was called from boarding school to stay with my sick father, and as I was neither mussel nor fish, they kindly took me in. The oldest and the youngest singer had the honour to hold the black board.

During WW1 the "Comiteit" looked after the sharing out of food sent from America. This was done in the Convent Chapel. Marie knew all those people shown in the photograph Their names from left to right - Jeanne Fonteyne, Julia van Houcke, Leon Engelrelst, Julien Herrebout, Pieter Landuyt, Leonie Hudders, Leon van Poucke, Romanie Bellaert, Leon van Houcke, Marie Calliauw & Réne Serlet.

A photograph "illegally" taken during the occupation WW1 by the schoolmaster J.Creytens from an upstairs window. It was strictly forbidden to take photographs or to have possession of a camera. All the bicycles were called in, requisitioned. A group of cyclists waiting to obtain a pass. This happened in front of Commune Hall, some were allowed to keep their cycles, but had to give up the tyres !

The joy at the end of the war manifested itself with a grand deliverance feast with a long procession which you see here in parts. It was the beginning of a new era.

The Last Boat to leave Ostend *
(probably May 20th - 25th. 1914)

The following is a typescript of a narration made in 1983 by Maria Ida Aleda Julia Grimer *née* Bockaert, prompted by her son John Arthur Grimer. The narration is about her life, and fleeing from Belgium as the German army occupied her country. Her story is recorded on Sides (a) and (b) of a ninety minute tape. Maria died aged 103 years.

For many years the tape remained only as an aural record until August 2006, when I made a digital copy of the tape onto CD, from which Joyce Southern Grenfell made a sympathetic typescript. The difficulty she found in making her copy was at first having to spend many hours listening to Maria's voice, how she shaped her words, (Maria spoke rapidly), her repeated answers to the prompts made by her son John, memorising all that was said as best as she could.

Maria was a Belgian woman who spoke fluent French : therefore her accent was strong and had to be understood and mastered before a text could be considered. However, Joyce (my wife) made a noteworthy rendition from the CD, a task which took her some two full weeks of listening and writing down the text in free hand, which she then copied onto her computer.

Then one evening our friend Peter Warden, who happened to be staying with us during a holiday, asked if he could listen to the CD while reading Joyce's version. Peter, a *bel esprit* was educated at Lancing College, speaks fluent French, and has extremely acute hearing. Strict silence was essential during this session because the volume of sound from the CD is very low.

After he had listened and read he asked if he might take the CD and a copy of Joyce's printed text home with him to work on it. Joyce agreed. His copy is almost identical to Joyce's version, and he was able to supply the French proper nouns.

* the title is mine, Ed.

Maria Grimer's Story - her early years:
" The last boat to leave Ostend."

John - "My mother is now going to talk about her memories of her earlier childhood, growing up in the little village of Oedelem, where her father was a country doctor...."

John - " Maman...!

Maria - " What ?...What, dear ?"

John - "Well, off you go..."

Maria - " About what..?"

John - "About your early childhood.."

Maria - "I went to a very nice boarding school in the Wallonie because, as we lived in Flanders... near Bruges, and my father wanted me ...to get me educated in the French atmosphere because he did not like us being brought up in the Flemish part of Belgium where they did not speak French, and he thought French was a very important language, and we should *emmulate?* no good"... *(assimilate?)* And he put me right in the Wallonie? Then I became a boarder, left home. And I was very happy there. I spoke French fluently within the first term, and, not only that, I studied very hard because my father said it cost a lot of money and, "Don't waste our money, you must study hard that you get a good position and that in your life you can become an independent person." "

John - " How old were you then ?"

Maria - "I was very young, I was nine."

John - " And that was when you went to Tirlemont Boarding School – how did you find the school, how did you like it when you went there...?"

Maria - " I liked the school...I liked the school, I liked the studies, I work very hard because I wanted to please my father. My father said "If you want to please me, you work hard." And I work very hard."

John - "Did you make any friends at the school ?" *(repeats question..Maria mistakes 'friends' for 'French')*

Maria - " They only spoke French, they spoke no other language, so I learned French very early, very young. Fluently... and, what was more, I came first of the class against all the girls of Wallonie that only spoke just one language and I had to learn, I had to battle with both. But they did speak no Flemish in Wallonie !"

John - "Were there any English girls there ?"

Maria - "Yes...At St.Tirlemont I met some very nice English girls ...from very good families, very many, because (to ?) lots of English people the Notre Dame was a very nice Order and they had Houses in England, and they sent the pupils of their high class schools to Tirlemont.

Now, as I was the eldest of seven children I did not go home for any holidays except the mid summer holiday. I spent all the Christmas holiday and Easter holiday in the Convent with the English girls and made great friends of the English girls, and they took me on, like, you know, my protectors and I learned to speak English, because they did not know more French than I did. But I learned to speak their language, because they talked between themselves in the holiday...In the holidays they were allowed to speak English...."

John - " So that was very useful to you when you went to England, later.."

Maria - " Yes...There was Elise Normanville who came from a very distinguished family who built a bridge in town...what town is it now ?... A Civil Engineer who built a big bridge in one of the big towns in ... I will have to look in the Atlas..."

John - " Not Sydney ?..where ? In Europe ?"

Maria - " In England...And they had two brothers, Benedictines, and their name was de Normanville... they really came from a French-extraction family."

John - "Is that the friend that you kept writing to in Rhodesia all these years ?"

Maria - "Yes, she just died last year.."

John - " She did ? How old was she ?"

Maria - "Ninety-one. That was the friend that came. Every big girl had to look after a little girl and she happened to be my big girl. I was there during the holiday, when all the other boarding girls had gone home, and she was sort of like my protector. And the English had parcels sent from home and I never had anything of course, seven children...they didn't have the time to think of sending parcels to me, and she said to the English girls.. "You share, everything we eat she have," and Elise was like a mother to me, she was a big girl looking after me. And there was Hilda, Naomi, three de Normanvilles. There was a P(r)owell ?, her father was director of the Port of Singapore, very high position, there were others, lots of them that I can remember, but the one I got attached to, for all of my life, was Elise Normanville. All my life I corresponded with her. Oh ! after the war I happened to call in at the convent she was brought up in England, St.Leonards-on- Sea. "

John - " Oh ! she was there, was she ?"

Maria - "That was a great . . . And I recognised the uniform and I said "That's funny, Sister, I had a friend in Tirlemont, a boarder with me and she wore the same tunic as the girls wear here ."She said, "What was the name of your friend ?" and I said, "Elise Normanville." She said, "Of course, they have all been here, Elise, Naomi, Hilda, Vita: fancy you knowing Elise Normanville." I said, "Yes, she was the big girl that looked after me." And they were amazed and, you know, they were rather fascinated by it, and they wrote to Elise and Elise came to visit me in St. Leonards. And she said " Fancy !" and she came to take me out. She took me out, she took me out to London, and I sat in a high cab, you know, with a horse..."

John - "A hansom cab."

Maria - " A what ?"

John - " A hansom cab"

Maria - " Yes," she said, "Now I am going to give you a treat. "...I was going to sit in a high cab...what do you call them ? where the man sits behind, and I was giggling so much, and she said " Look! What's funny about it ?" and I said, "The man is behind us and the horse is in front of us!" I was amazed, I was going around with my mouth open in London, a great big town; I had never seen much, you know. And I came to stay in her London home for three or four days, near St.Pauls, where she had family and scholars there. ...they were very high...Leamington Spa !! "

John - " Oh, It was Leamington..." (thats where he built the bridge)

Maria - "He was the Engineer of Leaminton Spa and he built a bridge there... And she took me out, and she took me to the theatre; she said, " Now I am going to take you to an English theatre" and she treated me like a friend, and she paid everything, and she sent me £5 for my fare, which was a lot of money in those days, and possibly a bit of pocket money - Oh! she was like a mother to me. And all my life I've remembered this; and all her life she's remembered me. That was..that was something wonderful of God, wasn't it ?" "She wanted to become a nun once, but she was a Novice but she had to come out, that was not her vocation. She married, she had a boy who was killed the first week in the war, who was a flying man in your war, John Bailey [Davey ?]. She married Mr Bailey [?] That was the same family; that was very wonderful!"

John - "To get back to school, you stayed there until you heard your father was ill ..You stayed at Tirlemont until you heard that your father was ill, till he sent for you?"

Maria - "No, one day the Reverend Mother called me to her private room and said, and.. that year I was top of the class, had all the prizes and the crown of excellence, the gold crown with little gold beads...and she said, "Now you've got to be very brave, girl , you've done very well, don't tell anybody but you are having the excellence crown of the year.. because you have earned it, you have deserved it, and we are so sad that we are going to lose you...because your father has claimed you to come back home, to go back home, and I cried because I was so looking forward to go in the next form, it had always been my ambition...Elise had been in there. And the Reverend Mother said "Well, my dear, your mother is very ill and has had to go away, and your father has nobody except little children and a housekeeper". All the children that were able to be accepted went to boarding school, except the babies, and they wouldn't take those, and my father had to get a housekeeper. My mother went away in a nursing home for a year and a half or two years, lost her mind. And my father had to have company of some human being that he could talk to. I was then , how old...?"

John - " Fourteen?"

Maria - " Fourteen ?, Fourteen...and he said, " Now," he said, "You have to take charge of the money 'cos I have a housekeeper, and you have to open the door and receive the patients and you have to do many things that your mother used to do but will no longer be there"- and I cried. And the Reverend Mother said, " Don't worry, dear, we will pray for you, and we will pray for your father, and your mother is very ill ". So I came home, with all my books, six prizes, big books, tied up and a crown hanging on it, and my father met me in Bruges, at the station, and then he saw me and saw what I had, I could see the tears in his eyes and he tried to carry my prizes and he couldn't, he was too weak. And he said, "It is terrible, could you hold them, could you carry them?" He had leukaemia.. And he said, "I have not got long to live, and I wanted to have one person home to whom I could talk and say things to remember" So that is why I had to go away from the boarding school, that was my life. And I stayed with my father, I did the pharmacy, I made the ointments, I received the patients. I had to open the door, introduce them to wait till my father came in, I had to do all the things that a dispenser does.. and I was fourteen, you know. ...a child.. But God gave me great intelligence and I accompanied my father on his visits and I did ride the horse, he taught me how to lead the horse. And I did everything for him till he died. I was with him two years, very sad. "

John - " And what happened then ?

Maria - "Just before he died he said," I have to ask your mother to come home, now in the nursing home, if she is well enough, could she come home, because he said, "When I die some body must be here..you are too young. And my mother came back home, only a little while before he died."

John - "And was she alright, your mother ? "

Maria - "She was never alright, and she was well enough to be able to live , of a sort, but she was never a mother to me - you know what I mean. She was difficult and I had a very sad life, because she seemed to resent me more than any of the others, because she knew how close I was to my father. We had two nursing sisters looking after him at my home, because my mother was unable, and the Nursing Sisters told my mother my father was dying, "Would she come in the room?", and she said she couldn't, she wouldn't come, and they came back.. and my father..and he told me to come near him and he held my hand, and he died holding my hand. And the Sisters said to me, "Oh, Let us take her away", but my father said ,"Leave her, leave her with me." And after he said, 'Leave her with me' he went into a coma..and died. And that's how he died, I have never forgotten that … in all my life." [Maria then broke down and became tearful].

John - "Soon after that, soon afterwards…. the war came, didn't it ?"

Maria - "Yes, the year after, the war came. And I was safe, I was really safe through the war. Joseph remembers all that, too, Joseph remembers, he was my -…'cos I had a great job to light the fires. "He was very good, he was at the college in Bruges and he came home over weekends, and he was my only person, you know, to talk to me, in a sensible way : and that's why he and I are so close, he knows what I am going through - he understands, and after my father died he took his bicycle, and he rounded up all the debts, the money that was owing, on his bicycle ; and my father bought him the bicycle because he was top of his class the year he died. And my father was so proud of him, he thought he was going to become a doctor, and he asked, on his death-bed, my brother promised to my father that he would look after all his little brothers, which he has done. To see every child to get married, to get a house, to get everything that a parent would have done. He was going to be a doctor. I wrote a letter to him. "When you die and go to heaven my father will say "Welcome! you have kept your word my son, you have kept your promise." And he wanted to become a doctor but when my father died he thought he could do more for his brothers and sisters by remaining not married, he stayed single and he had a vocation for the priesthood and became a priest. My father counted on him to become the guardian of his children. And he was only a very young boy, but he was always very clever, very intelligent, much more intelligent than I am. He writes books, he has a pen, you know,"

John - " You gave me one of his books, you gave me "Le don de Dieu." "

Maria - "He writes poetry, he has written books of poetry, books of them, lovely poetry. He was mad on poetry. He's written a book, you've got a book. He knows Dutch, Nederland; Flemish is not a language , if you speak Flemish properly it becomes Netherland; it's got a grammar. He speaks Nederland, he speaks French, very good French. He speaks Latin. He knows Greek, he can read books in Greek, what else has he got?. He is absolutely very clever, I am just like a washboard, next to him I am just nothing compared to him, very clever. He can talk in Latin conversationally. When he came here somebody say "How are you going to get on when you go to England, they can't speak French ?" He says "That is nothing, I will go to the Presbytery and I can speak to the other priests in Latin, I can talk to priests, no matter what language, as they all speak Latin.. So in came Father Reagan, a poor Irishman, and he spoke to him in latin and poor father Reagan stood there in amazement, he couldn't understand a word of it ! And he said "What country is this, the priests are supposed to speak Latin fluently, he says he can't under- stand a word I say to him !" He speaks Greek as well, he was a Greek scholar. I am a very ignoramus compared to him ! "

John - "And what happened to Laurent, Uncle Laurent?"

Maria - " Timon went to Israel and became a doctor with very good qualifications, very high up. Laurent became an engineer, and earned a good living, a very good living, Laurent is rich. Pia, she became a nun and entered the Philippines and her health broke down and they sent her home, because she was not fitted for any other work but missionary work. So she left, she left and she became just an ordinary woman and spent all her life as a spinster, looking after my mother, she stayed home with my mother till my mother died. So it was God's way of keeping somebody to look after my mother. She came to the convent and they said, "Well, you have an old mother to nurse, you go and do your duty by your mother, so your life won't be wasted." My mother wanted very much for her to marry, she had an offer to marry a doctor, but she say "No, I have made my vows and I keep my vocation," and my mother lived and kept Pia another fifteen or twenty years."

John - "And what happened to Walter, Uncle Walter ?"

Maria - "Walter was killed the first day of the war ."

John - " The first day…?"

Maria - "On the battlefield. He was a chemist, and he was called up straight away when the war broke out. And he was on the battlefield of V?, near Forplain ? And he was struck by a shell, he was very young, but was married with three little children. The first day of the War and they came in through there.. This was the Second War, and Joseph was on the battlefield too, as an almoner, what do you call them…"

John - "Padre, we call them Padre in England…"

Maria - " A padre, a chaplain ? They were both on the battlefield, first day, a great big battle and Walter was hit by a ?? and my brother was on the same battlefield to give him the last rites and saw him bleed to death. He was carried on a stretcher to the near convent and Joseph gave him the last sacraments and anointed him and he died, terrible that was, and I didn't know, for four years I didn't know he was dead. On the first day of the war, two of my brothers were on the battlefield, and one gave his life. And Joseph said he died a wonderful death. He told me all that he said Joseph said, "I take care of your children and see they get on.""

John - "Are those the ones that went to the Argentine ?"

Maria - "No, they're the other Bockaerts.. my uncle's children, not my father's children, the children of my father's brother, my Uncle's."

John - "And what did Timon do during the war ?"

Maria - "Timon was a young boy…not the Second War……Timon was working as a doctor somewhere, but I don't know where."

John - "And you had quite a busy time here in England, didn't you – in the Second War here in Wembley?"

Maria - "I stayed here after they were evacuated…Your father went up north and I stayed here with the two boys, the two young ones, Peter and Francis. I remember the bombs dropping all around Wembley, with the two boys and Daddy was up north, and people dying, all roads blocked to Sudbury Station, all the houses flat, many people die, and I was here all through the war alone, with the two boys, and we slept under the stairs, under an iron table.* Lots of things I had to face When the bombs came they built shelters out in the road but I said I will be just as safe under my iron table. I said, " Anyhow, if God wants us he'll take us from under a shelter as from under an iron table…! And we take it !" I have had a very interesting life. In each war I lost something … In the first war I lost my home, and in the second war I lost my brother - you know, killed, hardship with the children, and you were missing, how do you think I felt about that ? When you were missing… every night I cried, "Dear God only let me know if he is alive or dead!" I kept thinking every night I think of you as I was going to bed, and when the news came through I sat at the bottom of the stairs and I didn't know where I was – and I called Daddy and then we prayed very hard even though you were not dead, we knew you were alive ; because the news was not very nice, and you suffered. But I have got it all written down by Bob, I gave you the letter, didn't I?.. But Bob was very good, he has always been a good brother to all of them. Then the rumours of war, Germany and Belgium, and nothing happened. Then suddenly war was declared and I was on holiday. I was going to a new school to study to become a teacher, four years college. "

John - "How old were you then ?"

Maria - " I was fifteen, just fifteen, you had to be fifteen or you were not accepted, you must be fifteen and you have four years course. So I had prepared my trunk ready to go, the first week in September, for Brussels, I had, you know, obtained a post, you know, that was…wait a moment, my God !, I had done four years college…

see, I am thinking before the War. I had done my four years college and I had qualified with honours and I got my degree. And I had obtained a position in Brussels, in a nice…the Notre Dame Convent…"

John - " So you were nineteen years old, weren't you ?"

* We were all sheltering under the iron table, which was in fact a Morrison Shelter, positioned in our dining room. The Morrison Shelter was introduced in March 1941 and consisted of a steel table with a steel top and heavy gauge nets (which we didn't use) measuring 6ft. 6ins. in length, 4ft. wide by 2ft. 9ins. high. Its cost was £7. 12s. 6d., but was free to families earning below £350 per year. We used it during the raids; and after painting it brown mother used it for dress making, and for meals when we had visitors.

Maria - "I was nineteen, not fifteen, nineteen years, I am mixing up my going to my College. And everything was ready, my trunk was packed and my sister, Clothilde, who was fifteen, was going to go as a student to do the four years College that I done, to Antwerp, in the Notre Dame also. And the nuns arranged that with the money I earned my sister could go free, 'cos you remember, my father died at the age of forty five, leaving seven children. The eldest was myself, so my mother had to look after what she could pay for, and I had three brothers at the college of the Jesuits, and they cost a lot of money. So I say to the people in Brussels," Well, look here, how much am I going to earn ?" They say, "Well, if you like, as you have lost your father, and you have no more father and your mother is a widow with seven children, we will take your sister free in the college in Antwerp, to get her degree, the same degree as you've got ,(I got mine in Ghent), and you just have pocket money for yourself, "Would that be suitable ?", and I agreed 'cos I thought I must help my mother, I must help my sister and as long as I have a bit of pocket money… I have always been a very careful girl, never very spendthrift, always, being the eldest, knowing my father had died and we had to live on a very strict income… So that was agreed, so my sister was very pleased." "I had my trunk ready and she had her trunk ready, all ready to leave. On the first of September; now, the war broke out on the fourteenth of August, something like that, and everything fell in the water, well, it didn't fall in the water yet because we thought the war would be over in a fortnight. "

John - "And of course the Germans hadn't invaded Belgium then, had they ?"

Maria - "Hadn't invaded but had declared war on Britain and France in August, we were still free and could move about. So we got all these trunks got prepared, all ready, and, alright, things changed within a few days to such a pitch that the Germans entered Belgium. And we had the forerunners of the army in retreat, there was a battle or two in the South, and the retreating army came to lodge in our house, all the officers and the Lieutenant-Major. .Slept .., of course we had a lot of rooms, seven bedrooms, a big house. And they saw us two girls and they say, "You two, you've got to leave at once because tonight the Germans will be here and they'll occupy your house that we occupy now. You, a girl of nineteen and a girl of fifteen, you go to England. The last boat goes this afternoon at 2 o'clock"; it was then 10 o'clock. We had not got time to do anything, we had no money, I said, " We have no money, we have to go to the bank, how are we going to get to England ?" They say, "You don't have to have any money, the last ship leaves at 2 o'clock. You've got to go at once, just get the train there, get to Ostend, and you don't have to have any money, they've got to keep you or get you on the boat as refugees. The last lot are leaving, women and children only." So, in the clothes I stood , with enough pounds on me as I had, we left, Clothilde and I.. we were the last ones almost, on the boat. Because the Gendarmes with bayonets stopping anybody but women and children and, filled the boat up until it couldn't take another person, and they left, and it took all day to get to Dover because of the mines in the sea. We had to go all along the coast to Dover, a roundabout way. There was no water or food on the boat so we had nothing to eat, and the clothes we stood in.."

John- "Were you on the deck ?"

Maria - "On the deck, we were on the deck, the bottom was already full and we sat on the deck, and it was cold because you know at that time of the year, the evenings…the days are alright but the evening was cold and there was nothing to eat. And we arrived in Dover. It took twelve hours, about…It seemed to take all day. Whether it was night or day I don't know, but it took a long, long time to get to Dover." "When we got to Dover we all had to pass through an examination. They lifted up our hats, I don't know why - to see our hair or something. And they examined, a quick sort of examination, you know, and they passed us. But we came, on that same train was my cousin from Ghent, and he had a letter; his father was railway master of Ghent, and he had a letter for the consul in Dover to say his son and his two nieces, two girls, were coming ; could he see what happened to us ? And when we got to Dover he met us, he asked our name, told us who we were, and we didn't have to go through the refugee examination; he say he take us. So he took us and looked after us for a day or two, he said " I find somebody among my friends who will give you three a home" - and thats how we got to Gran's, 71 Folkestone Road, 71…the reverse of 17…, and Mr.Grimer looked after us, and Mrs.Grimer was a darling, like a grandma. When I had been there for couple of weeks I started worrying and said, "Look here, I am nineteen.

I have got a degree, I do not want to be a charge on anybody. I've got to earn my living." They say "Yes, but you can't earn a living till you can speak a bit of English. You will have to stay a bit with us and we have to talk to you." I had learned a little bit of English at school of course, but you know what that is like. When anybody talks to you, you don't understand anything. So we got into the swing and we were there till Christmas and at Christmas I said, "Look, I definitely can speak English now, I can earn a living and look after my sister", so they said , "Don't you worry we will find you a place, a situation" So Mr.Grimer looked through this newspaper and I said we are catholics, and they say "Yes, we know, we're looking for a convent where you could teach, and your sister could be a boarder so you wouldn't cost anything to anybody, because your salary would pay your sister's keep. " So I took that, and I agreed. We both went. And my sister was very sad because she did not like to be a boarder, because I was in another department you see, I was with the teachers and she was with the boarders, she was very homesick, and she cried a lot and she was unhappy. I said, "Look here, you have to get used to it otherwise you have to go back to the Germans and be killed !". And I said " Do you think I like it? I've got to work hard, I haven't got a minute to myself. I also have to learn English to be able to teach.. You can't teach French if you don't know a word of English to a class that doesn't know a word of French !." And she was very sad and very unhappy, and that was bad for me because I had my own troubles as well." "However, I taught there for how long ..?"

John Grimer - "That was Christmas 1914, you went there ? At St.Leonards near Hastings"

Maria - " I think I taught there, could have been a year, could have been more, could have been less…I don't know the dates, Yes, St Leonards, was a very chic convent, with all the Royalty of England and all the aristocracy of England ; their children were educated there." And Catherine ?? of the Belgians was there and the girl, Georgette, .. she took a fancy to me knowing I was Belgian, you know. She was very friendly to me, and kind to me, and there were such a lot of Belgians, the rich people that had come over, long before the trouble really started …in fact the girls were there at boarding school for, you know, the end of their education. So I was there, I had to work very hard..Taught there, work all day!"

John - " Did they pay you ?"

Maria - "No, no pay, no payment, they say, " "But in your free time you can give private lessons that will pay you and that would give you pocket-money." "But that was hard work."

John - "So they didn't pay you but they put Clothilde up, they paid Clothilde's fees…in other words you worked to keep Clothilde there…"

Maria - "My sister was there, free, so I gave private lessons…and… Very chic people, and one woman paid me a guinea, for every lesson a golden guinea…she gave me a sovereign. I used to collect sovereigns in a little box. And she was a very rich woman, her husband had been a very famous doctor, and died, and she was a widow, and I think she was looking to get married again, and she wanted to learn French and I used to teach her, and for every lesson she gave me one guinea, and a guinea in those days was a lot of money…because for three guineas I bought a lovely purse. So that went on. Well, in the meantime my brother had gone to Holland with his little boys, he was a Seminarist when the War broke out; he had a vocation to the priesthood .And they didn't take seminarists. He had no army training, seminarists don't do their army training, they can go straight in the Seminary."

John - " When the war broke out ? So he took the younger boys, Uncle Laurent and Uncle Timon and Pia?"

Maria - " 'Cos I couldn't take Pia to England, she was only a little girl aged seven. And he took them to Holland, north Holland, And they allowed him to stay with the children for a few months 'till he he [sic] could find a home for them, before rejoining the Seminary…because he had to make all the arrangements for the children to be looked after. So, when the children were looked after..that took about six or seven months..and he said to me "Is Clothilde happy in England?" I said, "No, she cries, she's always crying, she's very unhappy, she can't get used to it like I can, she's much younger"..And he says "Well, it's good thing, it's the way of God, he says, because I really must get back to the Seminary. I want to become a Priest, I've already had nearly a year away, I can't leave them. Perhaps Clothilde would like to come to Holland… where Holland speaks the same language as Belgium." So Clothilde, Oh ! she was delighted, she was going back to Holland, the only thing she said "To leave you, you've been so good to me, I don't like you to be all alone! "…"Don't worry about me being all alone, I am twenty, I know my ways and I can make plenty of friends.. Don't worry, you go to Holland." So she bought me a little album, Farewell, with her little bit of money she had and said goodbye to me. And of course I was sad to see her go. But Joseph was delighted. She was then sixteen…no she was then fourteen, she was always the friend of the maids…because she always helped the maids with the housework and I hated housework.

I liked books, and piano, and never would do anything, Because I said, you can't order me, you're the maid ! But Clothilde got round them, and they gave her little sweets and things, on the quiet ! And she loved housework and… the maids took to Clothilde and not to me..so she was glad, she was going to do the housekeeping in Holland…Fourteen, and she was very good, that is to say she could cook, she could do the things she never could do, and she was much better in the kitchen than I was. I hated the kitchen, I was studying, so Clothilde went to Holland. "

John - " Holland wasn't in the war, of course…It was neutral..You could go across by boat quite easily "

Maria - "Clothilde was very happy, she was going back to Holland…with the help of Mr Grimer, the Grimer's because he knew the ways, he knew the Consul, he was a friend of the Consul, and they got Clothilde to Holland, free…Joseph was delighted, Joseph could go back to the Seminary and Clothilde brought up the other three. In the meantime, two of the boys grew and joined the Belgian Army when they were of age, nineteen or eighteen, through Mr Grimer. When they were of age, they joined the Belgian Army that was fighting in France.. in the South of France, on the east coast of France. "

John - "Laurent was one..Uncle Laurent and the other…Timon?

Maria - "Timon was always recalcitrant, when Joseph left for Holland, always he said , No…he stay with the Germans, he was not frightened; that is to say, he went to the van Dammes who had the brewery, my mother's brothers,, my mother's home.. There were four women, two men.. Timon never went to Holland. Timon became a doctor later, he stayed in Belgium during the war, he was only [?], and Walter, three. And Pia stayed behind…I was in England and Clothilde go back to Holland,…and Clothilde was delighted and she made a nice home for them, and cooked, you know, and they were refugees, they got money from the, you know, from the government."

John - " And your mother stayed in Belgium with Pia, with Timon. ? Where did you go, in England, when Clothilde left?"

Maria - "When Clothilde had gone, I said to the Nuns, " Look here, now my sister is gone, she is no more expense to you, I would now like to earn a proper salary, I would like to look for a situation, advertise for a post . And I did and I got a post. The Head of a big school, a private school, in Epsom, came to interview me and saw my credentials and I showed my Diplomas. And she said, Yes, she'd be glad have me to go to teach French and the Piano to the juniors..and that was what I was teaching in the Convent. So I went to Epsom; I stayed a bit in the Convent longer, not straight away after Clothilde left, a bit longer. The Nuns wanted to pay me a salary, but it was not a salary that kept me. Also I wanted my freedom, you know, so I went to Epsom and I had the Spanish 'Flu there, and they looked after me as if I was a princess, they had a Doctor coming every day to see me,… they put me in a nice room in the infirmary and got me through the terrible 'flu, people died, red crosses on the doors, Spanish 'Flu, people died like flies; I caught that when I was there. I did my time.."

John - "What year ? Was that the end of the War?"

Maria - " I can't remember the year, the War was still on."

John - "Had you seen anything of Daddy in all this time? Dada?"

Maria - "Oh no,. a lot happened in the meantime. I spent my holidays in Dover..And Daddy was a soldier, and called up, and he came home on leave and his brother also came on leave and his brother was a sailor. I was fascinated by the sailors, nice uniforms, and Daddy was only a private soldier, it was not his career. I was a bit stricken by the sailors and Grandpa … The sailors were rather fascinating, nice badge, nice uniforms, and sailors were rather 'flash!"

John - " You were stricken by the sailors?!"

Maria - The little Grandpa said to me ," Mary, you know, don't make a mistake; it's Artie who is the good boy !" He said, "Sailors ! A girl in every port!" "Don't say that to me, a girl in every port ! I was a Catholic… that was it as immoral!" " He's never told a lie, that boy, Artie"

John - " Oh dear, oh dear!"

Maria - " I said, he's a very good boy and he's become a Catholic. Well , that immediately appealed to me, a Catholic! A sailor had no religion. And, well, but Clothilde also became fond of Artie. But in the meantime Clothilde left for Holland and that was the end. There was only Artie left and I left. Well, he was a Catholic and anxious to talk to me, he was always very scrupulous; he found 'comfort'.."Don't worry about that, that's nothing, that's not a sin ! You're in the Army" Yes, but he was on leave.."God doesn't want impossible things." He was very scrupulous ! Lucky he married me, I was never scrupulous! Canon ?? said, when he went to confession, "You do what Mrs Grimer says you can do, don't worry so much! " He told me that himself. And well, so I got engaged to Artie after I had known him…"

John - " When…about 1916?"

Maria - " Couldn't quite say…about 1916…I think it was before, must have been '15."

John - " Then he was in France at the time, was he?"

Maria - " He was then still in England, and then he left for France, and I didn't see him.. From France he went to Greece and from Greece he went to Jerusalem, to the entry of Jerusalem in thing's army…General Allenby.. I didn't see him, I saw him once, he had one leave in four years, one leave I saw him and, of course it was heartbreaking."

John - " You would get letters?"

Maria - "And every day they were allowed to send a card with their name on…I mean, not every day, every week, that they're alive. But they were only allowed a letter now and then, when there was mail that was going.. Look at the places he went, he was in ..in the Dardanelles, he was in the entry into Jerusalem, he was in the battle of the Somme, he was in the other big battle… Passchendaele ! he came through Flanders, he was almost near Bruges…when the Armistice… But I was engaged to him and couldn't go out with boys; I had to wait. When he came out of the army we got married straight away."

John - " Now, what year was that?"

Maria - "The war was over, 1919 or 1920, the Armistice. He wasn't immediately free you know, he had to wait, but he was one of the first coming home 'cos they needed him at Whitehall, at Whitehall, because he did accountancy, he was an accountant. He was one of the first batch coming home, and as soon as he came home we married, and we hadn't got any money, much. That was my life, my young life…!"

John - " Thank you very much, Maman! I've heard it before but I wanted to put it on tape .. because I want to play it to my pupils in class..they're reading a book about the First World War."

Maria - "Arty was so pleased to meet a Catholic girl because he said he feels he could never get married unless he married a Catholic! He had so many scruples you know!"

photograph 1914 - "Final Year of the Students, Ecole Normale, Mont- St.Amand, Belguim."
<u>from left to right</u> - top row :- Marthe de Ro (died 1916). Mary Ronse (went to California).
Marie van Belle. Emma Grenier. Maria Bockaert.
<u>sitting down</u> :- Leontine van Nieuvenyse (now Revd. Mother at Visitation). Godelieve Morel (Carmelite nun).
Marthe Ronse (sister to Mary, went to California). Galuelle Claeys (died 65).

<u>further information relating to Maria's story</u> :-

Wallonia is simply defined as the southern, French-speaking half of Belgium which comes under the administration of the Walloon government, in contrast to Flanders in the north of Belgium where they speak Flemish. Belgium has four distinct linguistic areas - Flanders (the majority of the north), Wallonia (the majority of the south), the two German speaking cantons on the eastern border between Wallonia and Germany, and the officially bilingual area surrounding and including the capital city of Brussels.

An 1892 Patent Application for improved ladies waist belts, corsets etc., was made by a William Louis Normanville, of 6 Clarendon Crescent, Leamington, complete with diagrams.

Louise de Normanville went to Rhodesia where she stayed for many years. Maria taught French at St.Leonards-on-Sea Convent and she kept in touch with Louise, (who lived into her nineties), all her long life.

There are two pictures of Robert Grimer (Uncle Bob - my fathers brother*) in the 1910 - 1911 football team of Dover Grammar School. Arthur Grimer's name can be found in the Dover Grammer School Archives as well. It mentions him leaving to become a boy clerk in the Civil Service. (Google.)   * added by John Grimer.

"CHILDHOOD AND "MISSPENT YOUTH."
John Grimer

Whenever I ask John Grimer what his earliest memory is he invariably draws reference to certain boyhood pranks and episodes from what he calls "his misspent youth." His youth was certainly not spent in idleness; he worked to earn his living, and the work he followed was quite varied. He served no apprenticeship, followed no trade, nor listened to any words of wisdom from his father who had laboured hard to send his children to private schools, when he himself survived after experiencing the horrors of the First World War.

John Arthur Grimer was born in his parents house on Saturday the 16th.day of September 1922 in Wembley, Middlesex, home to the famous Wembley Stadium - the scene of the more important football matches and other sporting events, including the Horse of the Year Show held there each autumn. He was the second child born being the issue of John Arthur Grimer & Maria Ida Aleda Julia née Bockaert. The four children born in order was :-

Robert Walter Grimer	(1920 - 2000), married Marguerite Foakes (b.1923).
John Arthur Grimer	(b.1922), married Jean Loretto (1918 - 2005).
Peter Grimer	(b.1928), married Margaret Howick (1935 - 1995),
Francis Joseph Grimer	(b.1932), married Patricia Alison Neal (1931 - 1986).

(Francis & Patricia had issue nine children, and at at the time of writing fifty-six grandchildren!)

Before John drew his very first breath his mother remarked to the person who carried out the delivery "very blue," and that same person had to slap the infant on his back many times before he did draw in that vital initial breath of life. John Arthur was a sickly baby.

His first memory was when he was aged between one and a half to two years of age being left in Great Ormond Street Hospital, London. His mother recalled that occasion by telling him how he clung to her like a cat. When he came out of that hospital he was placed in a cot upstairs and his elder brother Robert, who would have been aged about four at the time used to empty the contents of the chamber pot over him in the mornings saying as he did so "I baptise thee in the name of the Father, the Son, and the Holy Ghost." Their mother eventually caught him in the act and gave him a sound smacking.

However he progressed from there I suppose as in the way of most infants, but when he reached the age of about three or four years they found he couldn't walk properly; there was something wrong with his right leg, probably a development of polio. After several doctors and orthopaedic specialists had examined the defective limb he was eventually deposited in his Uncle Timon's clinic in Belgium. There the limb was encased in a sort of lace-up cast, but for how long John did not know; but he must have spent a year in bed. Eventually the leg did heal itself. What he could remember was that he did not return to England, and walking again, until he was aged between four or five years. But by then he did speak French as well as he could speak English.

John found it was good to return to his parents house in England once more and now he was able to join in with all the vigourous activities with Robert again, who took great delight in teasing him. John could still remember how he used to go up to the top of the garden where there was a large poplar tree, and Robert would send him down to the house to shout at mother who was busy washing the kitchen floor with a mop. John would shout at her "Beast, devil, rotter, skunk" after which he would make a hasty retreat back to the poplar tree. He did this several times. In the end mother took hold of her mop stick and came roaring out of the kitchen. John was terrified but she passed him by and ran straight on up to the top of the garden to where Robert was and gave him a good walloping.

John went on with his story. About the age of seven, after several attempts in little private schools where I had learnt absolutely nothing, I did a term at Alperton Elementary School of which all I can remember was sticking bits of coloured paper on to a sheet of white paper.

My mother was then expecting another child, which would have been my brother Peter, and so I was sent to Visitation Convent at Bridport, where I was sad and miserable. I would have to go to the top of the house to where the toilets were and cry bitter tears and look out at Primrose Hill and the train which took my mother away from me. It was my first real feeling of homesickness, as I had been too young to feel homesickness at Uncle Timon's clinic in Belgium.

I spent two years at Bridport but came home for holidays, which was lovely. Then I would have to go back, and the dreadful smell of the Convents' soap, (probably carbolic soap) would bring back all my misery. The nuns were very kind to us. However, they used to bath us and take us for crocodile walks to West Bay, and once to a magical place called Eype which was further along the coast, where we would collect winkles and baby crabs which they would boil for us and we could eat later.

There was a rather big nun called Georgina, a strong Dutch girl wearing a complete nun's habit with a starched front. I can remember tapping this as I got out of the bath and I must have spoken to the other children because one day the Reverend Mother and Sister Georgina called me into the office where with stern faces the Reverend Mother said "Grimer, No.56, (we all had numbers in those days), what is this we hear, you have been telling the children that Sister Georgina is hollow and not to be frightened of her." Well, I suppose I had thought this starched breastplate which the nuns all wore sounded hollow when you touched it, and had told the other children that Sister Georgina was really hollow ! Well these two nuns were looking sternly at me and I was really frightened, and suddenly they burst into peals of laughter and the Reverend Mother brought me to the desk and gave me some sweets.

Eventually, I suppose, I came back from the convent, and my father who didn't earn very much money, but managed somehow to send all his children to schools where you paid fees; all except for Robert who, being more clever had got a scholarship to the Wembley Secondary School where he stayed. Peter and I went to the Cardinal Vaughan Memorial School at Holland Park, London as paying pupils where they fiddled me through what passed for the 11 Plus in those days : although quite frankly I was a very late learner and never learnt to read properly at Bridport. I put this down to the fact that as a child I chewed a lot of lead soldiers and animals which might have affected my brain, anyway I had five years at that place which practised a strict narrow and oppressive regime with a martinet of a headmaster, one Monseigneur Canon John G.Vance, who was headmaster from 1928 - 1948. Doctor J.G.Vance was a sadist, but I believe he got his comeuppance in later life (was he not removed abroad) : but one was regularly thrashed. When the teachers went out of the room (we all stayed in the same classroom whilst the teachers were perambulating about) where there was a school monitor, and if you dared talk while the teachers were out of the room your name would go down in his little book. If your name went down three times in the course of one week you were paraded before the headmaster and sentenced to a thrashing which was administered by Father Clayton, who taught geography : but your hand would swell up quite considerably if you had six on each hand, and you could not write for the remainder of the day. By the time you went home the swelling had gone down and the evidence was not to be seen. (In his autobiography Norman St.John Stevas made no reference to the school, one can understand why!). One teacher, known as "Bulldog" would go purple in the face when he got angry, and on one occasion threw his blackboard cleaner (a wooden baton on which was affixed a felt strip) at my brother which opened up a gash on his head which needed stitches. Frequently one was made to kneel on coconut matting during the lunch break, and the school monitors made sure you remained in that position.

At both the Cardinal Vaughan School and at Ealing Benedictine Priory I had three school friends who became well known in their various professions. One was Edelson a rugby player, another was Norman St.John Stevas MP., and lastly there was Richard Greene, a star of films, in particular Robin Hood, which was made into a TV series that ran from 1955 to 1958 showing a total of 143 black and white episodes, each lasting 30 minutes. (Today all available on DVD.)

I survived all that but did absolutely no work, whereas my brother Robert did lend me his history note books; which were beautiful, and by mugging up these I was able to pass my history exam, and for the last term before I took my school certificate : thanks to my mother encouraging me and helping me with my French and my other subjects for about six weeks before the exam. I had had four or five disastrous reports with my father telling me to pull my socks up, and saying "Where the tree falls so shall it lie my son." I eventually, much to my parents surprise, managed to get five good O levels with credits, which enabled me to go on and take my school certificate, and fortunately to go to another school, which was a lovely school called Ealing Priory. It is still there but now called St.Bennett's, a branch of Downside, and is run by Dominican fathers and lay teachers. I remember Dom Adrian Morely in particular, the head master, a lovely man who took us for European history. We would go into his office where there was always a large box of Balkan Sobrannie cigarettes on his desk which he would offer to us eight boys. "Do have a cigarette boys, I would rather you smoked in here rather than out in the street which has been your wont in the past." So we smoked with him and promised him we wouldn't smoke in the street any more. (During WW2 the Cardinal Vaughan school was evacuated to Beaumont College, Windsor.)

There was a cadet force there which I rather enjoyed. You had to polish your boots and your brown leather strap on your uniform, and march up and down carrying rifles. Father Brooks wanted me to go to Sandhurst and told my mother so. However, that didn't come to pass and at the end of the year I took my higher school certificate in English, History, and French. The later was easy because I already spoke French with my mother, and I managed to get good grades in that. In order to show my ingratitude I did a dreadful thing; I ran away from home with another boy called Mike Cahill. I stole some French money from my mother's purse which she kept on her dressing table. Our aim was to go to London Docks and stow away aboard a ship bound for the South Sea

Islands. Well, we had been reading Conrad and Ballentyne, and I was fascinated by those stories about South Sea Islands and getting a boat to sail away in. Being aged sixteen we must have been very callow and stupid youths to even contemplate such a thing, but we thought we would go to London Docks and get on some ship. We met up on Burns Avenue, as Mike lived up at North Wembley, and we got on a train and went to Limehouse. We soon discovered that it wasn't easy to board a ship, even as stowaways. So after much to-ing and fro-ing we eventually boarded a train out to Ryegate in Surrey where we got jobs working for twelve shillings a week in the local claypits where I believe they were digging for Fullers Earth. We slept in a haystack, but for only three or four days. There was a little corner shop where I remember shoplifting a bottle of horseradish which I put into my pocket. But the lady in the shop must have seen me do it and reported the incident to the police.

The next time we went into the claypits to work there was a policeman waiting for us and they took us out where they had two police cars. We were bundled into the front of a car with the driver only to find our respective mothers sitting in the back waiting for us. As we drove away we listened to our mothers each blaming the other for us being led astray by their son. However, my father seemed quite unmoved by the experience, and my mother also kept rather quiet. Then to my amazement the school said it was alright and that they would have me back again. That must have been before I took my A levels in 1939, and during the summer of that year I had a marvellous time at Caen University, in France; I and four or five other English lads who met some German lads and we had some really great times together.

It seems strange as this happened just before the war, and in Caen of all places which was so dreadfully destroyed in the second front. We used to walk around the town and visit the bars and the bordellos, but never had the courage to do anything in the latter. But we had a marvellous time and after no work and much drinking we were awarded a huge highly impressive certificate for minimal attendance at lectures "Diplome de la langue et de la Literature Francaise," and to my lasting regret I've lost it. The only thing I have now is a very modest piece of paper which was an emergency teaching certificate which is nothing much to look at compared with the immense scroll from Caen University which was really something, and I should have had it framed.

However, it is now the summer of 1939, and war is threatening. My father, my brother, and I are digging up the back garden to install an Anderson Air Raid Shelter as the threat of war intensifies all the time.

My father, perhaps to place me somewhere safe, decides to send me to Exeter University which was an outpost of the London University in those days. Duly I arrived and celebrated my seventeenth birthday there and stayed in Kilmorrie Hall, in Pennsylvania Road, Exeter. I met two young Welshmen who attended courses there, and I proceeded to for the following year to cut all my lectures and spend all my time in Dellers coffee shop with its delightful gallery listening to their quite famous string quartet whose repertory included the Beethoven String Quartets, as well as the popular quartets of Mozart, Haydn and Schubert. I also visited Bobby's Coffee House in that charming pre-war city, went on lovely pub crawls with the other students, and did absolutely no work at all. I was supposed to be taking intermediate latin, so that I could proceed to a history course. However all to no avail !

There was a Saudi prince there who had a little MG car, and he was a lovely chap, and one of our greatest delights was to go for a drive with him in his car, and it was gorgeous. We visited the Washington Singer Labs where we could dance with the female students from Hope and Lopez Hall. At the end of a glorious year; which saw Dunkirk and the 1940's, together with soldiers returning through Exeter without arms and some without their trousers. They landed all along the south coast of England in what we thought would be the end of the war. We listened to Lord 'Haw Haw' on the radio in Kilmorrie Hall telling us all sorts of rubbish about England, and how we would soon lose the war. However this propaganda did not impinge very much on us, and in the end of the summer term I was told by the university authorities that there was no point in me continuing there with my studies, and I, instead of returning home decided to join the Forestry Commission on Dartmoor, and together with another young chap we went to a village called Lustleigh, near Bovey Tracy, on the south-eastern edge of Dartmoor. Our job with the Forestry Commission was cutting tress suitable to make pit props, which were then dragged away by horses. Pit props were not only for use in the development of the coal mines, but also used in mineral mines which were being worked up to full speed to produce all that which was so urgently needed (particularly wolfram), for the manufacturing of aircraft, ships, tanks, armaments, and the like. But I had marvellous 'digs' in a romantic cottage known as "The Mill," with Harry and Gladys, a wonderful couple.

We didn't make a very good job with our tree cutting work, and at the end of a week had earned something like twenty five shillings between us. The foreman then took us off piece work chopping down our own trees, and put us on the general gang work which gave us enough money to pay our rent. With this my friend decided to return home, but I decided to stay on being entranced by the lovely scenery, as well as with my comfortable digs at "The Mill," a cottage which had originally been a mill by a stream in the village of Lustleigh.

Then one day my whole life seemed to come to an abrupt end. There was a railway station at Lustleigh, and there it was that I witnessed a train steam in and two girls of the W.L.A. (Woman's Land Army) alighted to join our team of forestry workers. One was tall, blonde, and very beautiful, who I thought probably was a peroxide blonde typist. Then one day standing in a queue at the fish and chip shop in Bovey Tracy, I turned around and there was this girl beside me. Flushed with excitement, as well as being well fortified with Dutch courage and a more than adequate amount of cider, I looked at this girl, took her in my arms, and kissed her. This daring move of mine must have impressed her because on subsequent days she seemed never to be far away from me, and very soon we found ourselves wandering away together into the woods; and for the first time in my life I found myself hopelessly in love. We spent all our free time together during that hot momentous summer of 1940, exploring the idyllic beauties and the bleakness of Dartmoor, Becky Falls, Hay Tor - where we slept out one night with nothing but a can of beans and nothing with which to open it with.

The girl was Jean Loretto, a beautiful blonde part Cornish girl whose family on her mothers side owned Liscawn Farm, at Crafthole, in the Cornish parish of Sheviock. She was older than myself, I being aged seventeen years, and she aged twenty one years. So it continued, that hot glorious summer which shone forth its joy and etched into my memory as no other memory in the whole of my life. Eventually I decided I had to go home. Jean had just finished her degree at London University and had got a place to take a post graduate diploma of education. So instead of going back to Bristol where London University had been evacuated, the department of education was evacuated to Nottingham where there was a university, and I wanting to stay with my beloved as long as possible persuaded my poor father to enrol me as a student at Nottingham University: having made such a miserable mess of my time at Exeter. After some persuasion my father relented, and sent me up there with an allowance of three pounds a month which was a lot of money in those days for a student. So to Nottingham, and to Jean I went where I was able to consort with my beloved who was staying in digs in Burton Joyce, and I obtained suitable digs nearby; but usually managed to slip into her digs when ever the occasion arose.

Once again I was absolutely unscrupulous about doing no work at all, my whole life now was taken up with my complete infatuation with Jean. But after the first term my father enquired from them a report of my academic progress, and receiving a very adverse answer he withdrew my allowance of three pounds a month, and I had no option but to find work - easy enough after 1940. I had to leave my digs and so Jean and I somehow drifted apart.

I went into Nottingham where they had smoke coming from oil burners at street corners which was supposed to form a smoke screen over the whole city to deter German bombers. I don't know if it worked, except it gave me severe bronchitis. I got digs with a very nice family called Briggs, and a job working in the Nottingham lace industry dragging great skeins of machined lace over gas burner jets in the bowels of a large factory, being in the company of ghastly crude old women, and me being young had to put up with their coarse ribaldry, as well as having to walk for miles trying to buy a packet of cigarettes. From the age of eleven I smoked rather heavily, and buying 2d. packets of Woodbines whenever I could get the money, I simply had to have some ! That, together with the smoke filled streets of Nottingham which must have made the people of Nottingham rather unhealthy I left the city, and got a job navvying in the countryside digging ditches for Callender Cable Company at Langar Aerodrome near Derby. Here I worked with many Irishmen who dissuaded me from my initial enthusiasm of digging too fast, and where the foreman constantly came down to berate us all, calling me a "long nosed c.... and other things. (Most of those Irishmen had fought in the Spanish Civil War).

Then followed a succession of jobs which proved to be nothing more than manual labour, I now being a travelling navvy. Jobs throughout the Midlands, laying concrete runways for aerodromes (concrete often woefully under strength - a racket). Doing demolition work in the bombed cities - in Birmingham I nearly got bombed myself. Always moving on to where there might be an extra pound or two. Sleeping in railway stations, on park benches, Rowton Houses (the Poor Man's Hotel) and at the Salvation Army Hostels - where I was mixing with the 'down and outs' and sometimes very disreputable people, and often woken in the middle of the night by a policeman's' torch - looking for wanted men; criminals, and deserters. The food was rather horrible in those places, especially as the war was on, but I preferred to spend my money on beer and cigarettes than on food, so I am afraid I must have been pretty filthy and degenerate. Occasionally one could get a bath in a Rowton House: but I wasn't all that keen on washing anyway.

By the end of that year, 1941, after working all over the country I finished up in London and found work with Ind Coop brewery delivering barrels of beer to pubs round about King's Cross; and every time we rolled in a few barrels the publican gave us a free pint of beer or porter, so we were all rather merry by the end of the day - the driver included ! But there was little traffic on the roads in those days. Then I heard on the grapevine lads were wanted to work in the London tunnels, as "pit ponies," pushing away the trucks of excavated clay. The work was in compressed air, but the pay was amazingly good, between ten and twelve pounds a week. Our tunnel was in George Street, the miners sometimes, if the day was very wet, had to work at the face in compressed air then they would put big concrete rings up and bolt them together and so slowly the tunnel would progress. We worked both day and night shifts and I can well remember during the break in the middle of a night the ganger foreman taking out a great handkerchief turned into a crown and anchor board, and the miners, many of them Irish, would spend what seemed to be vast sums of money on the board and would lose ten or fifty pounds at a time which to me seemed absolutely amazing. I never indulged in this myself. I believe our tunnel later became part of the Jubilee Line.

Often in the morning I would walk into Covent Garden Market, or other markets near by where I would buy oysters. In those days I would swallow these down raw with some beer, but since those days I have not been able to bear even the sight of an oyster.

It was now January 1942, and I had enough money to rent a room in a cheap boarding house at Earls Court. Jean and I had long since drifted apart, but now I had a room I again got in touch with her. She paid me one brief visit and was not much impressed by the squalor of my appearance and surroundings, so I didn't get any further visits from her and we continued to drift apart. I spent the whole of that month in the London tunnels, but in about February 1942 my father, who was working in the office of the Ministry of Labour, discovered my whereabouts and persuaded me to come home. There I was cleaned up, rehabilitated, given my elder brothers old clothes, properly fed, and in return I did jobs for my mother. I laid a concrete path with some large flat stones set in it, up through the garden. My parents were very forgiving and kind to me.

But early in March of that year I was called up into the Royal Air Force.

1939 - 1945
Summary of John's WW2 service

March - April 1942 - A.C.R.C., at St.Johns Wood where John was nick-named "Gristle." Here John embarked on aircrew training (no.1804070). April - May 1942 - I.T.W., Newquay. June 1942 - E.F.T.S., RAF. Anstey, soloed in a Tiger Moth after nine hours instruction. Various navigation, gunnery and bomb aiming courses. Spring 1943 - RAF St.Eval, Cornwall, map reading in Whitleys over the Bay of Biscay, anti-submarine sweeps. August - December 1942 - Various holding stations around the country, no serious flying training due possibly to too many recruits for the training resources. Spring 1943 - Bomb aiming & gunnery course, quite intensive at RAF Millon, passed out top. Considered too scruffy for a commission but appealed on account of my results but eventually I was accepted. Pilot Officer Grimer (138336), 21 years old. Summer 1943 - various navigation courses on Ansons. Bomb aimer on Halifax Mk 1A. August 1943 - Honeybourne on Whitleys again. Early September 1943 - (RAF.Ricall) conversion course to, and bomb aimer Halifaxes. No.77 Squadron, RAF. Elvington, Yorks., fourteen operations with same crew. Shot down April 23rd. 1943. Parachuted. POW, (no POW number probably due to hospitalisation in Rheims Military Hospital.) September 1944 - liberated by General Patton's 3rd.Army. Weighed under six stone. September 1944 - Flown home in US. DC3. Sent to 101st. US Hospital, Taunton. October - November 1944 - RAF Hospital, Locking. December 1944 - Medical re-habilitation Unit, Loughborough. 1945 - 46 - Various admin. jobs - RAF.Church Fenton, RAF.Yatesbury (E.V.T. Officer), RAF.Mount Wise, Plymouth. Summer 1947 - March 1948, M.R.E.S work in American zone of Germany, and British Sector of Berlin.. March 1948 - Demobbed.

WARTIME
"Won't it be simply wonderful to be together again after this palaver is over."

"I was awaiting call-up which came early in 1942, in February and I then joined the RAF. To begin with we went to the Air Crew Reception Centre in St.John's Wood, and I actually stood on Lord's Cricket Ground - on that hallowed turf !

There we were given kit-bags and various items of uniform, and then we were taken to our barracks nearby to the cricket grounds. It was there that we had to do seemingly useless tasks and taught how to box fold our blankets and to place them centrally at the head of our beds. After about a month of our initial training we had learned to march and drill, and so we had to march down a London street (which I believe was The Strand) where we stood in ranks, at ease, while having to listen to a speech given by Sir Archibald Sinclair. We heard the RAF March played by the band for the first time, and we were given a white flash to wear in our caps to signify that we were to become air crew.

Air Ministry, Whitehall - 21st.March 1942
A MESSAGE OF WELCOME

You are now an airman and it gives me great pleasure to welcome you into the Royal Air Force.

To have been selected for air crew training is a great distinction. The Royal Air Force demands a high standard of physical fitness and alertness from the flying crews. Relatively few attain that standard, and I congratulate you on passing the stringent tests.

Not only have you passed these stringent tests, but you have been recommended for immediate entry into training, instead of returning to civil life to await your recall. You are exceptionally fit. Work hard but live temperately, and make yourself proficient at your flying job."

"In wishing you success in the Service of your choice I would like to add this: the honour of the Royal Air Force is in your hands. Our country's safety and the final overthrow of the powers of evil now arrayed against us depend upon you and your comrades. You will be given the best aircraft and armament that the factories of Britain and America can produce. Learn how to use them."

Archibald Sinclair   SECRETARY OF STATE FOR AIR.

"From London we moved to Newquay for further training where we enjoyed glorious weather in the early spring. We also enjoyed the course, we were taught how to take a Browning machine gun to pieces, and given endless hours of 'square bashing" and marching down through the town. We were barracked in an hotel overlooking the beach and the island, and for six weeks we were proudly looking forward to becoming Spitfire pilots, but I believe they were flooded with too many recruits, because for the following few months I can only describe it as an attempt to keep us occupied as we were shifted from one RAF Station to another, being mainly requisitioned hotels along the South Coast. I remember one such hotel all having to dive under a desk when a German plane came low over the sea and dropped a bomb which just missed the hotel and smashed into a house behind. We all went out and helped in the ruins, and that was my first sight of a little child who was killed by this particular bomb. I can recall a chain of us passing one little dead infant, just a quiet small bundle, passed from one to another, as we extracted them from the ruins.

From there we went to various other holiday and seaside towns giving lectures all the time. I can remember a particularly pleasant stay in a Harrogate house, probably owned by gentry. But eventually came the time when we actually had to learn to fly and so we went, some of us, to a little grass covered aerodrome called Anstey, near Birmingham and Redditch, and there I learnt to fly a Tiger Moth. It was a marvellous and thrilling experience. I was convinced I was going to be a Spitfire pilot, but I had never flown a plane, or even driven a car, but after eight and a half hours I was able to take off alone in a Tiger Moth and it was glorious after having got up in the air, but feeling very frightened at being on my own for the first time I lost sight of where the aerodrome was; but I followed the instructions - left hand turn at 500 ft. and then another left hand turn at 500 ft. and I eventually found the aerodrome and made a fairly successful landing. I was quite sure then that I was going to be a Spitfire pilot, and all the girls would be after me when I had my wings, but it transpired not to be, we were all hauled out on the parade ground where I believe about six of us were told they would continue as pilots, and the remainder told that we would be air crew, air gunners, navigators, wireless operators, bomb aimers, or whatever, but not pilots. I was so disappointed that I really contemplated desertion; however, good sense prevailed, and I then proceeded to go on the various navigation and gunnery courses at various aerodromes and flying schools around the country.

We finished up flying all over the country in Ansons, and to Scotland learning to map read, learning how to wind down the undercarriage of the dear old Anson and then getting it up again, which was very hard work because Ansons had no automatic undercarriage. I can remember on one occasion on a low flight over Ireland, looking down and seeing a lady on a bicycle with a basket which apparently contained eggs, because the poor soul fell off her bike as we swept low over her, and I could see the basket and the eggs smashed all over the road.

After that we went to RAF Millom in Cumberland, (John's Royal Air Force Observers and Air Gunner's Flying Log Book,(DRM 1767) for Grimer J.A., of Unit No.2 (O) AFU., Millom, in Cumberland, dated 22nd. March, 1943, lists Flying Officers results of AB. INITIO GUNNERY Course and Remarks; together with his AB INITIO A./B. Course at the same training wing, dates from 12th.November 1942 to 22nd.March the following year. The Certificate of Qualification of 1804070 Grimer J.A., qualifying him an Air Bomber, and also ascribed him as Pilot Officer, Service No.138336, dated from 22nd. March 1942, Unit No.2 (O) A.F.U., Millom.) and there with Polish pilots flying Boulton Paul Defiants. We had gunnery courses where we sat in the turret behind and we had to fire at a drogue dragged by a Lysander aircraft to find out how many bullets you could get into it. This was not easy because of the curved trajectory each bullet made as it left the Browning machine gun. But eventually I managed to hit the drogue quite a few times. Then when flying in an Anson from the same aerodrome I scored good marks for bomb aiming, in fact I scored higher marks than most of the other pupils, so when we came to the end of the course, and it was 1943, they called out some of the lads to be offered commissions. I was not offered one myself although I had the highest scores for both gunnery and bomb aiming, and naturally I felt so dejected by their decision that I went in front of a board, consisting of a Warrant Officer and some other officers where I asked them why I wasn't given a commission as my results were the best of that course. Their reply was "Grimer, you are very scruffy, and therefore not fit to be an officer." It was true. I never had been very presentable, I suppose what with my careless upbringing and my complete lack of any liking for clothes, although I had a pork pie hat that I was rather fond as a teenager ! (RAF No.1804070 AC1. Grimer, J.A. When he achieved Pilot Officer status, his Service number was changed to RAF No.138336.)

After some deliberation and chewing the cud they did say I could have a commission, but I would have to smarten myself up a lot. With this good news I was allowed leave and so I went home to my mother who was so proud of me that she took me to Hope Bros: who were also agents for schools uniforms, and stockists of RAF uniforms made in a material of better quality with a finer cut than those of standard issue So with my mothers help I was fitted out with all I would need as an RAF officer, and my mother being so proud insisted on me having my photograph taken.

Well, after about a weeks leave I was posted back to the RAF to continue my training, and now commissioned I went first of all to St.Eval in Cornwall where we learn't to fly Whitleys, again training, but also doing Bay of Biscay sweeps looking for enemy submarines. When back in the mess it was always very crowded and we had to sleep all over the shop, some of us even on the billiard tables.

The types of aircraft I flew in were Ansons, Defiants, Whittles, and Halifaxes, in that order.

After that I was sent to an RAF Conversion Unit, (this was now into 1943), at Long Marston near Honeybourne, which was an operational Training Unit, and again we were flying Whitleys and Ansons. I don't think we flew in Wellingtons, but they had Wellingtons on the station, and that continued well into the summer. Eventually we did go to a Conversion Unit to convert from Whitleys into heavy four engined bombers, and it was there we were crewed up for the first time. The pilot would choose from amongst the rest of us the men for his crew, and so it transpired that Squadron Leader Bond chose me because I suppose of my gunnery and bomb aiming results. The others he choose was Charles Hobgen, or Charlie as we called him, being the navigator. Johnny Johnson to be the wireless operator. Jock Mason as mid upper gunner, Jack Waddilove to be tail gunner. So we all crewed up into Halifax's, and S/L Kenneth Bond, who was much older than the rest of us, was actually a squadron leader from RAF India, who had come back to England, it being his desire, to take part in the war.

S/L Bond didn't make a very easy job of flying a Halifax, and his landings were pretty awful; we were often badly bumped about so much that we soon lacked respect for his flying ability when it came to landing: but otherwise he seemed to be a very efficient pilot. I soon realised how little he thought of me because he frequently told me to get my hair cut, and not to look so scruffy. But we stayed together. S/L Bond always remained somewhat aloof from the rest of us and didn't use our Christian names, only our rank and surname; unlike many other crews which was all on Christian name terms

The now famous No.77 Squadron I was attached to was based at RAF Elvington, near the city of York, and it was to this place where we were posted in September, I believe, which was to be our squadron home. In October 1943 the squadron converted to Handley Page Halifax B Mark 11's. That ill-fated mission which is so vividly described was flown in a Mk.1A, because it was not until the following month of May that the Mk.3 came into force at RAF Elvington [internet source states 8th.September 1943]. Let the historians sort this out. Anyway, we settled in at Elvington and it was there I met the people who remain so clearly etched in my memory."

On the 24th.November, 1942 John started flying operations. His log begins :-

Date	Hour	Aircraft Type and number	Pilot	Duty	Remarks	Flying Times
24/9/42,	14.10hrs	Anson 47	F/S Wait,	Air Bomber.	B.3 course. Wind on C.S.B.S	1.40 day.

(a facsimile copy of the above Log Book 66074 can be seen in Appendix 1)

Our first real operation was over Frankfurt early in October (or late September) and S/L Bond was very pleased because the photograph that had to be taken after you had dropped the bombs showed the air photograph of the aiming point to be the best taken by the squadron. He was very proud of the fact that his bomb aimer, however scruffy he was, was a very good bomb aimer.

We continued for six months in that squadron with S/L Bond, but being a flight commander he didn't have to fly as often as the other crews, so during that six months we could count how many planes failed to return. We usually put up between twelve and fourteen planes during each operation, and on some occasions they all came back. But more often than not one or two were missing, and on one occasion four of our aircraft failed to return. So we would listen to the weather forecast. If it was very bad and the ops were cancelled or "scrubbed" we were all delighted and so we all traipsed into the town of York to visit the various inns and continued to live a riotous life as we did in the mess. We didn't get into any trouble for any of these escapades they seemed to tolerate our behaviour. My best friend on the squadron (because Charlie, my best friend in the crew was not then commissioned, so I didn't see much of him until after the war) was Pete Cadman. Pete Cadman's was one of the rare crews who we saw to complete their tour of thirty operations in the six months I was there, so it doesn't take much arithmetic to work out your chances of surviving. Dear Pete Cadman did finish his tour of ops and we had an uproarious party. I can remember it well, and he then travelled down to Oxfordshire to fly Oxfords, that was a training plane, and after Pete had been there a fortnight he was killed in an accident to the general dismay of us all.

On one occasion Group Captain Leonard Cheshire VC., OM., DSO & 2 Bars, DFC., gave us a visit with his American wife, a very coarse lady who sang coarse songs at the piano. It was something to have actually met or seen the legendary Group Captain himself, who was the youngest Group Captain known. In 1959, he married Sue Ryder, (Lady Ryder of Warsaw, C.G.M., OBE.), formerly of the Special Operations Executive, and famous for her work in Poland with concentration camp survivors.

We continued with our ops., and on my fourteenth op. with this crew; having bombed Berlin two or three times, and Leipzig; which was our worst one, and various other German cities we were taken off bombing German cities to bomb French targets, in preparation for the Second Front. It was on our mission to Laon in north eastern France that we were to bomb the railway marshalling yards there, and I believe we were flying at about 1000ft. when we were over Laon, after an uneventful channel crossing where we didn't see much Ack Ack or night fighter activity.

But just after I had dropped the bombs I could clearly see them hitting the marshalling yards and then as I looked up (you had to continue straight and level for a time to be sure you had your photograph of the bomb burst) I saw a great 'Roman candle' of fire straight in front of us and I quickly switched on my oxygen mask intercom to warn the crew (actually it was underneath us, and firing upwards in front of us) and before the bullets all ripped through the fuselage of the plane setting it on fire from the petrol tanks, and the whole thing was ablaze, we being right at the front were out of the flames for the most part and my one thought was to get out as quickly as possible. Charlie who sat over the escape hatch with his table was miraculously not hurt at all, but the wireless operator was in much distress having his leg hanging off, almost as though several cannon shells had been through it. Charles and I dragged him out, clipped on his parachute, lifted the escape hatch, and threw him out. He did manage to pull the rip cord and he did land alive in a field. Then Charlie went out, then I got my parachute to go out too when I found one of the lugs wouldn't work but hoped that the other lug would. I then followed Charlie as soon as I could. We had no communication with the pilot all this time. Subsequently I found out that the pilot had stayed in the plane. Perhaps he thought he could land it, I don't know. The engineer got out unhurt, the tail gunner got out unhurt, and both of these two managed to find their way back to England; one via Switzerland, and the other via Spain. The mid upper gunner also had very serious leg wounds but he managed to get out too. He and the wireless operator were later to join me in hospital in Rheims.

Anyway, having got out I felt that I had been shot in the eye. Actually the bomb site had disintegrated in front of my face with bullets going through it, and a splinter had cut my eyelid open. I believed I would be blinded as there was blood on my face, but when I got onto the ground I found that my eye was perfectly alright, I could see through it, and tried to stand up. But before that as I floated down in my parachute I could see the plane burning, it had gone off at a tangent, not nose diving, and I drifted down for some time before landing in some trees. I looked down I was fairly high up where I could see the reflection of stars, (so it must have been a clear night), in the water below me). So I undid my quick release thinking I was over a river or canal, and I plummeted down I suppose twenty or thirty feet and landed in a puddle, where I dislocated my shoulder and broke my left ankle. I tried to stand up but found I couldn't. I then discovered I had been seriously wounded in a leg, the blood was streaming out of it, making the cut on my face as nothing.

Farewell party for W/C Roncoroni - taken after I was shot down, but I remember some of the faces.
© photo RAF Elvington Museum

Front row believed to have been all killed. © photo RAF Elvington Museum

only known photograph of Capt.Bond © photo RAF Elvington Museum

"Wing Commander "Lofty" Lowe, later Group Captain. He was followed by S.S.Bertram who was one of the pilots in the Swordfish biplanes that attacked the Scharnhorst and Gnies He never flew with us."
© photo RAF Elvington Museum

I knew what to do and so I removed my belt and made a tourniquet out of it to stem the flow of blood but still I found I could not stand up, so I crawled dragging my leg behind me and proceeded to crawl out of the small copse with its many puddles and mud, and eventually after an hour or two I found a road which led to a few houses, rather a hamlet where I proceeded to yell out that I was an English airman which brought some response because one or two windows was opened and people told me to shut up. But I managed to reach the door of a house after another endless crawl where an elderly couple took me in and gave me some raw eggs to eat, after placing my wounded leg up on a chair. I loosened the tourniquet every twenty minutes or so otherwise the flesh would mortify.

The next day I was so ill and feverish, and fearing that I would die from septicaemia I asked the old French couple to contact the Germans, which would give me a chance of being hospitalised where I might get away with my life. They did, and in the course of time a German motor cycle and sidecar arrived

One of our crew, Bob Johnson, the wireless operator, was seeing a lot of Helen, a WAAF stationed at Elvington who, being attached to the MT Section drove a bus which ferried crews to and from the operational planes. Bob and Helen fell in love with each other and I have often wondered what happened to them.

Our temporary tail gunner (F/O Jacks DFC) emigrated to Australia after the war and, could still be alive. [See photograph of F/O Jacks (see p.30), taken sometime during the 1990's]

Although the Flight Engineer Sgt.Victor Clare had bailed out on that ill-fated raid over Laon on the 22nd of April 1944 he survived and managed to evade capture, reach Switzerland, and live to fight another day. It is a dreadful thought that an air gunners life expectancy during WW2 was only two weeks, and some 20,000 such gunners were killed. Flight Engineer Clare seemed to have had some luck when he found himself after the war, back in dear ol' Blighty. But it was not to be for long : Victor Clare remained in the RAF, but when flying a redundant Halifax aircraft to be scrapped, it crashed killing him and the pilot.

Here is the story as told by Ian Robinson.

The Crash of Halifax Mk.2 JP 203 on the 8th.June 1945

(as recalled by Ian Robinson, pilot.)

" With the end of the European war in May 1945 most of the Halifax equipped squadrons from all Commands, Bomber, Coastal, Met., but not the airborne forces 38 Group, were flown into the Handley Page repair depot at Clifton near York for disposal, i.e. dismantling and subsequent scrapping of aluminium.

We, Handley Page, were still however continuing to carry out major repair, overhaul and modification to the later mark of Halifax ie.V11, CV111 and A1X. The CV111's were ultimately used on the Berlin airlift and the Mk.1X was developed for airborne forces and freight carrying.

June 8th on a pleasant sunny morning I proceeded to flying control to collect that days Met. forecast, time circa 10.00 hrs., each day we continued to receive yet more Halifaxes for scrapping, already several hundred or so were lined up nose over tail on the airfield. On this particular day we had two aeroplanes for air test scheduled mid day.

Whilst in the control tower we noticed a Halifax approaching from the east with its port outer engine feathered and at about 250 yards from touch down some 150ft high, the control caravan on that day manned by ATC. commenced firing red Vary flares. I think there was some small obstruction on the runway.
We assumed that the pilot reacted to the red flares opened up the three remaining good engines and attempted an over shoot. I sensed immediately that he lacked both power and height to recover and was about to crash. In my state of panic I jumped into our RAF Hillman car and, with the hand brake still on drove madly beneath the Halifax which was losing height all the time. (In hindsight I have no idea what I could have achieved).

To the east of the airfield, the direction in which the aeroplane was travelling, was the City of York with some 100,000 inhabitants, and in particular JP 203 was heading towards the largest council housing estate in the City. Some 500 yards into the estate was a Catholic Church of contemporary design including a cross on its steeple at the eastern end.

The stricken Halifax hit the cross with its port wing tip and crashed miraculously into a small allotment behind a public house called the New Imperial. The area in which JP203 crashed was little more than 1/3rd of an acre, the air frame disintegrated with the centre section and undercarriage against the end of a row of houses. By the time I arrived at the crash site some civilians were trying to rescue the crew, sadly both pilot and flight engineer did not survive.

With saddened heart I returned to the Handley Page Flight Office and reported the events to our Test Pilot T.V.'Mitch' Mitchell. By then the time was about 11.30hrs. and we were due to fly an A (airborne) Mk111, I asked my skipper if I could be excused from flying as I was pretty upset at my experience. 'Mitch', I suppose, wisely insisted that I accompany him as Flight Engineer and that we do the job in hand. Reluctantly we boarded NA 218, carried out the air test followed by a similar exercise on MZ 336 later that day.

For nearly fifty years I remembered this episode in my aviating career with tremendous sadness: as in my humble opinion the accident should never have been allowed to happen. The disabled Halifax should have been given permission to land. At most Remembrance Day services I recall this incident and wondered who the two RAF aircrew were who tragically lost their lives unnecessarily.

On November 11th.1994 I was presented with a research file from our Newsletter Editor, Norman Spence. In itself not an unusual occurrence at Y.A.M as we frequently receive some fascinating WW2 stories at Elvington . . . on my desk was a story about a Halifax Flight Engineer Victor Clare (Sgt) about his escape through France after being shot down on 22nd. April 1944 after a raid on Laon. That night two Halifaxes were shot down, we searched for squadron numbers involved, they were 419 RCAF 6 Group and 77 Squadron RAF 4 Group Elvington York. I had also received, week ending 11th. November the Roll of Honour of 77 Squadron prepared meticulously by Y.A.M member and friend of 77 Squadron Association., Roy Walker.

On the night of 22nd.April 77 Squadron lost Halifax LK 710 whose skipper was Squadron Leader K.Bond, Navigator Flg. Officer C.Hobgen, Flight Engineer Sgt.V.Clare DFM. Whilst all this information arrived on my desk, within days Norman Spence then informed me that Victor Clare escaped through France, returned to England late 1944 and it was he who was killed in the described incident at Clifton, York, in June 1945. He is buried in the cemetery in the city of York. "

"Flight Sergeant Clare was awarded the DFM on his return to England in 1944, sadly to lose his life on a non-operational ferry flight."

Ian Robinson, 15th.November, 1994. Yorkshire Air Museum, Elvington.

Wombleton Aerodrome became operational during WW2, but not as a base for any squadron during the war, but the home for No.1666 Heavy Conversion Unit (No.1666 HCU): one of more than thirty such establishments in Britain at which hundreds of aircrew were trained to operate in four-engined aircraft. No.1666 HCU, Wombleton, was part of the Royal Canadian Airforce's No.6 Group, Bomber Command; and, as at all similar establishments, its young, mainly inexperienced, crews were required to fly their training sorties in war-weary Halifax and Lancaster bombers.

One of the aircraft involved was a Halifax 11 1a: HR723 which, immediately prior to arrival at Wombleton, had served as M Mother with No.77 Squadron, at Elvington: on four occasions carrying out successful operations when flown by Cecil Manson - from Cottingham, near Hull - and his crew, his navigator being another Yorkshireman Clifford Smith from Yeadon, Leeds, who, sadly, with two others did not survive the war.

On October 27th. on a night training exercise HR723 was subjected to severe icing and was abandoned by its crew over North Wales; six of them descending successfully by parachute; a welcome fate not to be experienced by their wireless operator who due to the incorrect attachment of the parachute failed to survive the descent.

By an amazing coincidence, their aircraft came home to earth for the last time on Pydew Hill, near Llandudno Junction, barely a half-mile from the home of Jack Whitely who flew in it earlier, as mid-upper gunner in Cecil Manson's 77 Squadron crew!

YORKSHIRE POST, October 13th. by Gerald Myers of Tranmere Park.

50,000 airmen died during operations carried out in WW2, plus 9,000 who died in training.

Bill Jack

Charles Hobgen

THE "RED TAP"

John Grimer married Jean Caroline Loretto, a teacher at Liskeard Grammar, tall, blonde and very lovely. As children in West Looe after WW2 we believed she was a film-star who had come over to England from Hollywood. I well remember many pairs of children's eyes admiring her form and beauty, (the girls whispering together as their eyes ravished her clothes during those austere days of wartime rationing) every time we saw her pass us by.

John and Jean lived in a cottage by the bottom of North Road, (once known as Horse Lane). The terraced cottage featured a tap affixed on the roadside wall by the doorway which the newly-weds soon painted pillar-box red; and named the house " The Red Tap." Later the cottage featured a coal-bunker...! But that's another story.

Jean Grimer had bought No.2 North Road in February 1948 - shortly before John was demobbed. The auction price, £750, appeared in The Cornish Times as the highest price ever paid for a fishermans cottage. Even with a mortgage of £400 & John's RAF gratuity they were only able to make up the shortfall on the mortgage - with a generous "loan" from John's parents.

Next door to " The Red Tap " lived Alfie Martin, known as 'Onions,' a local boatman, and his wife Alma. She came to Looe from London with her sister Hetty, and they both worked in Service until 'Onions' swept Alma off her feet and married her. They had no issue so they adopted a boy whose mother had died. The lad was Laurence Arnold, known as "Ginney," and so they brought him up as their own. Alma was aged sixty three years when she died. John Grimer would take "The Times" in to her to do the crossword after John had finished with it, and often she completed it. Then Alma found she was suffering from cancer, but she bore her illness with fortitude even tho' she lost much weight. Eventually she had to stay in hospital where John and Jean still visited her and took the newspaper in to her as usual. But after their last visit they told her how they would see her tomorrow, but Alma replied "I will die tomorrow, Tuesday after- noon" - and she did.

Lily, Alfie's sister, called her brother a scamp: but I have heard other adjectives used to describe him! Yet he was a likeable person, and often did acts of kindness for the poor. Lily and Alfie Martin had a sister Muriel who had her tonsils removed. The operation went wrong and she lost her sight and her sense of speech and hearing. The poor girl died when aged 19 years. Their father, Jack 'Pincher' Martin, had been a crewman on the royal yacht Britannia, and there is a photograph of him aboard the royal yacht standing alongside King George V11.

John and Jean lived in the "Red Tap" until 1953 when they had "High Windmill" built at the top of the hill known as Bay View Road, where John still lives.

The Story of the Coal Bunker
(A light-hearted tale with which to end this chapter in WW2 history)

During the early part of 1950, the cottage, known as the "Red Tap," having nowhere to store coal, John Grimer built a small bunker on the front of the cottage. After building the bunker (a wooden box with a sloping hinged lid, the whole no bigger than a modest dog kennel), the council complete with the new planning regulations descended on him like a ton of coal !

In a long battle in the press John quoted names of important locals who had also built before permission was granted. Eventually he was allowed to keep the bunker. Sadly, in these days of central and electric heating the bunker is no more, and the incident is now long forgotten, recriminations versus a carefully composed, but light hearted banter,

John's letter appeared in the Press dated 27th.May 1950.

"Sir, - With reference to my letter. . . and the report of the Looe Urban Council's discussion of it, may I make five points?

1. Mr.F.Clarke admits that he did not obtain planning permission (page 5, column 1, line 36). Further, I did not suggest that Mr.Clarke's garden and extra step were not on his own property.

2. Mr.H.P.Stokes "anticipated permission," which, may I suggest, is so close to obtaining permission in retrospect as to be the same thing (page 5, column 1, line 149).

3. Mr.F.Curtis has not, perhaps, read my letter too carefully, seems to be owed an apology. The public right-of-way is no longer blocked, since the Council (i.e. the ratepayers) has now built a footpath around the shed at West Quarries (page 5, column 1, line 91). (I hasten to add that I have no desire that the ratepayers should defray the cost of my coal bunker. All I wish is that it may be left standing, since it improves the appearance of North-road).

4. The Chairman of the Council said that I had written to the Press without waiting for the Council to consider the matter (page 5, column 1, line 55). I should like to point out that the Council did have the opportunity of considering the matter before it appeared in the Press. The Clerk of the Council received my letter on Saturday, 15th of April, with a request that it should be discussed at the Council meeting on Monday, 17th of April. At that meeting, the Chairman said he did not consider the Council should be "stampeded" into discussing the matter (page 6, column 4, line31), although I had informed the Council that copies of the letter had been sent to the Press. The first Press account of my letter appeared on Tuesday, 18th of April. After carefully checking my facts, I find that on average, Mondays preceeded Tuesdays - even in Looe.

5. With regard to the Chairman's remark that it was "a poor show" if one cannot build on one's own ground (page 5, column 1, line 58) I heartily agree. However, I have recently ascertained that that is just what one cannot do nowadays - without planning permission.

In my original letter, I merely pleaded that I had acted in ignorance, and that I should be the first to plead guilty if I had done wrong. After all, it appears that the intricacies of the regulations in the Town and Country Planning Act are such, that even the Authorities are not over-familiar with them.

Finally, I had taken pains to state that all the instances of work done were for the benefit of Looe, and never suggested that the shed at West Quarries was an eyesore, and that it should be torn down. I was thus much surprised at the manner in which the Council discussed my letter, the main object of which was to plead that my case should be given reasonable consideration.

J.A.Grimer, No.2 North-road, West Looe, Cornwall. April 25th, 1950."

Alfie & Alma Martin *née* Stapelton, & her sister Hetty. Next door live John & Jean Grimer, his Austin 7 car can just be seen.   © J.Southern Collection.

and the Hill's

Catherine Hill was the youngest of four daughters, being the issue of John Hill and Catherine "Carrie" who farmed Liscawn at Crafthole, a village within the parish of Sheviock on the SE Cornish coast between Downderry and the Rame Head. The four daughters were Dolly, Molly, Barabara, known as "Aunty Babs" and another who died young with TB. : but they had no son to carry on the farm. Carrie, Molly, Dolly, 'Aunty' Babs who lived in Downderry. Carrie was the only one who left home. Today, the noble old farmhouse known as Liscawn is an inn. The Hill family graves can be seen in the churchyard at St.Mary's parish church, Sheviock.

1891 Census : Liscawn Farm - Simon Hill (b.1824) of Sheviock, farmer aged 67 years & Emma *née* Giles (b.1834) of Devon, & their issue - John Giles Hill (b.1859) farmers son. Clara Hill (b.1860) daughter-in-law, Charles Hill (born 1876), farmers son. Grace Vigurs, a domestic servant and Mary Cook a grand daughter who was staying in the farmhouse.

Dolly Hill, of rather plump proportions, married "Uncle Channings who worked as Capt. of Torpoint Ferry, while she ran the post-office at Crafthole He loved to spent his free time in his shed at the bottom of his garden where he could gaze out over the sea while he smoked his pipe : a habit he was not allowed to enjoy indoors.

"Aunty" Babs married Albert Bersey, a traveller for K.G.Foster who bought beef, livestock on the hoof, for the meat market. They had no children. The Bersey's were farmers and butchers at Crafthole. Other Berseys included William Bersey head gamekeeper for the earl of St. Germans. Wesley Copplestone Bersey who farmed Minards. Others farmed at Trerulefoot, while Albert W.Bersey lived "up the hill at Downderry."

Molly Hill married Arnold (whose surname is now forgotten), but he died aged 84 years while starting his car by cranking the starting handle.

The Loretto's

For convenience I will begin my rather brief version of the Loretto family story with Jean's grandfather, Henry. The family name is said to originate from Our Lady of Loretto; the Holy House in Loretto where Mary was the Protectress of Rome. Henry came from co.Sligo in Northern Ireland and was a pianist of some repute who had helped to establish the co.Sligo fiech festival. He also taught piano and frequently gave piano recitals, as well as playing in string ensembles should a piano be required. He presented a Silver Cup (the Loretto Cup) for the winner of some piano competition, and it happened that Jeans' daughter Frances entered the competition and won, so her name can be seen inscribed on her grandfathers cup.

His father or grandfather, an Italian, had been a pianist who taught music. A further Loretto was a violinist who lived at Peacehaven in Sussex, a town where the Meridian Monument stands on the actual Greenwich Meridian line. Jean's father again was an Irishman, Carlo Claude Loretto who married Catherine Hill, a Cornish girl and farmers daughter in Sheviock parish.

During WW1 there were many troops stationed at Tregantle Fort (in a neighbouring parish to Sheviock), and one of them was Carlo Claude Loretto. He and Carrie met up and eventually they married. But six of their children were born out of wedlock, Alec being the last born before the couple married. Lots of eyebrows were raised at the time because of the amount of children they had Eventually this family lived in Ware in Hertfordshire. From there they moved to Caterham in Surrey - about nine miles south from Croydon. The youngest five were born at Ware, the remainder born at Redhill, again in Surrey. So Alec was born in Redhill, as were the four younger ones. It might be that growing up in wartime England was very restrictive, one could not get petrol to travel, the whole country was literally under siege. So in 1945 when war ended, these ten children left England very quickly. John went to Rhodesia, Min went to New Zealand, Eileen (who became an academic in biology and botany), Tony, who later in their life went to New Zealand. Alec eventually settled in New Zealand, another went to Australia for two years and then returned. David eventually went to New York, Michael is a professor at Birmingham University, Maureen became a nurse, and then, with Richard went to Canada where he enrolled in the Canadian Air Force, and later became an air line pilot.

Jean Caroline Loretto was born on the 4th.day of December 1918 at Hanley Castle in Worcestershire, a small town with a 17th-cent. brick built church. The family called her "Carrie" after her mother, a pet-name she hated, so she always used her first name, Jean. Jean was the eldest of a family of ten children. Between Jean (b.1918), the first born, and Richard, the last, was a twenty year period. So Richard and Jean never knew each other in the same way as children of a closer age when brought up together..

Top row - John, Jean, Walter, Eileen. Middle row - Michael, Carlo Claude Loretto, Min holding Richard, Carrie Loretto née Hill, Alec. Bottom row - David & Maureen.

The first of the children to die was Walter who served in Merchant Navy during the war, married late in life, and settled in Vancouver. Jean was the second, she died in August 2005, then Min who died in September 2007, and was buried at Bideford. Alec flew over from New Zealand to attend her funeral.

But the children proved to be a successful at their respective occupations, and all, except Jean, emigrated to other countries.

Alec Loretto wished to follow a career as a musician and so learned to play the clarinet, studying the instrument at London University for three years. But wanting to venture into the pre-Mozart musical repertoire (pre-clarinet days indeed !), he had to settle for the nearest equivalent instrument; the recorder. But after playing all available recorders from known manufacturers he found qualities within each of those instruments which failed to satisfy his discerning mind. The outcome, after failing in his search to find a perfect recorder, was to set up in business and make such instruments.

Carlo's sister was Nita Loretto, a cellist who played with a string quartet, and often her brother would play the piano if a piano quintet was to be performed. John and Jean went to see her when she was dying near London. Her brother inherited the contents of her will, which included her treasured cello. During WW1 he served in the newly formed Royal Flying Corps (the forerunner of the RAF which was formed in 1921), where he achieved the rank of a lieutenant.

But Carlo moved to Caterham in Surrey where he worked as a school teacher at New Maldon, as well as in other schools. Although he brought up his ten children in a strict manner, and being agnostic, he refused to allow them any religious education when at school. He was also a sadist and subjected his family to acts of cruelty, hard beatings were often regularly given. Yet he was not lax in subjecting them to an upbringing of culture by putting each of them to play a musical instrument, taking them to plays and concerts of classical music, as well as taking them from Caterham to Brighton on bicycles; camping along the way. He acted as a complete martinet with his wife, yet those who knew him, especially those who had been his pupils, spoke kindly of him, showing much respect for him, and telling of his great love for poetry and music.

When asked why he had served in the Royal Flying Corps during WW1, his answer was very practical "Would you be wanting to be up to your knees in mud in the trenches of France?"

When Carrie became pregnant with her eleventh child her doctor found her child to be deformed and so her pregnancy was terminated. The situation in the household had by then reached a point when something rather drastic needed to be done in order for them to live a more settled and normal life. The older children got together and demanded of their mother to divorce her husband - and eventually she did.

This rather unprecedented request brought to my mind an occasion when John was telling me about a wedding he once attended, when a young girl in the congregation asked her grandad had he ever thought of divorcing his own wife? His reply was "divorce never, murder often!"

After the divorce Carlo remarried - but died in his seventies.

Jean Loretto was brought up at Caterham Valley in Surrey, living at No.20 Markville Gardens. She obtained a scholarship for Whyteleaf Grammar School for girls, and then went on to King's College London University where in 1940 she obtained an upper second degree in geography and geology. During the war the London Institute of Education had been evacuated to Nottingham University, where Jean completed her Teaching Diploma. Her best friend at Caterham was Joyce Hall who published art books.

In the summer vacation of 1940 Jean joined the Womans Land Army (W.L.A.) and was sent down by the Forestry Commission to Lustleigh parish, in Devonshire, on the south side of Dartmoor. Jean, accompanied by a W.L.A friend, had the job of measuring the thickness of small trees in coppice woods, marking those suitable for cutting to make into pit-props for the mining industry, which was rapidly being geared up for the war effort.

For some time Jean worked as a teacher at Great Tree school in the parish of St.Martin by Looe. There the headmaster was Mr.Keast, with whom she never got on with, and disliked him both as a man and as a teacher. Mrs Keast did the cooking to provide the lunchtime meal for the staff as well as the children. Jean said how "Mrs. Keast was a treasure, and I shall always remember her as the provider of the finest meals I have ever experienced."

John, Frances & Jean   © John Grimer

Jean and her grand daughter Ishani.

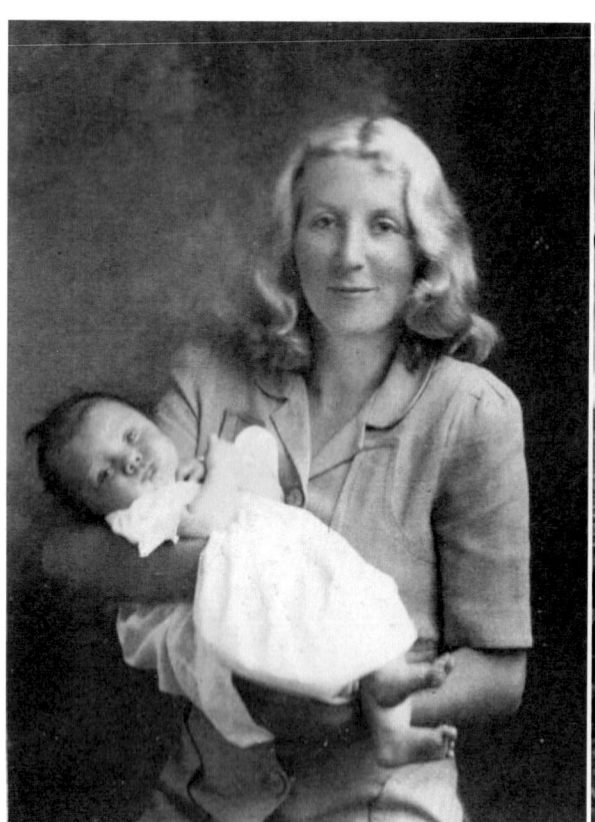

Jean & Frances 1944

"Frances & friend" The shed cum stable was where Major Ross kept horses. Margot Fonteyn often collected a horse from the shed when she went holiday riding, usually with a different male companion each time she came

John and Jean's Wedding at Liskeard

F.O.Grimer had several 48 hour passes, which meant he could usually travel down to Cornwall by train on weekends to see his adorable fair maid who occupied the very essence of his mind : so it wasn't long before they decided they had better get married. He had called around to the school where she worked and managed to obtain a brief meeting with the head master, Mr. Travers. After he introduced himself, he said to the headmaster, "Sir, I have come to ask you if I may marry one of your mistresses ?" Mr.Travers kept a straight face while he went to fetch Miss Loretto into his study, but he first went into the teachers rest-room where many of his staff were having some lunch, and told them how a young man in RAF uniform wanted to marry one of his mistresses, and immediately burst into laughter ; as did the remainder of the gathering !

Their wedding day at Liskeard.

They married on Friday the 15th.day of October, 1943 in Greenbank Chapel, Liskeard, the service of Holy matrimony provided by the Revd.Mr.Clifford Buckroyd. As the happy couple left the church they found to their very great surprise all of Jean's pupils crowded outside waving, clapping, and cheering. Mr.Travers had allowed them to leave class and to make their way down to the church "in a quiet and orderly manner." As the couple stood for someone to take a photograph; John dressed in his uniform, a black American GI stopped to look at the joyous occasion and shook the hand of F/O.Grimer, saying "I wish you bags of joy boy !"

John had to borrow a few pounds from Rob Willcocks so as he could buy a cheap wedding ring in Liskeard. That ring did service for fifty years before he bought her an expensive wedding ring to celebrate their golden wedding anniversary.

There was no honeymoon, only a long train journey back to camp where he found his name on orders to report to the CO., for which he received a months extra duties for marrying without the CO's permission, and signature to do so.

It was at this point that I asked John how his mother took the news of him marrying a woman who was not of Roman Catholic persuasion, but an agnostic. Had he fore warned her of his intention, and who of his family attended to wedding ? John replied that only two people were in attendance at the ceremony, one was Mrs.Bersey, Jean's aunt, and the other was the black American GI referred to above. (Mrs Berseys' husband was a frequent shooting companion with the earl of St.Germans over the Port Elliot estate. The Berseys had no issue).

Regarding my second question - it was six months after the wedding before John told his mother he had married. John replied that he and Jean had travelled up to London and called to see his mother. He knew what her reaction would be and he dreaded the confrontation; but it had to be done. Maria answered the door. Neither John nor Jean would go inside but remained standing on her doorstep. It was then that John told her they had married - six months ago! Mother was silent, speechless with shock, but her words were cruel, cutting. "If I had been informed that you were missing, shot down over enemy territory and feared dead, such news would not have hurt me as much as hearing what you have just told me, that you have taken a wife outside the bounds of the Roman Catholic church."

After John was shot down over France and taken POW, Jean moved to London where she stayed with family and friends. She gave birth to her daughter Frances, in the basement of Charing Cross hospital on the 27th.June,1944, at the height of the V1 rocket attacks on the capital. Yet her mother-in-law was kindness itself, she helped Jean and her baby all she could, in fact she could not have done more. Those dreadful words she had uttered soon proved to be a prime example of 'the biter-bit,' (or the biter being bit?) the double-edged sword which had struck back at her after she heard that her son had been shot down over France and was feared dead.

In very old age Maria entered into a residential home for the elderly. The home was Visitation Convent with its own hospital wing and was part of the Convent at East Finchley. John often visited her and when she was able they would walk together in the spacious grounds. The garden featured a grotto where a statue of Our Lady cut from Cararra marble stood, and Maria would stand and recite the Magnificat in latin, and then kneel to pray. "I'm so happy, I'm so happy," she would repeatedly say. But John did recall how he had once opened a door inside Visitation and entered a room by mistake. He had heard many voices from inside which suggested a party was in session. But in that room he found a number of retired priests smoking, drinking whiskey and Guinness, as they watched horse racing on a television set. They were having a grand time loudly urging the contestant of their choice to be the first past the winning post.

Maria spent twelve years in the home. When she was aged 98 years she fell and broke her hip. The following year she broke her other hip. But her general health was excellent, no doubt helped by having a bottle of Guinness every day !

When John was liberated from POW hospital in September of that year the family moved back to Cornwall - where Jean began teaching again when her child was old enough.

Throughout her teaching life Jean taught in a wide range of schools, infant, junior, secondary modern, grammar and comprehensive - all in East Cornwall. In 1941 Jean obtained a post at Liskeard Grammar School in which she remained until shortly after her marriage. In 1966 she was offered the post of Senior Mistress at Bodmin Grammar School, but withdrew from this appointment in order to have a year's sabbatical at Dartington Hall, which she thoroughly enjoyed.

Perhaps her happiest time teaching were the eight years she spent at Pelynt Primary, followed by five years at Fowey Grammar School. She retired from teaching in 1983 at the age of 65 years.

School - Thirty years

The chapter in the life of John Grimer when he taught at Looe Comprehensive School should be written by a more capable writer than myself. It is a subject that should be written which undoubtedly would prove to be a worthy addition to the bibliography of books about Looe. Consequently I will only put together a very potted account, and then by using articles about the school written by ex-pupils. Subsequently, because of John Grimer's age the need to go to press now is prudent!.

John's first teaching job was at Saltash. He worked there for only one term teaching ages from seven until eleven. The headmaster was Mr Bidgood. John could remember nothing regarding his term there except that the headmaster had a very pretty daughter!

For one term only he became supply teacher at Four Lanes End School by Millbrook. To get there he took a Western National Bus to Higher Tregantle (where he kept his bicycle in a barn); henceforth he cycled along that narrow and twisting road to Four Lanes End. The school stood on a hill which then took the traveller on to Cremyll where the road ended. If it rained he wore a cycling cape, but when the wind blew hard he very quickly became soaked through.

He taught in a temporary capacity for one term at Callington Grammar School under Dr.Kent the headmaster. He took digs at Kelly Bray with an elderly couple. He found both school and headmaster a delight and loved his time there. He taught children English and French from the age of eleven.

He began teaching at Menheniot School in 1950 under Mr.Rundle, the headmaster, where he taught a class of some thirty kids, aged from seven to eleven years, for two years. He cycled from Looe to Menheniot every day and eventually learned to recognise many of our wild flowers he found growing in the hedgebanks of the lanes he followed. John claims that his success at that school was due to William Appleby's wireless show "Singing Together" after which he read them stories by Enid Blyton. It was while he was at Menheniot that he began building and using his Puppet Theatre, and got the children making the puppets.

He began teaching at Polperro School in 1952, and stayed there until 1957 when the newly built school at Looe was completed.

At Polperro the school kept a small menagerie with an aviary at the rear together with many hives of bees. The Cornwall County bee-keeper was Squadron Leader Harrison, who would visit the school to give talks on bees. He told John that the Rosebay Willow Herb was the best plant for bees to visit because it produces the finest honey. Harrison claimed that the willow herb filled "the June gap."

He developed his puppet theatre until it came to the notice of others in the teaching profession, until eventually he put on shows at Truro. One of his pupils was Brian Howells, who was a dwarf; yet his sister was normal. But John gave Brian a role to play in the puppet theatre, he stood him on the table where he portrayed the giant in Jack and the Beanstalk!

Back row - Fernley Boxall. Clive Puckey. Richard Hicks. Godfrey Bryant. David Palmer David King. Middle row - Ivor Skentlebery. Barry Ginster. Daphne Nettlinghame. Doreen Trengrove. Elizabeth Roose. Marilyn Pope. David Puckey. Front row - Anthony Joslin. Brenda Penter. Brenda Rowe. Shirley Nettlinghame. Jenifer Palmer. David Johns. Two in front - Adrian Peneter. Peter Gerry.

Back row - David Kelly. David Palmer. Fernley Boxall. Anthony Joslin. ? Keith Hoare. Peter Libby. Colin Beal. Middle row - Heather Julian. Janet Fisher. Colin Joslin. Michael Harvey. Roslind Ritchie. Margaret George. Mary? Ritch. Front row - Brenda Rowe. Peter Gerry. Robin Puckey. Neil Libby. Christopher Curtis. Terry Buckley. John Blatchford. Noreen Langmaid.

Looe Comphrehensive School.
A few familiar faces of the pupils are Duncan Bond, Sharron Williams,
Mandy Webb, Julie Marks, Susan Johnson & Andrew Bone.

NOAH
Produced in March 1961

Written in 1929 and first produced in England in 1934 with John Gielgud as Noah. It has since been performed on all the principal stages in Europe but remains in essence a play which depends largely on mime and simplicity.

Its cast in order of appearance :-

Noah, Peter Pascoe	Tiger, Stuart Raddy
Bear, Duncan Bartlett	Japheth, Raymond Blannin
Lion, Roger Little	Shem, Peter Cripps
Monkey Barbara Bentley	Ham, Kenneth Jay
Elephant, Linda Rowe &	Mamma, Pauline Richards
Christina Dignam	Ada, Wendy Holten
Cow, Jean Ramsey &	Sella, Jennifer Cripps
Judith McKinley	Naomi, Rosemary Hendry
Lamb, Anita Moore	Man, Raymond Reynolds
Giraffe, Marion Passmore	Savages, M.Benny, T.Raddy, P.Bewshea,
& Sylvia Pengelly	M.Wojcik, W.Gibson, D.Wilcox.

LOOE COUNTY SECONDARY SCHOOL
DRAMA CLUB

NOAH by André Obey

WEDNESDAY & THURSDAY
MARCH 22nd & 23rd. at 7.30 p.m.

ADMISSION 2/6d.
CHILDREN 1/-

THE RIVALS, Sheridan
Produced in December 1963.

Set in Bath in about 1775. The entire action of the play takes place one afternoon and evening. Its cast:-

Sir Anthony Absolute	Neil Jennings
Captain Jack Absolute	Raymond Blannin
Falkland	Jeremy Bonner
Acres	John Pengelly
Sir Lucius O'Trigger	Paul Weldon
Fag	Andrew Symons
David	Robert Hocking
Thomas	Roger Little
Boy	Peter Barton
Mrs Malaprop	Marilyn Pearn
Lydia Languish	Cherry Dann
Julia	Julie Pearn
Lucy	Barbara Bentley.

Promp - Judith McKinley. Lighting - Roger Little. Wardrobe Mistress - Anita Moore. Stage Manager - Andrew Slee. Make Up - Miss Phillips & Mr Owen. Producer - Mr Grimer.

Marion Pearn was strong minded, a lovely actress. Colin Bussell was a good performer in Androleas and the Lion. Peter Pasco was my leading actor followed by Petroc Dan. The school had a Chess Club, and Justin Webb once beat John at the game. Rita Tushingham's daughter came to Looe Comprehensive School.

During September 1957 the newly built Secondary School at Sunrising, East Looe, opened its doors. Consequently some out-lying schools, Pelynt, Lanreath and Duloe, closed with their pupils being daily bussed into the new school, while Mr.Raymond Dan from West Looe school, and Mr. John Grimer from Polperro school also moved into the new building bringing all their "livestock" with them!

Mr.Grimer recalled the occasion -

"In September 1957, after five years happy teaching at Polperro all age Primary School, I was transferred, together with the secondary age pupils to the great new Secondary Modern School in Looe. We gazed in awe at the gleaming corridors, the great assembly hall, and at the shiny new desks and Venetian blinds in the classrooms. At break time the lads and lasses from Pelynt, Polperro and Looe mingled together en masse for the first time. It was all very peaceful - unlike erstwhile meetings of some of these youngsters at venues such as "Barcelona !" "

"The pupils were rapidly put into streams and I, perhaps being the least qualified of the staff, possessing only a one year post-war emergency teaching certificate, was put in charge of the "C" stream. I was allocated the library. This was a magnificent room - chairs, tables, highly varnished shelves and cupboards - and not a single book ! After an appeal to children and parents we soon accumulated an assorted collection of several hundred books and a dedicated team of older girls, classified - card indexed - and issued borrowers' tickets for these. I remember those lasses with much affection."

"And so the next thirty years slipped away. In time I became Head of the English Department, Deputy Head, and for one memorable term Acting Head. I had always resented the 11+ and selection: the stark contrast between 280 pupils and twelve non-graduate teachers at Looe, and the 150 pupils with thirteen all graduate staff at Fowey Grammar School where my wife taught. Further there existed no school leaving qualification for Secondary Modern pupils at that time. Because of this I entered those who wished, in the 1960's, for the College of Preceptors examination - and many left school with a worthwhile certificate. Perhaps the work I enjoyed most with young people was the production of plays during the twelve years from '59 to '71. Many of these students were very gifted and several went on to become professional actors - a tradition that has continued at the school to this day."

"Over the years the school has grown and flourished, become comprehensive - with special Arts status."

"Superb extra buildings have sprung up - a Sports Hall, Science labs, a Performing Arts centre - an extra classrooms extension to replace the leaking prefab huts, introduced when pupil numbers grew. My only sadness was the demise of our swimming pool built with our own money raising and actual manual efforts, in the 1960's - and the scene of many enjoyable inter house swimming galas in the last week of the summer term."

"Now 86 years old I look back on my years at Looe School with great pleasure - years that gave me, a post war "foreigner," the opportunity to come to know and to love the people of Looe."

LOOE COMMUNITY SCHOOL CELEBRATES 50 YEARS (1957 - 2007).
by John Grimer.

Husband of the Year

"The Sunday Independant's "Husband of the Year" competition was won by 51 year old Cornish schoolmaster John Grimer. He wins a prize of £50 as the top West Country spouse. . . "

"John Grimers reaction to being told he was the West Country's Husband of the Year was to turn to his wife and tell her "Your a terrible fraud. We've had more rows than you've cooked dinners." Out of scores of entries for the competition Jean's letter caught the imagination of the judges for its mixture of humour and deep affection and respect.

Now John - "I've got to face all those jeering kids at Looe County Secondary School" - collects the prize of £50, and goes on to compete in the national contest.

Jean [says] "Our marriage got off to a terrible start and later after the ceremony at Liskeard our honeymoon lasted only 72 hours before my husband (a young RAF officer) had to return to his unit. A few months later he was shot down and taken prisoner. Our baby was born while he was in captivity and when he was repatriated be weighed just over six stone and was lucky to be alive."

"He is now a well-loved and respected teacher, having taken the Emergency Teacher's Training Course after the war, and can turn his hand to practically anything in school and at home. He is head of the English department and has produced plays, and made the scenery. He teaches French, had helped to introduce driving lessons, has a large hut-cum-garage in the grounds, has helped umpteen kids pass GCE's and O-levels, and been their friend and counsellor for years."

" Do we have rows and arguments ? Let me tell you we have them at storm proportions and things have flown about more than once. But like most people we have weathered them over the years and come through smiling. . . "

"The one thing that worries me is what some of my pupils are going to say. They're going to have a field day at my expense when they read about this."

What follows is not simply a tribute to Mr.Grimer from one of his pupils, but one of his pupils supporting his old school, now titled Looe Community School, which was endeavouring to put together plans to be considered a specialist school for the performing arts.

The tribute itself was written in March 2001 by John Garvin, once a pupil at Looe Comprehensive School, and who went on to become a professional actor.

It is with his kind permission that I include his untitled tribute.

"The year was 1983.

It was raining and the classroom was thick with the smell of school dinners.

Wet coats and scarves lay stretched across the radiators, slowly steaming up the windows and allowing us to write our names in the condensation. The window frame was buffeted by each blast of rain that hit it and we sat behind our desks praying for four o'clock to come quickly. I was thirteen years old and it was the first day of a new term at Looe Comprehensive School. It was afternoon's double English lesson. To make matters worst, our new English teacher was the infamous Mr.Grimer, one of the longest-standing staff members and without doubt the most feared and strict teacher of the school.

"Who have you got for English this year?" Students in the year above would ask. "Mr.Grimer." Their eyes would immediately radiate pity. "Old Grim himself... best of luck to you."

We heard Mr.Grimer long before he entered the classroom. Some poor unfortunate was late for his history lesson further down the corridor. "Walk. Don't run boy ! Can't you see the floor is slippery ?" "Sorry Sir" "You ! Stop running !"

The classroom door actually shook and the windows rattled to his shout. He was in a bad mood. The class glanced at each other nervously. The door burst open and there he stood, peering over a large pile of old and faded books, the spines either missing or torn. "Well don't just sit there staring... somebody start handing these out at once !"

Three students closest to him all jumped up at once and soon, in front of each of us was a battered old copy of the play Androcles and the Lion, by George Bernard Shaw. I particularly remember my copy because on its front cover was a badly drawn cartoon of a gruesome ogre with glasses. The words "Mr.Grim" were scrawled underneath. Immediately I was nervous that I would be mistaken as the artist. I quickly swapped my copy with the boy who sat next to me when he wasn't looking. I opened the front cover. It was the first play I had ever seen. And it was to change my life forever.

"Right !" shouted Grimer. "Everybody off their seats and stack all the tables and chairs in that corner, quick as you can." This was unexpected. We had all been bracing ourselves for two hours of unrelenting torment and boredom. Now here we were being instructed to dismantle a classroom. "I'm going to play the lead villain in this piece" announced Mr.Grimer with a glint in his eye. "The rest of you I'll give roles to as we go along."

And there we were. Twenty teenagers looking on in a combination of disbelief and awe as this ferocious old man transported us through time and space for the next two hours. We were no longer in a stuffy classroom with the rain pouring down the windows. We were in the glorious Roman Coliseum, bathed by sunlight and the roar of the spectators. We were Centurions glorious in victory, eagerly awaiting the Mighty Emperor (Mr. Grimer) to give the thumbs up or down as to whether our fellow classmates should live or die by the sword (improvised classroom rulers were used as props).

One of the class was chosen to play the part of the lion. Mr.Grimer (quite deliberately) mis-casts the quietest, most timid girl in the class, who mewed feebly when the script demanded a roar. Giggles of the other students were silenced instantly by a glare from Mr. Grimer.

"Hmm. And what exactly was that supposed to be girl ?" "A lions roar Mr.Grimer Sir." The girl blushed nervously. "I've heard mice roar more ferociously. You can do better than that girl."

As means of demonstration he proceeded to roar with such an intensity of volume that all our friends from classrooms the other side of the school asked after school : "blimey... who got done by Grim ?"

Encouraged by this, the girl cast as the lion screeched out a loud roar, which sounded like nails running down a blackboard. It was really truly excruciating and had us all clamping our hands over our ears. The door suddenly jerked open as the Headmaster himself peered in, curious as to what all the noise was about. Another staff member had tipped him off that our class was running riot, unsupervised. He was just about to start bellowing at the screaming, roaring girl when he noticed Mr.Grimer, still on all fours, perched upon his desk impersonating a lion. With a look of utter confusion he said nothing and quietly closed the door behind him. We applauded the girl's efforts unreservedly and she grinned sheepishly at us all, proud of the fact that she had scared away the Headmaster himself.

The play continued.

My best memory of the afternoon relates to a single moment where the character I was playing had to slap the face of a captured slave. By this point we were all swapping parts so often we had lost track of who was who. I realised with horror, four pages before the event, that it would be Mr.Grimer himself that would be on the receiving end of my violent act. The four pages crawled closer and closer until there I was, confronted face to face with the most feared teacher in the school, with a stage direction issuing the following instructions : "The slave is slapped violently across the face. . . and after turning the other cheek is slapped even harder."

The script is quite specific. You could have heard a pin drop. "Well, what are you waiting for boy ?" "Nothing sir. . . am I really to do this ?" "What's it say in the script boy ?" "That you get hit Sir." "Then go ahead. . . ." Before the words were out of his mouth I slapped him. Hard. There was a sharp gasp off all the class. Then there was a silence in which you could hear a pin drop. Slowly Mr. Grimer turned his face back to me with a red, hand-shaped welt against his check. His glasses were hanging off his ears. His eyes glowered menace.""Call that a slap boy. . . My auntie could do better. Try again." As the script dictated he slowly turned his face and offered the other cheek.

"Go on. . . hit him !" A voice from the crowd. "Slap him senseless !" The class was on it now. . . the encouragement building to crescendo. "Whack him !"

"Go on my Son !" "Do it !"

I slapped him hard around the face and watched in dismay as he careered across the floor, fell over a table and landed in an undignified heap under the blackboard. The classroom erupted with cheers and applause and banging of tables and chairs. I was elated. "By God that's a fair right hook you have on you boy no mistake." Mr.Grimer pulled himself back on his feet and winked surreptitiously to me. "I'd hate to end up in a real fight with you and no mistake. No need to re-do that particular scene I think. . . Let's move on."

Two weeks previously I'd been ready to leave school because my life was being made a misery by a couple of guys who'd decided to start bullying me. From that moment on all that was to change. I was the guy who floored Grimer. I was untouchable.

I always suspected that Mr.Grimer knew I was having a hard time with bullying and cast the play so I could belt him one. It was the first time I realised that drama works on many levels. It can transport us to different places and more importantly, it allows us to become different people.

The following year I was delighted to be asked to take part in the School Play. I could not believe my luck when Mrs.Rennie, Mrs.Lord and Mr.Webb asked me to play the lead in "The Mouse and His Child." For the first time in my life I knew what I wanted to do.

In all the years that followed as a professional actor I was often asked the question "To what do you owe your success ?" My answer has always been the same. "I was lucky" I reply. "I've always known exactly what I wanted to do ever since I was thirteen." As a professional actor I would always, before every opening night, venture out into the centre of the stage and look into the empty auditorium. It was a routine I had developed to help combat the first-night nerves and I must have practised it in every theatre up and down the country. During those moments I would quietly take myself back to the start of my journey in Mr.Grimer's class and remind myself that its all the same thing. I just get paid for it now. One of my proudest moments of my life was when the teachers from Looe School came to see the show I was in at Plymouth Theatre Royal. It was a way of me saying thank-you to them. . .

John Garvin

Ettie Sweet served the school dinners, she was the wife of Jack Sweet the school gardener, with Mr Husk who taught gardening.

The pupils never wanted custard with our pudding or fruit pie, because Ettie served it by pouring it onto our plate from a jug, and the drips remaining on the spout of the jug after each pouring she would remove with a finger and then lick her finger clean. She would do this after every application. During WW2 Ettie packed parachutes at Sheffield for the bomber crews.

"Mrs Jean Grimer was to change my life. I know this was a long time ago. . ."

"Looking back reminds me how hard the teachers tried to educate me, when all I wanted to do was play football, go rowing and have a good time with my friends. Every day started the same: up, run down the hill to LePoidevin's newsagents to deliver papers to Station Road, Sandplace Road and up Shutta towards the school."

"My first term at school was probably the most important of my life. Mrs Grimer somehow inspired me to believe that I could learn if I tried. Although no longer with us, to me she is responsible for who I am and what I achieved in my life. Her husband, Me John Grimer, was later to pass his love for books to me and I still relax with a good book, the way he read Wind in the Willows, changing his voice for each character was pure theatre."

"During my time at the school I remember the teachers Mr Austin, Mr Evens, Mrs Dan, Mrs Bassett and Mr Dan (he died whilst our form teacher) who told great stories about the Second World War. They all did their best but Mrs Bassett could never get me to sing in tune and I still can't."

"Rugby was important to Mr Austin and although not the best team we did try. Playing Liskeard on the pitch right in front of their school was always memorable, this game was something to look forward to and winning was all that mattered."

"School is a time for so many first time experiences, many of them too personal to write about but my first love was always special. . ."

"To all those who are returning to Looe for the first time in many years, yes it's changed but so have we and this school made us what we are and be thankful for that." Armand Toms.

Several other articles were also contributed to make up the booklet, but as time is not on my side it is unfortunate I cannot use any more of them.

~~~~~~~~~~~~~~~~~~~~~~~~~~~

It is often said that young men who volunteered into the RAF had only one desire : to fly Spitfires ! No one wanted simply to be a member of a crew aboard a large bomber; except as a pilot. Yet for every large bomber the crew consisted of seven members :- pilot, navigator, wireless operator, engineer, bomb-aimer, mid upper-gunner, and tail-gunner in Halifaxes. The bomb-aimer also covered as co.pilot. No crew member really liked to admit to being a bomb-aimer, especially after the formation of Bomber Command, and the retaliatory bombing of enemy cities and civilians, so as the bomb-aimer was usually the co-pilot, they would identify themselves as being the latter.

Among the operational duties over enemy country was dropping, or planting mines in river estuaries and the approaches to the more important ports. This was colloquially known as "gardening trips," planting mines.

Bomb-aiming improved with the fitting of the Mk.14 bomb-sight, which was quite a sophisticated device.

The traditional PPI (Plan Position Indicator) radar we know of today came about with the development of centimetric radar through the klystron and magnatron. This was still in development during mid-1942, and didn't see operational service until late 1942 / early 1943 (IIRC). This system was known in the RAF as the H2S radar, and could be used for navigation. They were fitted initially to Bomber Command Halifaxes, Stirlings, and Lancasters, and to Coastal Command Wellingtons. He never used an H2S set which was operated by the navigator assisted by a former bomb aimer. But they did have GEE. "A navigational aid. Three widely separated radio stations transmitted a train of synchronised pulses, in a set order, from which a decoder in the aircraft could calculate the time differences between the two other beams, and the central master. From these time differences was calculated the distances of the aircraft from each slave and the master. A point where each constantly moving line crossed the other gave the position of the aircraft. The navigator, by reference of a GEE map, could obtain a reasonably accurate fix while at a maximum distance of 400 miles. The accuracy of the system improved at a shorter range."

NO TIME FOR FEAR, **Victor F.Gammon, 1998, p.80.**

No.77 Squadron Halifax S - Sugar

"Serial No.LK710 - Manufacturer : Fairey Aviation Co.Ltd., - Contract No.: ACFT / 891, - Reg No.HA1 / E11 / 41, - Delivery : Batch LK680 to LK711 delivered between 11/10/43 & 20/11/43, - Order Qty : 96B / Met Mk.V's, - First Unit : 77 Sqn."

"Sqn : 77 sqn Unit Codes : KN-S - Base : Elvington - Date : 23/04/1944 - Target : Laon - Time Up : 22:20hrs."

"Details : Left base without incident, to attack rail yards at Laon, France. Aircraft was shot down from height of 7000ft. by enemy night fighter (Ju88 ?),[later alleged to be an Me110] which raked the Halifax from aft to fore and from directly below (probably Schrage Musik ?) as no one on board saw it ! S-Sugar crashed approx 5km S.W of its target of Laon. Sqn Ldr Bond was sadly killed and is buried in Clinchy New Communal Cemetery, remainder of crew baled out, one was subsequently captured & taken POW, the remainder evaded capture." [incorrect].

www.57rescue.org

Operations Log of Squadron Leader K.E.P.Bond, & his aircrew whilst serving with R.A.F. No.77 Squadron.
Compiled by Roy Walker.

"Roy Walker, is the author of "Some of the many" - 77 Squadron (1939 - 1945) and of "77 Squadron - Honours and Awards - 1939 - 1945." On my [?]. behalf he very kindly carried out some research at the Public Record Office from which he compiled the following account of the bombing operations flown by Squadron Leader K.F.P.Bond, RAF and his crew during the period between 4th.October 1943 and 22nd.April 1944."

<u>4 / 5th. October 43</u>   <u>JD461-0</u>   FRANKFURT   <u>T/o 1742</u>   <u>Down 0127</u>

Route: Base - Beachy Head - 50.20N 01.35E - 49. 34N 07.52E - Target - 50.16N 08.45E - 50.20N 01.35E - Beachy Head - Base.

Bomb-Load: 1 x 1,000lb M.C. - 1 x 500lb M.C. both with T.D. 0.025 - 450 x 4lb Inc. Ordy. - 90 x 4lb x Type - 24 x 30lb Ordy.   Nickels : 2C. 78.

The primary target was identified by green flares seen to drop about four miles before arriving, then seen to cascade. Bombs seen to fall in a built up area. Heavy flak slight to moderate at target, but other defences were very active with night fighters in evidence. Landed BASE. (M/UG - Sgt L. Jackson.   F/E - Sgt J.F.Shirley) Opposition unrecorded. These reports did not commence until 11. 11. 43.

<u>8 / 9th. October 43</u>   <u>LW264 - K</u>   HANOVER   2243   0502
Route: Base - Hornsea - 53.20N - 03.50E - 52 - 55N - 08.00E - 52.40N - 09.40E - 51.56N - 09.18E - 52 - 35N - 03.30E - Hornsea - Base   (Microfilm very poor)

Bomb-Load: 2 x 1,000lb M.C. T.D. 0.025 - 720 x 4lb. Inc. Ordy. - 30 x 4Inc. X type - 32 inc. Ordy.   Nickels : 3C - 72.

The primary target was attacked after being identified by red and green T.L.s divided into two lots, east and west of target. There was low cloud over the target, visibility fairly good. Bombs were dropped at 0136 on one red in east section. The bombing seemed scattered, quite a number of bursts on the eastern side, only small fires were seen. Slight to moderate flak at the target, searchlights numerous. At 0133 / 0135 height 17,500 ft. a Wellington (1 chute) and a Halifax (4 chutes) were seen shot down. Landed BASE. (M/UG - Sgt D.F. Tittley F/E - Sgt A.D. West) (N.B. In after years Don Tittley became the Ass'n's Chaplain until his death in 1994).
Opposition unrecorded.

<u>22 / 23rd. October 43</u>   <u>LW290 - U</u>   KASSEL   1800   0013
Route : Base - Southwold - 52.15N 03.00E - 51.49   03.51E - 50.30 06.10E - 50.33N 07.15E - Target - 52.36N 08.29E - 53.13N 04.32N - 53.20N 03.50E - Southwold - Base.

Bomb-Load : 2 x 1,000lb M.C. T.D. 0.025 - 720 x 4lb Inc. Ordy. - 30 x 4lb X Type - 24 x 30lb Ordy.   Nickels : 2C - 72.

The primary target was identified by yellow markers, reds and greens. Bombs were dropped on reds seen to cascade. A large number of good fires taking hold, well concentrated around the markers, giving off some thick black smoke. Defences quite moderate, S/Ls were numerous working in co-operation with flak and fighters. At 2104 a Halifax was seen to be coned and then going down in flames. Landed BASE.   (M/UG - F/Sgt F.W.Walters)

Opposition : Slight heavy flax in loose barrage mainly West and North of target, 22,000ft. Light flak being 'hose-piped' up to 16,000ft. DESSAN - moderate to intense heavy flak. BREMEN - A great deal of light flax (red tracer) up to 15/16,000ft., extending over a wide area. FRANKFURT - moderate heavy flax in barrage form : also light flax defences at known places in Northern France, Southern Belgium and at the French coast it was fairly active. A fair number of searchlights were rendered ineffective because of cloud conditions at Leipzig; a good number operating through large gap in cloud at Frankfurt. They were also active at Amsterdam and along the French coast.

28 / 29th. January 44   LK710-S   BERLIN   0003   0802

Route : Base - Flamboro' - 55.10N 07.00E - 55.10N 10.00E - 54.30N 12.30E - Target - 52.10N 11.00E - 52.40N 08.55E - 53.40N 04.00E - Flamboro' - Base.

Bomb - Load : 1 x 2,000lb H.C. inst.- 2 x 5,00lb inc.(Cluster) - 24 x 30lb Inc. - 180 x 4lb Inc. - 90 x 4lb. Inc. No Nickels.

Primary target identified by Wanganui flares - six or seven concentrated Bombs dropped from 17,500 ft on MPI of five flares seen in bombsight, concentration of markers very good. At 0317 a terrific explosion was seen lasting some time. Fires were seen under the clouds. Landed BASE. (M/UG - F/O M.A. Mason and subsequent operations, unless otherwise stated)

Opposition : In the target area heavy flak in moderate barrages up to 22,000ft. Light flak self-destroying up to 15,000ft., shot effectively at sky markers in moderate amounts. Flak defences at West Danish coast (inc. Sylt), FLENSBURG, LUBECK and ROSTOCK active. One balloon at 17,000ft. south-east of target area reported by aircraft ' S.' Searchlights at target numerous but ineffective (except for silhouetting purposes) due to cloud, big cones reported on West Danish coast and others at Lubeck and Rostock.

15 / 16th. February 44   LK710-S   BERLIN 1737   0038

Route : Base - Flamboro' - 55.25N 0700E - 55.10N 10.00E - 54.30N 12.30E = Target - 52.10N 11.00E - 52.40N 55E - 53.40N 04.00E - Flamboro' - Base.

Bomb - Load : 2 x 500lb cluster Inc. - 32 x 30lb Inc. - 450 x 4lb Inc. Ordy - 90 x 4lb X Type - Nickels : 3C SG23.

Primary target identified by red and green T.I.s and red flares with green stars. 10/10ths cloud tops at 4,000-ft. Bombs dropped from 18,500-ft. on MPI of three very concentrated green T.I.'s cascading at 6,000-ft at 2119. On running up, one red flare was seen with green stars, then red T.I.'s followed by greens in target area. All markers were well concentrated although attack appeared to open early at 2118. Cloud prevented results being accurately assessed. Landed BASE.

Opposition : Moderate heavy flak, possibly slighter and predicted at first, changing to barrage for up to 23,000-ft. later. Slight light flax mainly shot at sky-markers up to 18,000-ft. Searchlights, if any, completely ineffective due to thick cloud.

19 / 20th.February 44   LK710-S   Leipig   2328   0627
Route : Base - Hornsea - 54.00N 04.40E - 52.40N 05.10E - 52.37N 11.52E 52.00N 12.55E - Target - 51.00N 12.00E - 52.40N 08.10E - 53.15N 04.00E Hornsea - Base.

Bomb-Load : 630 x 4lb. Inc. - 90 x 4lb X Type - 32 x 30lb. Inc. No Nickels this A/c.

The primary target was identified by greens dripping red, followed by green T.I.'s, there was 10 / 10ths. cloud at the time of attack. Bombs dropped from 19,500-ft. on centre of four green T.I.'s, cascading above clouds. Marking very well concentrated, a large glow of fires seen as aircraft left target. There was a small hole in windscreen in front of 2nd. pilot's position. Landed COLTISHALL.

Opposition : At target not more than a moderate heavy flak barrage at 18 / 22,000-ft. Slight light flak accurately fired at sky-markers. At 16,000-ft. at 53.15N 04.10E approximately, aircraft 'R' recorded flak ship in action with fairly accurate predicted heavy flak at 17,000-ft. Other light flax shipsa also in action off of Texel. Few searchlight belts, these ineffective because of 10 / 10ths. cloud. Cones in order of 50 beams were in operation in Gronigen and Ede areas for use of night fighters.

22 /23rd. March 44   LK710 - S   Minelaying   1803   0011

Route : Base - Flamborough Head - 55.00N 04.30E - 55.15N - 08.30E - 55.14N 09.40E - 54.57N 11.15E - 54.38N 11.20E - 54.36N 10.45E - 55.40N 09.00E - 55.50N 07.00E - Flamboro' - Base.

Bomb Load : Mines as stated below. No Nickels. Mines (1 x F616/6B, 1 x B230) were laid from 14,600-ft. at 2131 on D R from centre of ten red flares. Clear, visibility good. No green flares seen, reds spread over area from two to three miles. Landed BASE.

Opposition : 1. SYLT Heavy flak with searchlights ineffective due to cloud. 2. KIEL Heavy flak with searchlights. 3. FLENSBURG Heavy flak up to 20,000-ft. and above fifty searchlights. 4. ROMO(?) Predicted heavy flak. 5. AABENRA Predicted heavy flak and searchlights. 6. EBSJERG Fifteen red flak bursts and searchlights. 7. 54.36N 10.40E Two flak ships with two searchlights firing red tracer up beams averaging

12,000-ft. 8. South of ZANGELAND(?) Three flak ships, heavy flak. Also light flak at markers.

23 / 24th. March 44   LK710-S   LAON   1900   2210

Route : Base - Reading - Selsey Bill - 49.44N   00.15E - 49.02N   03.20E - LAON - 49.48N   03.40E - 49.44N 00.15E - Selsey Bill - Reading - Base.

Bomb - Load : 6 x 1,000lb M.C. - 9 x 500lb M.C. All with TD. 0.025. No Nickels.

Abortive 50.05N 01.12W at 2059, 5,00 ft owing to severe icing. Bombs jettisoned safe at 50.51N 01.18W at 2059, 5,500 ft. Unable to make concentration due to icing. Layer of icing 4,000 - 6,000 met fifty miles S of Base - unable to maintain height. Landed WING.

Opposition : LAON Slight light flak up to 6,000ft. Two heavy flak guns spasmodically up to 12,500ft. 2. ROUEN, LE HAVRE, BEAUVAIS, MONTDIDER, slight heavy flak activity. Rouen, one searchlight. 2. Abbeville area, two cones of ten / twenty searchlights. 3. Amiens, a few searchlights.

29 / 30th. March 44.   LK710-S   VAIRES   1902   0034
Route : Base - Reading - Selsey Bill - 50.00N   01.15E - Vaires - 48.45N   02.45E - 49.10N 03.00E - 50.00N   01.15 - Selsey Bill - Reading - Base.

Bomb - Load : 2 x 1,000lb M.C. - 13 x 500lb. All with T.D. 0.025. No Nickels.

Primary target identified by red T.I.s, clear but haze. Bombs dropped from 13,300 ft at 2141 on red T.I. which was disappearing in bombsight. Earlier on cascade at 2132, last one 2139, five or six small fires around T.I.s observed. One terrific explosion occurred at 2138 which bumped the aircraft and lit sky some fifty miles around. (Where landed not recorded, but flight time in line with those of other aircraft who returned to Base.

Opposition : VAIRES, 1/2 heavy flak guns and 1/2 light flak guns, former about 11,000ft and later fairly accurate. DIEPPE, slight heavy flak accurately predicted. ABBEVILLE area, searchlight belt apparently extended southwards. POIX area, 3/4 cones of six beams each. AMIENS area, eight/nine searchlights track-indicating.

30 / 31st. March 44   LK710 - S   MINELAYING (Rosemary)

DNTO - reason not recorded. (Aircraft) and crew are not listed on the Form 541 - DNTO appearing only on Form 540 - the monthly summary.)
Route : Base - Hornsea - 54.30N   05.00E - 54.06N   07.49E - 54.02N   08.14E - 54.30N 05.00E - Hornsea - Base.

Bomb - Load : Mines   No Nickels.

Opposition : Helioland defences more active than 18 / 19. 3. 44. Considerable heavy flak up to 16 / 17,000ft with light flak (including red tracer up to 15,000ft) some at markers, also about eight searchlights (which formed at one time into a cone) to a certain extent co-operating. One / two flak ships between Heligoland and markers and dropping point approximately. LANGEOOG, little flak activity.

9 / 10th. April 44   LK725 - F   LILLE   2135   02.24
Route : Base - Reading - Selsey Bill - 49.58N   01.10E - 49.35N   02.20E - Lille - 50.50N   03.00E - 51.40N   02.00E - Orfordness - Goole - Base. Bomb - Load : 5 x 1,000lb M.C. - 10 x 500lb M.C., Both T.D. 0.025. No Nickels.

The primary target was identified by seeing red T.L as aircraft went into attack. 7 / 10 ths thin cloud with breaks. Bombs were dropped from 14,200ft. at 00.41 hrs on MPL of three red T.I.s closely clustered and seem to cascade. A large explosion at 00.40 also one at 00.47 were seen. A fire that looked like an oil tank burning, also two buildings on fire. Attack well concentrated. Landed BASE.

Opposition : LILLE up to three heavy flak guns very slightly in action, also some light flak apparently at T.L.s - all from built-up area. French and Belgian coasts - slight heavy flak, Dieppe and Ostend areas. Searchlight belts - some light flak co-operating with searchlights. One searchlight in Dunkirk area.

12 / 13th. April 44   LL131 - R   MINELAYING   2110   0130
Route : Not detailed - 54.02E   08.14E (Drooping zone ?). Bomb - Load : Mines as stated below. No Nickels.

Detailed position located, mines (1 x C302, 1 x D404, 1 x F624 / 12, 1 x G714) were released from a height of 14,000 ft., after a timed run of 1 min 35.4 secs from red flares, visibility good. Landed BASE.

Opposition : Known enemy defences were active. Six sightings were made of enemy fighters, but no attacks developed. Conditions were good over the whole route.

22 / 23rd. April 44   LK710 - S   LAON   2100   FTR
(R / G - F / O W.A.Jacks)

Route : Baise - Reading - Beachy Head - 49.58N 01.10E - Target - 49.20N 03.50E - 49.44N 01.15E - Selsey Bill - Reading - Base. Bomb - Load : 5 x 1,000lb M.C. T.D. o.025 - 10 x 500lb M.C.

Opposition ; Medium flak at target, possibly six guns. Flak ship 4 or 5 miles north of Fecamp. Narrow belt of searchlights between Amiens and Rouen, or single line of eight. Two searchlights seen at St.Valery forming cone and going off at regular intervals. Fighter flares reported from target area back to east coast

Further information regarding the fate of Halifax S-Sugar and her crew.
This is part of the contents of a very informative letter received by John Grimer from Philip Froom of Crowthorne in Berkshire, dated 28th.November '05.

"Thank you for your letter dated 3rd.November and the loan of the enclosed copies of various documents, they were most interesting. . .

My research on Bill Jacks is coming on well - actually my research on S-Sugar and her crew is coming on well, the research on Jacks slightly less so, as with his death the trail has somewhat dried up. . .

I have a few questions which have come to light as a result of my researches which I would like to clear up if you could help? When S-Sugar was attacked, it was almost certainly by a Luftwaffe Night Fighter - a BF1 10-G4 flown by a certain Major Willi Herget of 1 / NJG4. His aircraft will have been fitted with both standard forward firing guns in the nose, but also with upward firing 20mm cannon in the rear cockpit

When S - Sugar was attacked, did the enemy fire come from below the aircraft and up through the floor (it sounds that way from Charles Hobgen's account of his chart table being cut in two), or did it come from the stern? If it came from below, did it come from stern to bow, or the reverse? I am assuming from your account of the 'roman candle' that it came from the bow and worked back down the fuselage to the stern. Reading Bob Johnson's account, he clearly says he knew he had been hit as "both his legs shot up with such force they hit the underside of his table." So I would very much like to understand from where the attack came if you can remember

With respect to the 'roman candle,' I think you said they were tracers? However, could it have been the muzzle blast from the upward firing cannon in the enemy aircraft? The reason I ask is that most experienced night fighter crews stopped using tracer, as it alerted all the bombers in the stream to the presence of night fighters. It also made them a target. So I wonder if it was his muzzle blast that you saw - in which case he must have been very close to you when he fired. etc. . ."

Painting of the ill-fated Halifax No.77 Squadron, S-Sugar commissioned by Charles Hobgen.

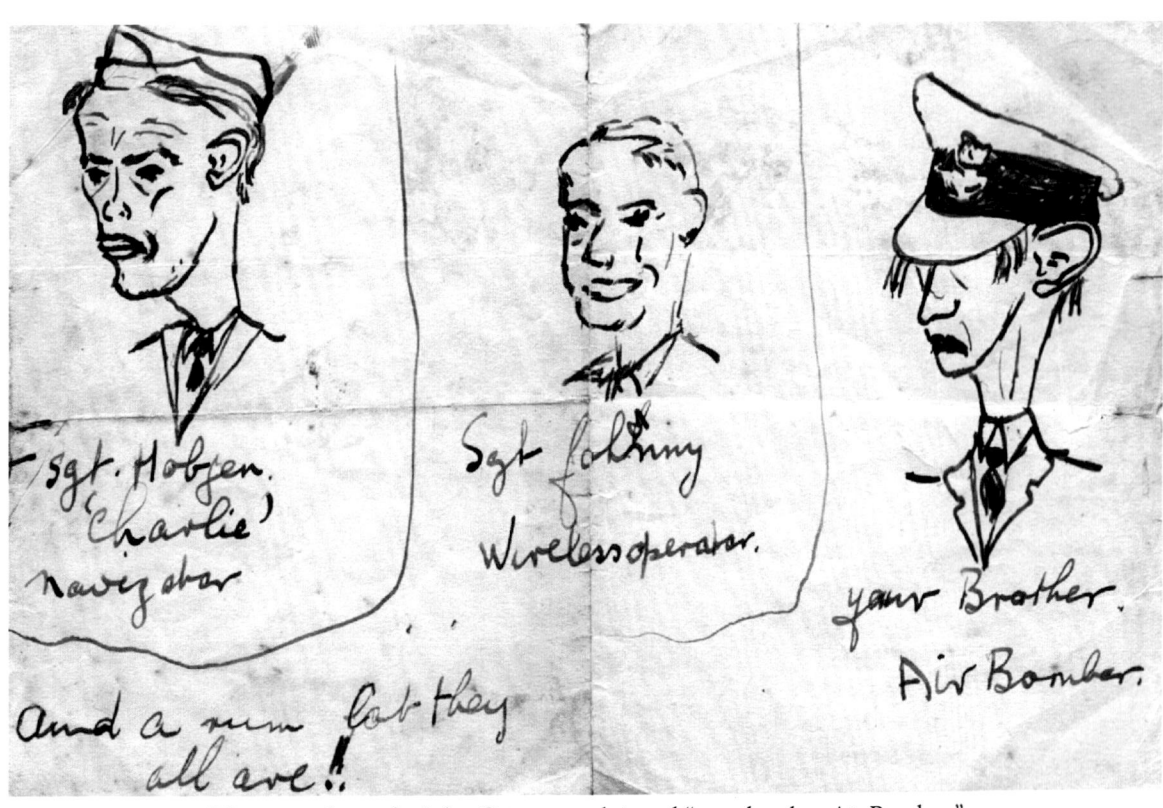

The crew, drawn by John Grimer and signed "your brother Air Bomber."
Sent to John's brother Peter 1943.

With Prejudice and Pride
by Charles Hobgen

Book 4 (PT2), Chapter 9.

"Again in the cause of clarity, I record that soon after I arrived on the squadron I was commissioned into the Royal Air Force Volunteer Reserve and became a pilot officer. After the war I remained in the RAF and was granted a regular commission. In 1948 I transferred from the flying branch of the Service - the General Duties Branch - to the Provost Branch. I retired from the RAF in 1975 having achieved the rank of group captain.

Flying Officer Mathew Mason did not arrive at RAF Elvington to join No.77 Squadron until 22nd. November 1943 and thus our crew flew on at least four operations with an alternative mid-upper gunner. Sergeant Victor Clare, our regular flight engineer, was absent on duty from the unit during two weeks in October and his place in our crew was filled by two other NCO's.

It will be helpful to the reader if I explain some of the expressions used by Roy Walker in the operations log he compiled for me :-

Base	RAF Elvington, Yorkshire.
T/O	Time of take-off.
Down	Time of landing.
M.C.	Medium Capacity bomb.
T.D.	Time Delay fuse.
Inc.	Incendiary bomb.
Nickels	Propaganda leaflets..
Opposition	Refers to the squadrons report on the opposition met by the crews during an operation'
Bomb-Load	Is the individual load for that aircraft and includes Mines.
PPF	Pathfinder Force.
Markers	Route marking flares dropped by PFF.
T.I.	Target indicators dropped by PFF.
S/Ls.	Searchlights.
Flak	Enemy anti-aircraft fire.
FTR	Failed To Return.

It was only after a crew had been with the squadron for a week or two that they graduated to flying the same aircraft on each operation - it became their aircraft. If, however, circumstances dictated otherwise, another crew might fly it when, for example, we were on leave, or were not on Battle Order.

From this it can be seen that we initially flew in, ' O ' - Orange; ' K ' - King; ' U ' - Uncle; and ' F ' - Freddie. Eventually, ' S ' - Sugar, (Serial Number LK710) became our aircraft and it was in this aircraft that we were shot down in April 1944.

More importantly, in using the same aircraft, a crew enjoyed the services of the same ground crew with whom a bond of trust and friendship inevitably grew and flourished. The pity is I cannot recall the names of our ground crew."

Halifax Dedication

"On May 12th. 2004, a service was held in the hanger of the Yorkshire Air Museum, to dedicate the re-build Halifax bomber with which most of us are familiar. The theme of the service which was attended by a few hundred people, was :-

> "Remembering the Service and the of all Air and ground crew who operated the Halifax bomber in the liberation of Europe and, marking the 60th. Anniversary of the formation of the Free French Squadrons at RAF Elvington."

"No.77 Squadron was mentioned briefly in the programme and it was when the Squadron left for Full Sutton, the airfield at Elvington would be entirely operated by the French airmen.

This was not quite correct for when 77 Squadron left the airfield a host of RAF men and women of aircrew, groundcrew and administrative staff remained at the airfield to assist the French. It is good that those present at the service included Rachel Semlyen, the original founder of the Yorkshire Air Museum and Ian Robinson, the late Chairman of Trustees etc. . . "

Newsletter, editor Vic Gammon.

A letter dated 23rd.April 1944, from Squadron Leader A.Webb, Commanding, No.77 Squadron, RAF.

"Dear Mr.Grimer,

It is with regret that I have to confirm my telegram informing you that your son Flying Officer John Arthur Grimer is missing from operations.

Your son was the Bomber of an aircraft that took off on an operational flight over enemy territory on the night of 22nd / 23rd.April, 1944. The aircraft did not return.

It may be several weeks before any definite news is received, but without raising false hopes I can tell you that a large number of aircraft members reported missing under similar circumstances ultimately prove to have made successful parachute jumps, and to be prisoners of war. I sincerely hope that this may be the case now.

It is desired to explain that the request in the telegram notifying you of the casualty to your son was included with the object of avoiding his chance of escape being prejudiced by undue publicity, in case he was still at large. This is not to say that any information about him is available, but is a precaution adopted in the case of all personnel reported missing.

Flying Officer Grimer has been with the Squadron for some time now, and has proved himself to be a very keen and capable member of an operational crew. He will be very much missed here, particularly among his brother officers.

Immediately any information is received concerning your son, you will of course be notified . . . "

re: 138336 Flying Officer J.Grimer.

"We have learned by cable through the International Red Cross Committee at Geneva in May your husband was a patient at the Military Hospital Reims and hope that you will very soon receive a letter from him in which he will send you a reassuring account of his health. Up to the present, we have received no information as to the extent of his wounds, but think you may be sure that he will be receiving satisfactory treatment and as soon as he is sufficiently recovered will be sent to a Prisoner of War camp. If you have received no other address for him, you might send a letter addressing it in the following way :-

Prisoners of War Post, *Kriegsgefangenenpost.*
138336 Flying Officer J.Grimer,
British Prisoner of War,
Military Hospital Reims,
C/o, Agency Centrale des Prisonniers de Guerre, Geneva.

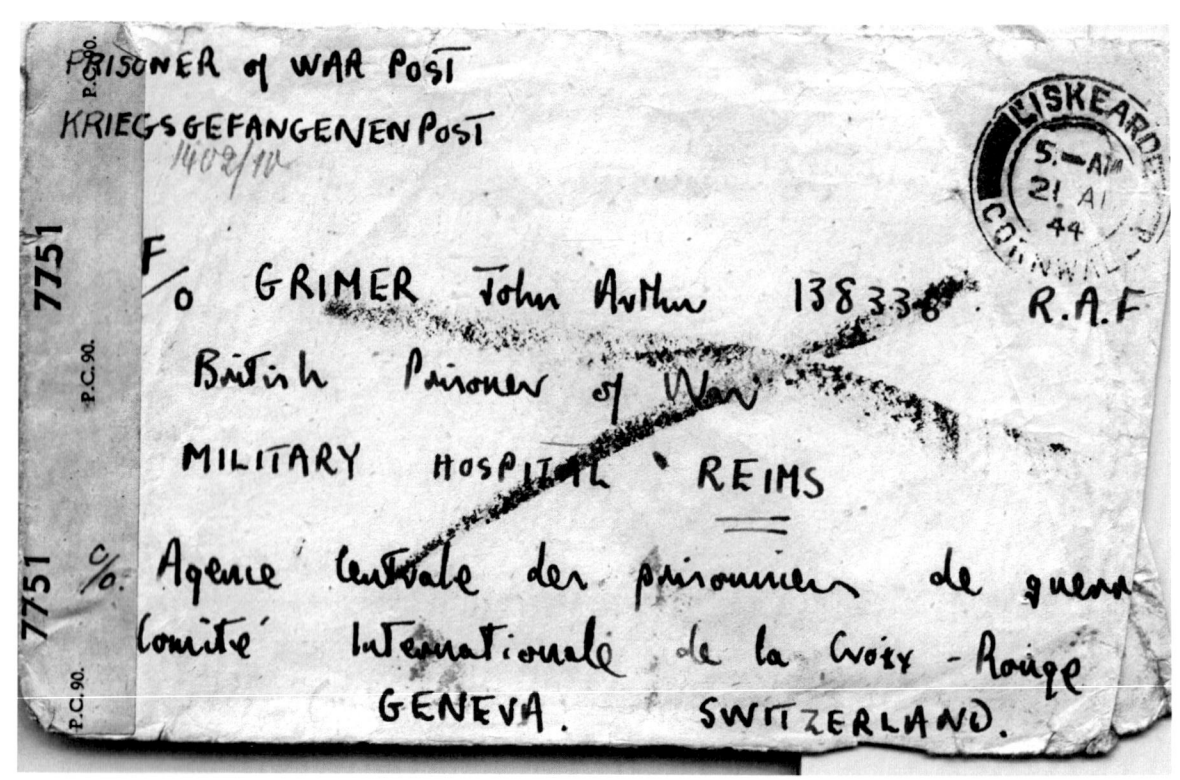

Letter from War Organisation of the Red Cross Society & Order of St.John of Jerusalem Prisoners of War Dept. St.James's Palace, London S.W.1. Dated 26th.July 1944, to Mrs.J.Grimer, 43 Hayes Way, Beckenham,

The envelope from above letter

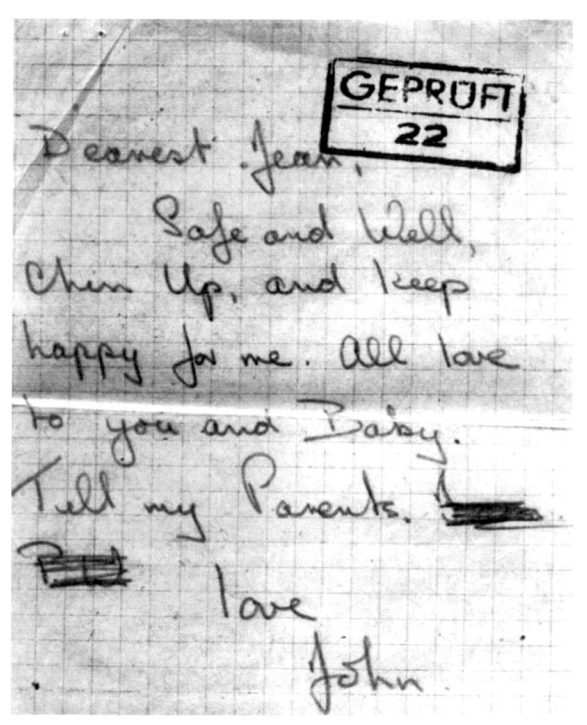

Letter to Jean Grimer from then F/O J.Grimer, POW.

DULCE ET DECORUM EST . . . ETC.
John Grimer, P.O.W

" . . . as I write [it] will be the Seventh Sunday before Christmas and Remembrance Sunday. There will be the usual sermons about what they died for - most of them wholly inaccurate : while most of the speakers will be sincere enough, few of them will have any personal knowledge of what it means to wake up, in the coming hours to lay your life on the line several times, and eventually to lie down, faintly surprised to be still alive.

I was moved to consider what I should say if, peculiarly, I should be asked to preach. In the opening months of the war there were few days in which I did not expect to be instantly blotted out; it was, therefore, with considerable surprise that in the early hours of a July morning I rose to my feet in the middle of a German potato field, apparently unharmed, while my aircraft blazed to the heavens in the next field. For me, as my first captor assured me with some sympathy, the war was over.

There is little to say about my war aims : to survive, if possible, and perhaps to play a small part in destroying something evil - how evil we did not then know. Names such as Belsen, Dachau, Auschwitz were as yet unknown to us. But I can tell you what we - my comrades and I did not fight for . . .

"We did not fight for a Britain which would be dishonestly railroaded into Europe against the peoples will; we did not fight for a Britain where successive governments, by their weakness and folly, would encourage crime and violence on an unprecedented scale; we did not fight for a Britain where thugs and psychopaths would murder and maim and torture, and never have a finger laid on them for it; we did not fight for a Britain whose leaders would be too cowardly to declare war on terrorism; we did not fight for a Britain whose Parliament would, again and again, betray its trust by legislating against the wishes of the country; we did not fight for a Britain where children could be snatched from their homes and parents, by night, on the old inquisition principle of secret information; we did not fight for a Britain where churches and schools would be undermined by fashionable reformers; we did not fight for a Britain where free choice could be anathematised as "discrimination"; we did not fight for a Britain where to hold by truths and values which have been thought good and worthy for a thousand years would be to run the risk of being called "fascist" - that, really, is the greatest and most pitiful irony of all."

"The words of the proceeding paragraphs I owe to a man who fought, as a lowly 'squaddie' throughout the Burma campaign; he spoke for his comrades of that time. Yet we have few means to proclaim, so far as the law allows, our fury and our frustration."

Roger Peacock. R.A.F ex - P.O.W. Association, *Newsletter No.49,* ed. Vic Gammon, (1994), pp.9 & 10.

A letter from above Red Cross Society dated 26th.October 1944, to Mrs J.Grimer at the same address:-

"138336 Flying Officer J.A.Grimer. We are so very glad to learn from the Air Ministry that your husband is now back in this country, and hope that he is making good progress from his injuries."

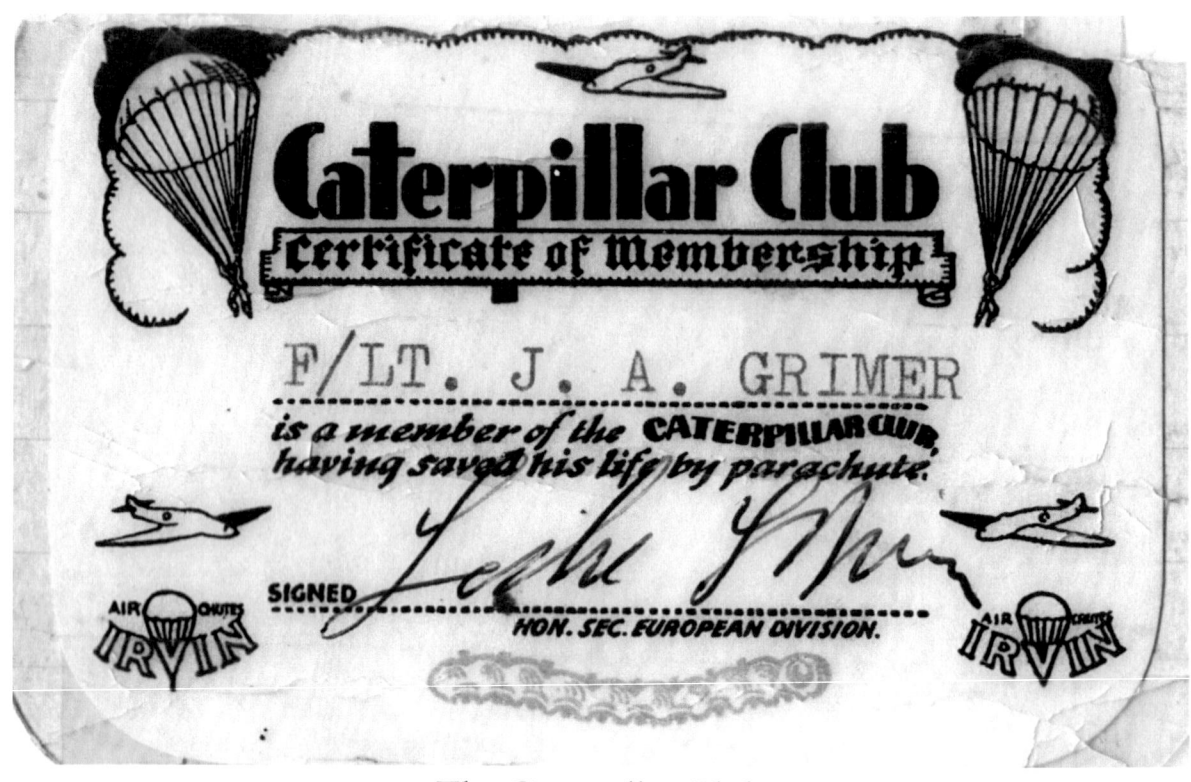

The Caterpillar Club

"It has taken a long time, but members of the exclusive Caterpillar Club are getting together at last. It was in November 1939, when Leslie Irvin, inventor of the free-fall parachute, suggested a reunion dinner for club members - all of whom must have escaped disaster by using a parachute. It should take place, said the American pioneer "in London after the war."

And tonight at the cafe Royal 400 guests, proudly wearing their solid gold caterpillar badge, will sit down together for the first time. Among them will be the club's only VC, former Warrant-Officer Norman Jackson of Hampton Hill, who was swept from the wing of a burning plane as he tried to put out the fire over Germany in 1944." - John London.

"The Caterpillar Club is one of the most exclusive aeronautical clubs in the world. To qualify for membership members must have saved their lives in an emergency with a parachute made or designed by Irving Air Chute of Great Britain Ltd. The European branch of the club was founded in 1926 and initially, had more than 30,000 members. The first reunion of the club was held 16th.November 1968. The following members of No.77 Squadron were present at the very first reunion of the club :-

C.H.Grace	N.A.Fearneyhough
J.A.Grimer	I.A.Kaynes
F.T.Kerr	R.L.Luce
A.E.Moore	A.P.H.Restarick
W.E.Sutton	R.J.Sage
J.W.Walsh	L.J.Ward
A.B.Wiggins. "	

Dulag-Luft was a transit camp about 30 miles NE from Oberursel. The camp became the main Nazi interrogation unit for Allied airmen. A mile to the W of the camp stands Kurklinik Hohemark, a hospital where wounded POW's were treated. Most of the captured airmen were interrogated at Dulag-Luft before being assigned to permanent POW camps. The very heavily secured camp covering some 500 acres, displayed its name in large white-painted boulders visible to British bombers warning them not to bomb the place.

In one of his letters (always written in pencil) dated June 4th. 1944, (they were allowed to write one every month) Grimer wrote that he has no regrets, and is lucky; but still "bed bound - the two men beside me have had amputations and they are very cheerful and excellent company. My wound is healing well and in another month or so I shall walk." In another letter dated July 2nd., "I got up last week, can hobble a bit each day. My wound is much better, otherwise I am fine. The Red Cross parcel once a fortnight is the milestone in our life here. We look forward to them eagerly, and their advent may best be described as a succession of childhood Christmases." He makes frequent mention of their child Frances, whom of course he has not seen, and frequently forewarns Jean that his appearance may be a shock to her due to his being emaciated, almost skeletal, and "with a lovely German crop and a real miserable straggly moustache."

In a further letter dated July 16th. he offers her self praises, and goes on to say "but honesty compels and the giving up of beer and the cutting down of cigarettes aren't such voluntary acts as I'd like you to believe." He further confesses to how they fill in the endless hours within their hospital room "with debates, general knowledge and anything from 'pins to polar bears' - and as you may guess - interminable women !" He was forced back to bed because his severe leg wound had burst open again "serves me right for walking about too much." But he went on "let me tell you some of the books I've read - *The Story of San Michele*, by Axel Munthe, is I think, one of the best books I've read for years. Also *See How they Run*, by Jerrard Tickell. For the rest I'm reading some good history books, poetry, and such a lot of pure unadulterated trash. Still, there's always something to read."

After about five months he was repatriated. Wounded prisoners were an un-necessary burden on maintaining a disciplined camp so they were got rid of as soon as possible, but only if their injuries made it impossible for POW's to return again for active duties.

He knew he would never regain sufficient fitness to fly again. His crew were no longer to be seen, nor any other familiar faces. Life had moved on during his absence and fearing for the success of his own future felt some reassurance when he eventually found himself posted to RAF Yatesbury on Salisbury Plain. The unit he was attached to consisted of officers and other ranks who were to become redundant with the ending of the war, so courses in re-training were the order of the day to find employment for all of those men.

The EVT [Educational & Vocational Training] scheme was set-up in 1946 in an attempt to re-habilitate wartime personnel, (now redundant with the war being over), into a job which they could carry out after returning back to civvy-street. The higher the rank, the more difficult it was to find those officers employment. F/O.J.Grimer (there seem to be two officers in the photograph) took to learning woodwork, a trade he was much interested in, and he soon was making pieces of furniture which are still in use today. The training was carried out by sergeant instructors who were ex-tradesmen.

Calne is the nearest village to RAF Yatesbury camp which sprawled along the road from Chippenham to

Marlborough to within walking distance of Avebury Rings. During those days our greatest delight was a meal of fried eggs bought from a nearby farm, coupled with the famous Harris sausage, pie & bacon from their factory at Calne, sadly now no more.

The site has since been cleared but one building remains, now used by the farmer. But before the unit was abandoned most of the equipment and stores were buried. John Grimer recalled that he witnessed boxes full of wireless valves and the like thrown into what looked like wells or old mine shafts, but probably were holes specially dug for the job.

After demobilisation John Grimer had to think of returning to work, badly handicapped as he was with a right leg which had the whole of its calf shot away. He was deemed thus to spend the remainder of his life walking with sticks and an iron clamped onto his leg. As he had spent much time in educational jobs, teaching and filling administrative duties it was obvious he was the right person for the teaching profession. One of his letters of reference proves the point :-

A letter from Headquarters, British Forces In Aden, M.E.F.,
dated 22nd September 1946,

"To whom it may concern :

Flight Lieutenant GRIMER has been known to me for the past year, during which period he filled the following posts :-

1. Staff Officer at No. 27 Group Headquarters for the general administration of Educational and Vocational Training within the Group.

2. Station Education Officer at R.A.F. Station, Yatesbury, involving :-

(a) The general administration control and development of educational and vocational training at the Station.

(b) Acting as advisor to the Station Commander on all matters relating to educational and vocational training.

(c) Teaching History and French to service men and women. Flight Lieutenant Grimer tackled his duties intelligently and enthusiastically and proved his ability to get things done. His powers of organisation were well above the average; his class-room work was good. [He spoke fluent French].

I always found him very loyal, hardworking, conscientious and reliable and a very likeable colleague."

(Signed) C.E.P. Suttle, S/Ldr.

<center>~~~~~~~~~~~~~~~~~~~~~~~~~~~~~~</center>

John Grimer received his letter of recommendation and a copy of his war service dated 21st. November 1949, which read as follows :-

"To whom it may concern,

J.A.Grimer (ex-Flight Lieutenant, Royal Air Force, No.138336) served with No.77 Bomber Squadron as an Air Bomber between October, 1943 and 1944, when I was commanding the Squadron.

The Squadron was operating with Bomber Command attacking targets on the continent.

Grimer flew with one of my Flight Commanders and had nearly completed a full operational tour (30 sorties) when on the 25th April, 1944, the crew was shot down over Laon, France.

Grimer was badly wounded but managed to bale out and was one of the few survivors of this gallant crew. His operational flying record was excellent.

As an individual I found him to be loyal, co-operative and intelligent, with a good sense of humour and a pleasant and likeable personality.

(Signed) J. A. Roncoroni W/C dr. R.A.F."

<center>~~~~~~~~~~~~~~~~~~~~~~~~~~~~~~</center>

After the war John worked for a year training with Brewers at Redlands, Bristol.

The *Western Morning News* dated Oct? 1991 reported "A Sad Post-script", concerning Wing Commander Steve Roncoroni, son of Wing Commander J.A. Roncoroni RAF, *above*, who had helped write about the 6 Shackleton bombers still on frontline RAF service forty one years after they first flew.

When Shackleton squadrons were based at St. Mawgan and St. Eval in Cornwall where Steve did most of early flying, they were familiar sights.

Steve was killed piloting a plane that mysteriously crashed into a hill on an island in the Hebrides, killing all his nine aircrew with himself. The navigator was a Plymouth man, Squadron Leader Jeremy Jane.

In command of what one of his men described as the battered old wrecks of No.8 Squadron which provided Britain's airborne early warning system, Steve held a great affection for the veteran planes of which many people were aware of their place in the history of a remarkable aeroplane, which apparently will be withdrawn next spring after holding the line for so long : the very last of the Shackletons will make a farewell flight in the Cornish skies they once dominated for so long.

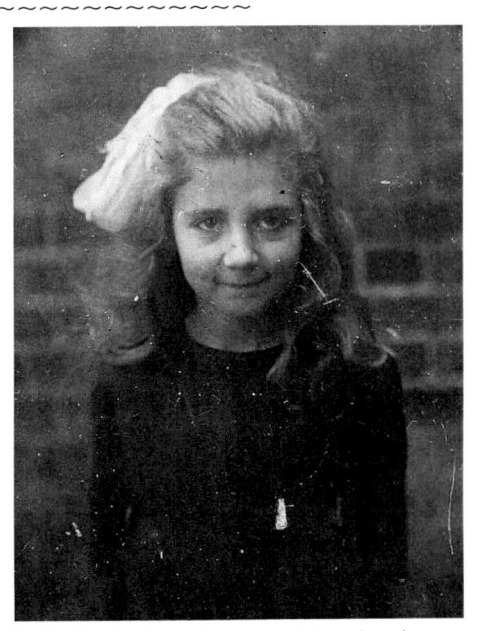

~~~~~~~~~~~~~~~~~~~~~~~~~~~~~

Catherine Loretto *née* Hill

Catherine Jean Loretto, eldest daughter

Peter & John Grimer early 2009 at Higher Windmill, Looe.

John Grimer became a member of the Royal Air Forces Ex-P.O.W. Association, whose chairman was Air Commodore C.H.Clarke.

John told me "the last words I heard my father say - was that I was "the first Grimer to have disgraced himself." This was of my becoming the Husband of the Year!

John recalled the turbulent times when speed was essential, and he was able to step aside when a vase, complete with a rich cluster of roses, and the water, came hurtling across the room to smash thro' a window. Red roses indeed - to afirm the love of the deliverer!

During their retirement John spent his time growing flowers, fruit and vegetables in his garden bordered as it is by the remains of an ancient windmill. The view from their house extends down over fields to Looe Island and the sea; with a distant sighting of the Eddystone Lighthouse on the far horizon.

In her retirement Jean was now able to devote all her time to her interest in the local community, serving on the East Looe Town Trust, the local council, and the district council where she chaired the environmental committee. In 1976 she founded and became secretary of the Looe & District Amenity Society. Many members became Friends of the Wooldown, a group which kept a vigilant eye on the protection and preservation of these fields (which were left for the enjoyment of the people of Looe) from tentative road and building proposals. On one occasion there was a plan to re-introduce sheep grazing and to reinforce all the boundaries with stock-proof fencing and barbed wire. It was even planned to make a corridor through "Three- penny-bit" field. An outcry ensued and the "Friends" cut and rolled up the wire and deposited it outside the office of the East Looe Town Trust.

When James Sargent was the Cornwall County Council music advisor he advised Jean to take a course on music at Dartington; which she did, and grew to love that place. She didn't play a musical instrument particularly well but she did play a recorder and performed with a group called the East Cornwall Recorder Consort. She organised the various music teachers around and they gave concerts in National Trust houses for some years. She also sang and played with the East Cornwall Bach Festivals, held in St.Germans Church, for over thirty years.

When on a visit to St.Ives she met Janet Axton who, with others, had pioneered the building of the Tate St.Ives, and whose book "From Gas Works to Gallery" inspired Jean to inaugurate a similar project for Looe when the Millpool gasometer was pulled down. This became known as the Millpool Project and Jean worked tirelessly organising meetings, canvassing support and persuading the council to finance a £25,000 feasibility study. The project was eventually turned down on the grounds of cost and doubtful profits.

For some years Jean suffered increasingly from rheumatoid arthritis and became bound to her bed by the end of 2003. She received every care from her husband and social and health services. She never grumbled or pitied herself and retained her mental faculties to the end. She died at her home on the 16th.day of August 2005.

John & Jean in their garden, standing where at one time had been the interior of a 17th.cent. windmill

NICKLE LEAFLET No.43, 1st.October 2008
No.77 (B) Squadron *Esse Potius Quam Videri (To be, rather than seen.)*

"John Grimer, bomb Aimer 1944, POW and having been seriously wounded on the Laon raid of 22 April 1944, as reported in Nickle Leaflet No.42. Congratulations on another superb Nickle. I was much intrigued to see the account of our being shot down on 22 April 1944.

Flying Officer Mason and Flight Sergeant Johnson spent four months with me in a hospital prison cell in Rheims until we were liberated by the troops of Old Blood and Guts Paton. Both Mason and Johnson suffered serious wounds involving amputations and although seriously wounded myself, I managed to emerge from captivity with my body more or less intact though, in the last few years my wounds have required extensive surgery.

Our Navigator, Charles Hobgen, was uninjured and was sent to Stalag Luft 11 at Sagan. Before this however, he was largely responsible for saving my life for after capture and being imprisoned in Laon (or was it Soissons?), Charles raised Cain with the guards and insisted that I be transferred to a hospital for treatment of my wounds. The upshot of this was that I was strapped to a motorcycle sidecar and taken to a hospital for treatment. I didn't meet Charles again until an association reunion in the early 1990's and it was very sad news for me when I learned of his death in 2005. I think I must now be the only survivor of the crew . . . "

END

The Grimer medal show-case

1. Defence Medal 1914 - 1918.
2. For Faithful Service in the Special Constabulary.
3. En Témoignace de Reconnaissance National [On Witness Recognition]1914 -1918. King Albert, [Leopold's father].

4. Civil Medal Presented in 1930 in Brussels. (Flemish inscription) " Thomas Ingledew Grimer uit dankbaarheid voor bewezen diensten aan de Vlaamsche Bevolking gedurende den Wereldoorlog 1914 - 1918. Brugge Den 13 - 7 - 1930, De Burgemeester Van Hoestenberghe." *trans.* Thomas Ingledew Grimer in thankfulness for what he did for the Flemish People during 1914 - 1918. Brugge 13 - 7 - 1930 from the Mayor Van Hoestenberghe. Around the upper border " Geschonken Door Het Gemeentebestuur Van Brugge." *trans.* Presented from the Consol from Brugge.
(Translation from the Flemish by Yvonne Toms *née* Peauwart at Looe).
5. 1915 Special Constable ville et portus Dovor.
6. Badge : Squadron No.77 R.A.F
7. Cap badge of the Civil Service Rifles (1914 - 1918).
8. Tunic badge, T.A.
9. The Great War for Civilisation (1914 - 1918).
10. Portrait of Arthur Thomas Grimer (1894 - 1974).
11. George V Medal (1914 - 1918).
12. For God & the Empire George V (1914 - 1918).
13. Flight Officer J.A.Grimer, pilots wings, (1939 - 1945).
14. The Air Crew Europe Star.
15. The 1939 - 1945 Star.
16. The Defence Medal.
17. 1939 - 1945 Medal.
18. A Tribute to the Air Crew of Bomber Command.
19. International Prisoner of War Medal.

~~~~~~~~~~~~~~~~~~~~~~~~~~~~~

Appendix One

LOG BOOK

Date	Hour	Aircraft Type and No.	Pilot	Duty	Remarks (including results of bombing, gunnery, exercises, etc.)	Flying Times Day	Night
					Time carried forward :—	14.50	
12/42	13.05	Anson 60	Sgt. Major	Air Bomber	B₃ 1000' HLB. 96 yds group conutd.	1.35	
2/42	19.45	Anson 60	Sgt. Page	Air Bomber	B₃ HLB. - no bombs dropped Weather u/s.	1.45	
					Sumary for December 42. Gunnery. 0.35 Bombing. 11.40 TOTAL 12.15		
/43	14.30	Anson 28	Sgt. Scutts	Air bomber	B₃ HLB. 6 bombs. 77 yds conc.	2.35	
/43	13.30	Anson 33	Sgt. Kader	Air Bomber	B₃ HLB. 6 bombs. 57 yds conc.	2.25	
/43	13.55	Anson 57	F/L. Ritchie	Air Bomber	Map reading. - Base - Whitehaven. M. of G. Silloth Whitehaven. Base.	2.35	
/43	10.50	Defiant 16	Sgt Matherson	Air Gunner	G.3. 200 rounds. 13 hits.	0.35	
/43	14.15	Defiant 5	Sgt Youens	Air Gunner	Cine gun exercise. 9 ft of film.	0.55	
/43	11.15	Anson 47	F/o Weicker	Air Bomber	Map reading. Base. Bardsly Port Maddock Aberystwyth. Base.	3.05	
1/43	10.40	Defiant 9	Sgt Matherson	Air Gunner	G3 6 rounds - no hits. - link stoppage	0.35	
					Total Time —	30.35	

Time carried forward :— 36.35

Date	Hour	Aircraft Type and No.	Pilot	Duty	Remarks (including results of bombing, gunnery, exercises, etc.)	Flying Times Day	Night
27/1/43	14.35	Anson 28	F/L Rippon	Air Bomber	LLB. 8 bombs dropped. errors. 37ˣ 24ˣ	1.05	
31/1/43	22.55	Anson 22	F/O Alston	Air Bomber	BS. 3 bombs dropped 62ʳᵈ computed		1.40
					Summary January 43		
					Gunnery 2.05 Nav. 5.40		
					Bombing 5.05 + 1.40(N)		
					TOTAL 14.30		
2/2/43	17.00	Anson 33	Sgt Thomas	Air Bomber	Duty not carried out	1.15	
3/2/43	16.25	Defiant 5	Sgt Mungall	Air Gunner	88 rounds fired G4. 2 hits	0.30	
3/2/43	11.45	Defiant 5	Sgt Mungall	Air Gunner	- no rounds fired -	0.25	
6/2/43	15.40	Anson 21	P/O Cameron	Air Bomber	Bg. LLB. 4 bombs 50 yd error	1.35	
7/2/43	13.55	Defiant 12	Sgt Kodler	Air Gunner	G4. 200 rounds. 7 hits.	0.30	
7/2/43	15.20	Defiant 12	Sgt Mungall	Air Gunner	G4. 200 rounds. 32 hits	0.35	
16/2/43	16.55	Defiant 7	Sgt Mungall	Air Gunner	G5. 200 rounds 12 hits	0.30	
20/2/43	02.15	Anson 25	F/S Jennings	Air Bomber	Map reading. 10/10 cloud on route		2.25

Total Time — 37.20 2.05

Time carried forward :— 37.20 2.05

Date	Hour	Aircraft Type and No.	Pilot	Duty	Remarks (including results of bombing, gunnery, exercises, etc.)	Flying Times Day	Night
1/2/43	12.55	Anson 37	F/S Major	Air Bomber	Bg. 4 bombs. 31 yd error	1.15	
1/2/43	08.00	Anson 30	F/S Stein	Air Bomber	Map reading	3.00	
5/2/43	17.10	Defiant 15	Sgt Forrest	Air Bomber	G5. 200 rounds. 45 hits	0.30	
5/2/43	15.15	Defiant 19	Sgt Rovens	Air Gunner	No Rounds fired Weather U.S.	0.25	
5/2/43	17.00	Anson 7	F/S George	Air Bomber	Map reading	2.05	
					Summary for February 43		
					DAY NIGHT		
					Navigation 5.05 2.25		
					Bombing 4.05		
					Gunnery 3.25		
					TOTALS 12.35 2.25		
					GRAND TOTAL = 15.00		
1/3/43	15.00	Anson 9	P/O Watson	Air Bomber	Map reading :- Base Whitehaven Base.(Weather US	1.05	
1/3/43	14.50	Anson 22	F/S White	Air Bomber	Map reading - Base Whitehaven Silloth M/F/G Base	2.05	

Total Time — 47.45 2.05

| | | Time carried forward :- | 47.45 | 6.25 |

Date	Hour	Aircraft Type and No.	Pilot	Duty	Remarks (including results of bombing, gunnery, exercises, etc.)	Flying Times Day	Night
5/3/43	20.05	Anson 22	Sgt Tomlinson	Air Bomber	Base. Whitehaven. Dumfries. Stranraer. Whitehaven base.		3.20
6/3/43	01.30	Anson 9	F/O Weicker	Air Bomber	B5. 6 Bombs. 212 yds at 10,000'		2.40
8/3/43	16.15	Anson 60	F/O Waters	Air Bomber	Low Flying map reading. Base. Dungannon. Armoy. Whitehaven Base.	3.00	
9/3/43	21.00	Anson 2	Sgt Tomlinson	Air Bomber	5 bombs. 160 yds. co-noted		1.40
11/3/43	20.00	Anson 23	Sgt Simpkin	Air Bomber	B5. 6 bombs. 20 yd group. converted		2.20
12/3/43	03.05	Anson 22	Sgt Shaw	Air Bomber	Map reading. - Base. Bardsley. Ballyhalbert. C.rch. Base.		8.10

Sumary of Course up to March 12

	DAY	NIGHT
Navigation	16.55	8.55
Bombing	26.40	8.20
Gunnery	5.10	---
TOTALS	50.45	17.15
GRAND TOTAL :-	68.00 hrs	

Total Time — 50.45 | 17.15

| | | Time carried forward :- | 50.45 | 17.15 |

Date	Hour	Aircraft Type and No.	Pilot	Duty	Remarks (including results of bombing, gunnery, exercises, etc.)	Flying Times Day	Night
14/3/43	10.25	Anson 16	F/S Adams	Air Bomber	Route:- Base Piercebridge Bellingham Glenluce Base. Low flying mapreading Vis:- good. 8 bombs B4 (3 sticks) 59 yd. group.	3.05	
13/3/43	11.00	Anson 60	Sgt. Scott	Air Bomber	B4. 3 sticks (8 bombs) 89 yd group	1.30	
18/3/43	14.35	Defiant 4	Sgt. Youens	Air Gunner	G3. 200 rounds	.25	
19/3/43	01.05	Anson 22	Sgt. Meiklem	Air Bomber	B3. 6 bombs 128 yds co-noted.		1.15
19/3/43	14.40	Defiant 3	Sgt. Munjad	Air Gunner	G5. 400 rounds.	.35	

Sumary for Course until 22nd/3/43

	DAY	NIGHT
Navigation	20.00	8.55
Bombing	29.25	8.20
Gunnery	8.10	---
	57.35	17.15

GRAND TOTAL   74.50 hrs.

Signed _____ S/LDR. C.A.I.

Total Time — 57.35 | 17.15

Date	Hour	Aircraft Type and No.	Pilot	Duty	Remarks (including results of bombing, gunnery, exercises, etc.)	Flying Times Day	Night
					Time carried forward :—	57.35	14.15
9.4.43	10.20	Whitley J	F/S Death P/O Steel	Air Bomber	Advanced dual	1.15	
10.4.43	9.55	Anson N	F/L Rawston W/O Lomas	Air Bomber	Base Leamington Bamford Northampton base	1.40	
13.4.43	10.30	Whitley J	S/L Pestridge Sgt. Occonor	Air Bomber	C+L dual	1.30	
13.4.43	2.00	Whitley J	Sgt. Occonor	Air Bomber	C+L Solo	1.00	
14.4.43	1500	Anson Y	F/O Vanexan	Air Bomber	Exercise 25	2.55	
16.4.43	14.40	Anson N	F/O Vanexan	Air Bomber	Exercise 25	3.20	
15.4.43	10.45	Whitley N	F/L Alcock	Air Bomber	To Honeybourne	0.15	
16.4.43	11.00	Whitley E	F/L Alcock P/O Douglas	Air Bomber	Advanced dual and formation flying	0.45	
17.4.43	10.15	Anson O	S/L Pestridge w/o C.White	Air Bomber	Exercise 24. Land Gatwick	2.30	
17.4.43	16.05	Whitley K	F/S Death Sgt. Tiplar	Air Bomber	H.L.B. Dual	1.10	
					Total Time	73.45	14.15

Date	Hour	Aircraft Type and No.	Pilot	Duty	Remarks (including results of bombing, gunnery, exercises, etc.)	Flying Times Day	Night
					Time carried forward :—	73.45	14.15
18/4/43	10.00	Whitley J	S/L Pestridge	Air Bomber	Exercise 22.	2.55	
					Summary for April 43. DAY NIGHT. 19.05 / TOTAL :— 19.05 /		
13.5.43	11.15	Anson N	W/O Nash	Air bomber	Exercise 21	3.20	
16.5.43	15.45	Anson N	F/O Vanexan	Air bomber	Exercise 24 Landed Stanton Harcourt	3.15	
19.5.43	09.50	Anson N	W/O Acres	Air bomber	Exercise 22	3.10	
					Summary for May 43. DAY NIGHT. 9.45 / TOTAL :— 9.45		
2.6.43	23.30	Anson N	Sgt. Wilde	Air Bomber	Exercise 16. Forced landing Wigesly		1.40
					Total Time	86.25	18.55

Time carried forward :— 86.25 | 18.55

Date	Hour	Aircraft Type and No.	Pilot	Duty	Remarks (including results of bombing, gunnery, exercises, etc.)	Flying Times Day	Night
3·6·43	12·00	Anson N	Sgt Wilde	Air Bomber	Wigsley Northampton Base.	2·00	
5·6·43	22·30	Anson N	F/O Vaughan	Air Bomber	Exercise 20.		2·40
10·6·43	10·30	Whit C	S/L Pestridge	Air Bomber	Air Test Honeybourne return Base.	·30	
16·6·43	23·40	Anson Y	W/O Nash	Air Bomber	Exercise 25 returned to Base. Plane U.S.		1·25
17·6·43	14·40	Whitley G	S/L Bond F/L Alcock	Air Bomber	Instrument Flying.	1·40	
20·6·43	14·20	Whitley P	S/L Bond F/L Alcock	Air Bomber	Air Test.	0·20	
20·6·43	15·10	Whitley P	S/L Bond	Air Bomber	Solo C+L.	1·25	
21·6·43	15·25	Whitley K	S/L Bond P/O Lomas	Air Bomber	Advanced dual and check	1·00	
21·6·43	16·30	Whitley K	S/L Bond	Air Bomber	Solo C+L.	1·35	
17·6·43	16·30	Anson Y	Sgt Wilde	Air Bomber	Honeybourne to base.	·15	
28·6·43	14·10	Whitley C	S/L Bond P/O Cromwell	Air Bomber	Ex 1. Sim bombing & LOS 1×2 H LB.	2·30	
29·6·43	10·25	Whitley C	S/L Bond	Air Bomber	Ex 3. Returned to Base. Engine trouble	0·30	

Total Time — 99·10 | 23·00

Time carried forward :— 99·10 | 23·00

Date	Hour	Aircraft Type and No.	Pilot	Duty	Remarks	Day	Night
29·6·43	12·50	Whitley N	S/L Bond	Air Bomber	Exercise 3 1×2. H.L.B. Sim bombing.	3·20	
30·6·43	11·25	Whitley E	S/L Bond F/L Alcock	Air Bomber	Exercise 5 Sim bombing	5·00	

Summary for June 43.
  DAY.   NIGHT
  18·15   5·45
TOTAL. 24·00

2·7·43	13·45	Whitley G	S/L BOND	Air Bomber	Exercise 9. H.L.B. 1×2.	5·15	
3·7·43	4·40	Whitley H	S/L Bond Sgt Casa	Air Bomber	H.L.B. 5 bombs.	1·10	
3·7·43	16·25	Whitley A.	S/L Bond	Air Bomber	H.L.B 6 bombs	0·55	
3·7·43	23·55	Whitley B	S/L Bond P/O Lomas	Air Bomber	Initial dual.		0·30
4·7·43	14·45	Whitley I	S/L Bond F/L Alcock	Air Bomber	L.L.B. 6 bombs.	1·00	
4·7·43	23·10	Whitley I	S/L Bond P/O Lomas	Air Bomber	Initial dual		1·05

Total Time — 115·50 | 24·35

						Time carried forward :—	116.50	24.35
Date	Hour	Aircraft Type and No.	Pilot	Duty	Remarks (including results of bombing, gunnery, exercises, etc.)		Day	Night
5.7.43	23.05	Whit. N	S/L Bond F/L Smith	Air Bomber	Dual C + L			1.40
5.7.43	00.50	Whit N	S/L Bond	Air Bomber	Solo C + L			0.30
5.7.43	02.00	Whit E	S/L Bond	Air Bomber	Solo C + L			0.30
7.7.43	23.15	Whit E	S/L Bond P/O Lomas	Air Bomber	Check C + L			0.25
7.7.43	23.40	Whit E W	S/L Bond	Air Bomber	Solo C + L			2.20
9.7.43	23.15	Whit K	S/L Bond	Air Bomber	Solo C + L			1.45
9.7.43	02.00	Whit K	S/L Bond Sgt Cass	Air Bomber	H.L.B. 8 bombs.			0.50
12.7.43	23.00	Whit F	S/L Bond Sgt Cass	Air Bomber	Ex 5 HLB. 2x2 one flash.			4.40
13/7.43	22.30	Whit F	S/L Bond	Air Bomber	Ex. 8. Landed Topcliffe owing to enemy activity.			3.30
14.7.43		Whit F	S/L Bond	Air Bomber	Return from Topcliffe to Base		1.40	
						Total Time —	117.30	40.55

						Time carried forward :—	117.30	40.55
Date	Hour	Aircraft Type and No.	Pilot	Duty	Remarks (including results of bombing, gunnery, exercises, etc.)		Day	Night
16.7.43	22.30	Whit. J	S/L Bond	Air bomber	Bomber Comand Bullseye. 2 traces. — (I.R.)			5.15
17.7.43	22.15	Whit F	S/L Bond	Air bomber	Bomber comand Bullseye. I.D.R. run trace.			3.00
19.7.43	22.25	Whit. A	S/L Bond	Air bomber	Exercise 9. 2x1 H.L.B. 1 flash 2, I.R. traces.			5.00
22.7.43	15.30	Whit. C	S/L Bond	Air bomber	'Warload'		2.00	
22.7.43	19.05	Whit. AC	S/L Bond	Air bomber	H.L.B.		1.00	
23.7.43	14.10	Whit. G (1st op)	S/L Bond	Air bomber	Air Test — Honeybourne.		0.20	
23.7.43	21.15	Whit. G	S/L Bond	Air bomber	Leaflet raid Montereau.			5.50
26.7.43	11.15	Whit. C	S/L Bond	Air bomber	Fighter Affiliation 9 bombs H.L.B.		2.30	

Sumary for July.
Day night.
15.50 36.50
Total. 52.40

| | | Total Time — | 123.50 | 60.00 |

Time carried forward :—						125.20	60.00
Date	Hour	Aircraft Type and No.	Pilot	Duty	Remarks (including results of bombing, gunnery, exercises, etc.)	Day	Night
8.9.43	13.15	Halifax H	F/O Garforth S/L BOND	Air Bomber	Ex. 2 and 3. D.C.O	2.00	
15.9.43	08.55	Halifax G	S/L Gaskell S/L BOND	"	Ex 2 and 3 D.C.O.	01.40	
17.9.43	10.25	Hal D+F	S/L Gaskell S/L BOND	"	Ex 2 and 3 D.C.O.	1.20	
19.9.43	13.30	Halifax G	S/L Gaskell S/L BOND	"	Ex 4 and 5 D.CO	00.40	
20.9.43	11.00	Halifax G	S/L Gaskell S/L BOND	"	Ex 4 and 5 D.C.O	2.00	
21.9.43	13.00	Halifax D	S/L Gaskell S/L BOND	"	Ex 4 and 5. D.C.O.	1.15	
21.9.43	14.15	Halifax D	S/L BOND	"	Ex 4 and 5. D.C.O	1.15	
22.9.43	05.40	Halifax D	S/L Gaskell S/L BOND	"	Ex 6 and 7. D.C.O.	1.00	
23.9.43	10.30	Halifax G	S/L Gaskell S/L BOND	"	F/A and Ex 8 and 9. D.C.O.	1.15	
23.9.43	11.45	Halifax G	S/L BOND	"	Exercise 8 and 9. D.C.O.	1.05	
24.9.43	09.00	Halifax H	S/L BOND	"	F/A and air to air D.C.O	1.20	
25.9.43	08.35	Halifax D	S/L BOND	"	F/A D.C.O.	1.35	
25.9.43	15.05	Halifax F	S/L BOND	"	Cross Country D.C.O	4.40	
					Total Time —	14.5.25	60.00

Time carried forward :—						145.25	60.00
Date	Hour	Aircraft Type and No.	Pilot	Duty	Remarks (including results of bombing, gunnery, exercises, etc.)	Day	Night
26.9.43	16.15	Halifax A	F/O Page S/L BOND	Air Bomber	3 eng. and 1/F. D.C.O.	0.45	
26.9.43	19.40	Halifax E	F/O Page S/L BOND	"	Dual and C, L. D.C.O.		1.00
26.9.43	20.40	Halifax E	S/L BOND	"	Solo C and L. D.C.O.		2.10
27.9.43	13.05	Halifax A	S/L BOND	"	Bombing and air firing. 6 bombs of 4000!	2.20	
27.9.43	19.15	Halifax H	S/L BOND	"	Cross country. D.P.C.O		1.30
27.9.43	21.05	Halifax H	S/L BOND	"	Bullseye. (recall.) D.P.C.O		4.10
28.9.43					Total. 1658. Con Unit. Day. 24.10. hrs. night. 8.50 hrs. Grand Total. 33.00 hrs Signed Peter Gaskell G/L. O.C.A.302.		
					Total Time —	148.30	68.50

Date	Hour	Aircraft Type and No.	Pilot	Duty	Remarks (including results of bombing, gunnery, exercises, etc.)	Flying Times Day	Night
1-10-43	20.20	"X"	S/Ldr Bond	X-C			4.20
4-10-43	17.55	"O"	S/Ldr Bond	OPS-Frankfurt	→		8.10
8-10-43	22.40	"K"	"	OPS-Hannover	→		6.30
7-10-43	14.25	"U"	"	Fighter Affil		1.00	
21-10-43	11.50	"R"	"		Air/Sea	.55	
3-11-43	17.22	"U"	"	B/A	OPS-Dusseldorf.		4.55
25-11-43	23.50	S	"	B/A	OPS-Frankfurt		6.50
26-11-43	15.54	S	"	B/A	Return from Wittering		
3-12-43	23.39	S	"	B/A	OPS Leipzig		8.25
19-12-43	11.55	Y	"	B/A	Local Flying	.50	

1944

Date	Hour	Aircraft Type and No.	Pilot	Duty	Remarks	Day	Night
21-1-44	13.55	LW 260	S/Ldr Bond	B/A	Air test.	1.05	
25-1-44	11.30	"V"	"	"	L.F.P.	.30	
27-1-44	18.45	"S"	"	"	H/O April.		2.40
28-1-44	00.05	"S"	"	"	OPS-Berlin.		7.55
7-2-44	15.15	"S"	"	"	A/A Firing.	1.00	
15-2-44	17.35	"S"	"	"	OPS-Berlin		7.05
19-2-44	23.30	S	"	"	OPS-Leipzig		6.55
20-2-44		S	"	"	Return to Base	1.10	
2-3-44	00.25	S	"	"	OPS-Meulan		5.20
22-3-44	19.05	S	"	"	OPS-Gardening		6.05
23-3-44	19.00	S	"	"	OPS Le Mans		3.10
24-3-44	10.45	S	"	"	Wing to Base	1.10	
30-3-44	19.00	S	"	"	OPS Vaites		5.35
31-3-44	11.00	S	"	"	Air test	.40	
9-4-44	21.25	F	"	"	OPS-Lille		4.50
10-4-44	15.55	X	"	"	Air test	1.05	
12-4-44	21.10	R	"	"	OPS Mining		4.20
22-4-44	21.00	S	"	"	OPS Laon-Missing		

B. Egan-Wyer S/L
O.C. No. 77 Squadron

Total Time on Sqd.   8.60 97.05

Appendix Two

M. R. E. S

(Missing Research & Enquiry Service)

AIR MINISTRY, P. 4 (Cas), 73 / 77 Oxford Street, London.
M.R.E.S Unit 4

F/Lt J.A.Grimer, Investigating Officer, Officer Commanding 13 Section.
The following Investigation Reports all bear the signature of F/Lt. J.A.Grimer,
Investigation Officer, Section 13. No.3, M.R.E.U., B.A.F.O.

25th.February 1947 -

Section Reference : G -1605.   Aircraft type & number : Four engined bomber.
Position of crash : 2 km.W.S.W. Geisingen.   Map reference : S/ 04/ 38.
Crew : S/L.Hill. F/O.Cummins. F/O.Newstead. F/Sgts.Dodds. F/Sgts.Hobbs. Two unidentified members. (F/S.Buckingham another.[closing bracket omitted].
Particulars of burial : Mass grave containing 7 members of crew at top, left hand corner of cemetery.
Cemetery & Map Reference : Geisingen cemetery S/ 06/ 39.

RESULT OF INVESTIGATION AND FINDINGS:

Information received from Herr Burkhart, the Burgomaster of Geisingen confirmed the crash of a four engined bomber approximately 2 km. West of Geisingen on the night of 30/ 31st. March 1944. The wreckage has long since been removed. The record of this crash has been sent to military Government Ludwigzburg and stated that 7 members of the crew had been killed three being identified as Hobbs, Dodds, and Hill. All had been buried at Geisingen cemetery. There had been no ceremony. The seven members of the crew were removed from the wreckage by the Wehrmacht and buried in a mass grave at Geisingen cemetery. (In the N.W.section). The grave was fairly well kept and surmounted by a rough wooden cross, inscribed :-

"HIER RUHEN   7 UNBEKANNTE   AMERIKANISCHE FLIEGER"

The "Americain" was a painting error, according to the Burgomaster and the Friedhof- master, and there is no doubt that the grave does in fact contain an English crew. The Friedhof- master a Herr Kulnle, who was on military service in Stuttgart during the war states he remembers that he was in Ludwigsburg on the night in question and saw the aircraft which was flying from the direction of Stuttgart shot down by flak at 4am. During subsequent investigations at Heutingsheim S/ 06/ 38 the Burgomaster Herr Lechele said that a "major" (nationality unspecified) was taken from the crash near Geisingen alive and taken to hospital at Ludwigsburg by one Walter Zeh (habitant of Heutingaheim). Walter Zeh could not be traced. There is no longer a military hospital at Ludwigsburg the records of the former one have been destroyed by the French, the staff dispersed, the major was presumably S/L.Hill. He was taken back to Geisingen after his death and buried with the other six members of the crew on 1/ 4/ 44. The cross bears the plote[sic] of no.5 graves registration unit. Could full information of this crew please be forwarded to this unit so that complete registration may be effected.

27th.February 1947 -

From No.3 M.R.E.U. B.A.F.O. A.M. Cas. Enquiry No: G. 1070.
Aircraft type & number: Halifax 111 LSW.505 "J".   Date & Time : 21st./ 2/ 44, time unknown.
Position of crash : Stuttgart and Zuffenhausen area.   Map reference: S. 0627.
Crew: two crews.   Particulars of burial: Section V111 Steinhaldan cemetery 14 bodies (details in report).
Cemetery & Map Reference : Steinhalden cemetery S/ 11/ 26.   Articles found : nil.
Any further action : Exhumation recommended.

161783 P/O.Wright, A.E.	157673 F/O.Chambers, W.J.
1390847 Sgt.Crosswell, L.M.	18022564 Sgt.Hayward, W.E.
132865 F/O.Atkinson, T.R.	960800 W/O.Mandall, J.B.
168515 P/O.Baird, J.H.	10602608 T/Sgt.Hannon.
632513 Sgt.Marshall, H.W.	1312876 Sgt.Mulcuck, A.L.
659104 F/Sgt. Stewart.	1874038 Sgt.Steward, A.L.
532588 Sgt.Duckworth.	Aus. 417335 F/Sgt.Campbell, J.J.

RESULT OF INVESTIGATION AND FINDINGS :

Investigation of the fate of the above mentioned crew started with a visit to the town-hall at Bad Cannstatt apart from a hearsay report that an aircraft had in fact crashed at Burgoby- koff no further information was far the coming. Further inquiries at Zuffenhausen and Stuttgart town halls brought no further light on these two crashes. At both places the Staffs had entirely changed since the end of the war and at the Stuttgart Rathaus whence all records of aircraft crashed had been sent all documents had been destroyed. A visit was then made to Steinhalden cemetery where all members of the above crews were found to be buried.

The cemetery had excellent records and the Friedhofmeister supplied the following information.

On the 24th./ 2/ 1944 a Wehrmacht truck brought 14 bodies of english airmen to the Steinhalden cemetery. Some seven of these were more or less intact and had been identified by the Wehrmacht as Baird, Atkinson, Marshall, Wright, Chambers, Heywood and Campbell. The identification particulars (discs etc.) of these had been obtained by the Wehrmacht. The other seven bodies were dismembered, but seven heads and torsoes were checked. A German Army document (re ? by the cemetery) confirmed these identifications and reported that both the aircraft concerned were shot down on the night of 21st/ 2/ 44. (time unspecified). This document also stated that all 14 bodies were buried with military honours at Steinhalden cemetery at 20/ 2/ 44. Living[sic] to the large sinze[sic] of the cemetery and magnitude of civil burials at that time, the grave digger concerned in the burial remembered little or nothing of this internment, although questions.[sic] All members of both crews are buried in section V111 of the cemetery, all lie in the front row.

Below is a diagram of grave positions and numbers:

Back row -   -   -   -   -   -   -   -   -

Front row:- Marshall   Chambers Wright   Atkinson   One   six unknown   blank   Hayward
     V111 8,55   V111   V111   V111   unknown V111   8,58 a   V111
     a   8.55   8,56a   8,60   V111   57, 57a, 58   8.60a
                                                                  8,59

Front row:- continued:- Baird   the grave of 1
                   V111 8,60

All graves have been used by No.40 Graves Registration Unit and bear that units plaque.

Each grave is surmounted by a white wooden cross bearing the name (if identified) and the state[?] of death. (In the case of grave V111 8,59. the painted date of date which is 14/ 9/ 44 has been crossed out in pencil presumably by AO Graves Registrations Unit and replaced by 21./ 2/ 44 in pencil :- This agrees with records of internment made at this time.

No further information regarding the plate[sic] of these crews, the manner in which they died, the exact location of the crashed aircraft is forthcoming. Exhumation alone will determine the individual identity of the 7 unknown and is recommended.

<u>27 / 2-6 / 2 1947</u> [sic] :- [report written in pencil]   "Exhumed by Topple" - hand written in top R/H corner of report'
<u>Cas. Enquiry No</u>: G 378.   <u>Aircraft Type & number</u>: Lancaster LM 259.
<u>Date & Time</u>: 4/ 12/ 44. Time unknown.   <u>Position of crash</u>: unknown.
<u>Crew</u>:- P/O (AF/L) Herbert S.   Sgt. Huston W.J.   Sgt. Maxwell J.D.   F/O. Cleary E.D.   F/S. Aspinall T.R. Sgt. Webb P.   Sgt. Whitbread W.R.
<u>Cemetery & Map Reference</u>: Klein Ingersheim cemetery. S/ 97/ 43.   <u>Articles found</u>: nil.
<u>Any further action</u>: Exhumation imperative.

RESULT OF INVESTIGATION AND FINDINGS

No trace of the crash of Lancaster LM 259 had been found in the Klein Ingersheim area nor within a circumference of 10 kms from that village. An interim report is submitted however, as a result of investigations on A.M. cas. enquiry no. G262, to which this case is referred.

It appears that Sgt Webb may well be the eight body which was found near the crash of Lancaster P.D. 375. From information received on AM cas. enquiry no.G.262 it appears most unlikely that the eighth body which was found 20 metres from the crash of the forward section of this aircraft is a member of that crew. No identification particulars were found on the body but a description of his charred clothing (sudcott[?] and battledress) it seems certain that he was an English airman. None of the persons in   ?   ?   in connection with case 9.262 has any recollection of parachute pack or remains, although this they admit, he may have been wearing. It seems probable that Sgt Webb (should this be his body) did in fact manage to leave his aircraft with or without parachute, over Klein Ingersheim and that he was killed on impact with the ground, or by the unfortunate coincidence of landing in the blazing remains of Lancaster P.D. 375. (which would account for his charred clothing, the destruction of his parachute, and the distance of 20 metres which he might presumably have crawled before death from burns - no other major injuries were found on his body which was intact.

This possible explanation is further confirmed by the fact that other members of Sgt Webbs' crew were seen and subsequently captured in the vicinity of the crash on the night of 4. 12. 44. (all members of Lancaster P.D. 375 were killed - all bodies were accounted for).

This eight body is buried with the crew of Lancaster P.D. 375 in Klein Ingershein cemetery. Exhumation alone will definitely establish its identity for further information on burial details etc., refer to case G 262. Should the crash or crash position of Lancaster L.M. 259 be located a further report will be submitted.

The Commonwealth War Graves Commission gives the following information -

Sergeant Peter Webb RAFVR., air gunner, Service No.3006137, No.227 Squadron, killed 4th.December 1944 aged 19 years. Son of Albert Edward and Josephine Emma Webb, of Streatham Hill, London. He is buried at Durnbach War Cemetery, reference 4.F.26.

At Durnbach War Cemetery can be seen eight graves of RAF crash victims all bearing the name Webb.

27th February 1947 - "Exhumed by Topple" [F/Lt.Topple, member of the team] hand written in pencil in top R/H corner of report)
Cas. Enquiry No : G.262.   Date & Time: 4/ 12/ 44   21.00 hrs.   Position of crash: Klein Ingersheim.
Map Reference: S/ 07/ 43.
Crew :- 103929 Capt.C.W.Hirstfield.   1607068 Sgt.A.D.Lorrain.   160033 F/O.P.Yorke.   A.429472 F/O.D.E.Murphy.   A.436051 F/Sgt.H.S.Jones.   1514804 Sgt.J.Mitchell.   1431938 Sgt.J.Storr.
Particulars of burial: 7 coffins in one mass grave. One coffin containing two bodies.
Cemetery & Map Reference: Klein Ingersheim cemetery S.0743   Articles found : nil.

RESULT OF INVESTIGATION AND FINDINGS :

Investigation of the above case at Klein Ingersheim led to the interviewing of the two Friedholmeisters employed in that village. Both these men were employed as gravediggers in Klein Ingersheim between 20.00 hrs. and 21.00 hrs. on the evening of the 4th. December 1944. It had been travelling from the direction of Heilbronn and had not been on fire until impact with the ground.

The aircraft had crashed in two pieces 150 meter[sic] apart, one part being the rear fuselage and tail assembly the other comprising the main plane, motors and forward section. (Both grave diggers were quite definite on this identification of the two parts of the aircraft, close questioning failing to reveal any possibility of any other aircraft having crashed in an near village on that day.

The wreckage of the aircraft has since been removed by the Wehrmacht.

The forward section, which had burnt out after the impact, contained 7 bodies.Five of these found sitting in the aircraft were charred but complete the two others were buried beneath the engines and dismembered. These seven had apparently come forward for crash positions as no rear gunner was found in the tail assembly 150 metres away. A further body (intact) was found twenty metres from the crash position of the forward section. Reference is made here to A.M. case C.378 in which a Lancaster was shot down by a night fighter over Klein Ingersheim on 4/ 12/ 44 and the mid upper gunner Sgt.Webb is believed to have been killed, the other six of the crew being captured. This is corroborated by a report from one of the grave diggers that yet another English airman was seen that night running away into a wood. He was captured two days later.

The eight who were dead were all dressed in flying kit and battle dress.Two were identified as Hirschfield and Storr (from identity discs). There was no record of Mitchell having been identified.

All were buried in a mass grave in the top left section of Klein Ingershein cemetery. The grave was well kept and surmounted by a cross with the following inscription :-

HIER RUHEN 8 ENGLISCHE FLIEGER

The grave bear the registration plate of No.SO Graves Registration Unit. The eight were buried in seven coffins. The two dismembered airmen who were found beneath the aircraft engines being buried in one coffin.

Further close questioning confirmed that there were in fact two bodies, both the graves diggers remembering that there were two heads.

Providing that Lancaster P.D.373 was not carrying an eight member it would appear that one of the mission buried at Klein Ingersheim night[sic] be Sgt.Webb (Ref. enquiry No.C.378).

Investigations are being carried out in connection with this and exhumation may prove necessary to effect complete registration.

<u>6th.March 1947 -</u>
<u>Cas. Enquiry No</u>: G 895. <u>Aircraft type & number</u>: Lancaster P.B.740. <u>Date & Time</u>: 4/ 12/ 44.
<u>Position of crash</u>: 2km. South-West Meinsheim. <u>Map Reference</u>: R./ 975/ 515.
<u>Crew</u>:- Aus.428353 (A/ F/ O) P/ O. I.B.Plumridge. 1894948 Sgt.J.L.Wood. Aus.432361 F/O. G.F.Sinden. Aus.432361 F/S.J.K.Perran - P.O.W. Aus.424797 F/O.C.D.Rawson. Aus.430654 F/S.C.L.George. Aus.433207 F/S.F.S.Haymann.
<u>Particular of Burial</u>: Five bodies in 3 coffins. Mass grave north-east corner of cemetery.
<u>Cemetery & Map Reference</u>: Meinsheim cemetery. R/ 99/ 53. <u>Articles found</u> : nil.

RESULT OF INVESTIGATION AND FINDINGS:

Investigation were carried out at Meinshein, and the Burgomaster Herr Ludeg? was interviewed.

He confirmed the crash of a four engined aircraft on the night of 4th.December 1944 at approximately 8 - 9 p.m.(the state[sic] was confirmed by two other members of the staff). The position of the crash was two kilometres south-west of Meinsheim in a field belonging to the farm of a Friederich Augenstein. All papers and records concerning the crash had been taken by the Luftwaffe prior to the end of the war.

Friederich Augenstein was then interviewed. He confirmed the state and the time of the crash which he had witnessed. The aircraft which had been flying from the direction of Reilbronn, was apparently hit by flak and came down in flames in a near vertical dive. After impact it burnt furiously for nearly ten minutes leaving little more than a heap of ashes. Her Augenstein arrived at the scene of the crash with some civilians at about 9.30 p.m. They found one whole charred body a few yards from the wreckage, and from the ashes, extracted various charred and dismemb- ered remains. No complete heads were found, but the presence of eight feet (in addition to the complete body.) led them to believe that there were in all five dead. The scene of the crash was then visited, but no further information was obtained. The wreckage had been removed by the Wehrmacht early in 1945, and the crash crater which had originally been two metres in depth was now less than a metre, having been ploughed over twice.

The five bodies were buried in three coffins. (the dismembered remains occupying two coffins), in the north-eastern section of Meinshein cemetery. Herr Augenstein was present at the burial, and says that there was no ceremony as the village had no pastor. The grave is situated apart from the rest on a piece of waste ground between the north wall of the church and the churchyard wall (it was thought at the time that it would be merely a temporary internment). The grave was indifferently tended and surmounted by a white wooden cross, inscribed:-

HIER   RUHEN   5 ENGLISCHE FLIEGER

The date of burial was 8/ 12/ 1944, the time 5p.m.

There was no record of any of the crews identity. Four identity discs and one watch, which had been recovered were taken by an officer in the Luftwaffe.

Herr Augenstein admitted that the crash may have contained six bodies and that from the condition of the charred remains he thought it quite possible that one body might have been almost completely cremated.

Exhumation is recommended to determine wheter the grave contains the remains of 5 or 6 members of this crew buried at Neinshein and consequently ascertain the fate of F/O.Sinden.

<u>25th.March 1947 -</u>
<u>A.M. Cas. Enquiry No</u> : G 179   <u>Aircraft type & number</u> : Lancaster Mk 1. R.F.1818 "G"
<u>Date & Time</u> : 22.30 hrs. 16/ 3/ 45   <u>Position of crash</u> : Frankenberg - Eastside.   <u>Map Reference</u> : S.505/ 43.
<u>Crew</u> : 150492 F/O. Dickey, D.G.   A.428714 F/Sgt. Irving, C.H.   A.429615 W/O. Neill,[?] W.A.   1665264 Sgt. Charles, W.J.   R.182952 F/Sgt. Brown, W.C.   1176177 Sgt. Nicholls, J.T.   1324158 F/Sgt. Henry, A.
<u>Cemetery & Map Reference</u> : Frankenberg S.505/ 42.   <u>Articles found</u> : Nil.

RESULT OF INVESTIGATION AND FINDINGS :

With reference to A.M. letter P.430626? 45/ S.7. Cas. (c)4 dated 12th October 1946, the attached information is confirmed as follows.

Lancaster RF 1818 "C" was flying in a west easterly direction on the night 16/17 March 1945 when it was attacked by a fighter, lost height and exploded in the air at a height of something over a thousand feet scattering the wreckage over an area of four square kilometres. The bodies of the five dead members of the crew were found hanging in trees in the crash area, three having half opened parachutes. From the extend [sic] and nature of their injuries however (one man with an opened parachute had half of his hand blown off) it seems almost certain that all had been killed instantaneously by the explosion in the air, and that their parachutes had been opened by the blast.

The main portion of the aircraft crashed on the East side of Frankenberg, and the remaining portions of wreckage did nothing but confirm an English aircraft.

The bodies were removed on the 17 March by the Wehrmacht and were identified from their discs. Herr Stein, farmer and daughter, Frankenberg saw the bodies and was present at the burial. There was no ceremony.

The grave is situated in the South-West corner of Frankenberg cemetery, it is excellently kept has a small cross, to which an inscription bearing the names of the dead men is now added.

The grave has been looked after by Frau Stein (Frankenberg). It is apparently always [sic] covered with flowers and wreaths. Frau Stein has received two letters from next of kin, and a letter of thanks on behalf of the relatives is being sent to her from this unit.

25th.March 1947 -
Section 13. A.M. Cas. Enquiry No : 178. Aircraft type & number : Lancaster N.G.336 "S."
Date & Time : 22.00 hrs. 16/ 3/ 45. Position of crash : 2 km. East Michelbach. Map Reference : 8. 5550
Crew :- 131067 F/O.Liefooghe,R.J. 2206216 Sgt.Jonca, T. 1398604 F/Sgt.Higgins, A.E. 53446 F/O.Hughs, R.R. 1205745 F/Sgt.Davidson, V.C. 1526667 Sgt. Anthony, F.E. 1896760 Sgt.Self, F.E.
Particulars of burial : Mass grave 3 coffins, S Hall cemetery.
Cemetery & Map Reference : Schwaebisch Hall S. 5946. Articles found : nil.
Any further action : Exhumation requested.

RESULT OF INVESTIGATION AND FINDINGS :

Investigations at Sulzdorf revealed that on the night of 16/ 3/ 45 a four engined British aircraft had crashed 2 km's. East of Michelbach on a hill named Latthaus.

Herr Ernst Duns, Burgomaster of Sulzdorf confirmed that a British flyer had stayed one day in the Rathaus after having been captured by the Volksturm. He had walked 3 kms. in a north easterly direction prior to capture. F/O Liefooghe's account of his walk to Sulzdor, the lady who gave him a glass of milk, the signpost pointing to Hall. The black and white board at Sulzdorf railway station (which he must have passed to enter the village) is confirmed in every detail, and although no one could remember his name, there is no doubt that the man taken to the Rathaus at Sulzdorf was F/O.Liefooghe.

Further Frau Hartman (the lady who had given him a glass of milk) remembered his ear injury.

A visit was next made to the Rathaus at Michalbach, where it was confirmed that the aircraft once down in flames and crashed at 10.p.m. Five bodies, all intact but burnt were found in and around the wreckage of the fuselage. Apparently little effort was made to identify them (it seems probable that exhumation would reveal their identity discs) and they were buried in a mass grave as unknown.

The old Friedhofmeister at Schwaebisch Hall who was in charge of the burial is now dead, and all papers at the Rathaus which may have had some bearing on the case were burnt at the end of the war.

The cross bears the date of burial 19/ 5/ 45 and although there are four other graves with unknown flyers in this cemetery, none of those were buried within 2 months of this date. The dead men were buried with military honours, a chaplain in attendance. The grave is neat and well kept, situated in the northern section of Schwaebisch Hall cemetery, grave No. XX 3-4.

The scene of the crash was then visited for further information. Again F/O.Liefooghe's account of the crash position and the nature of the terrain was confirmed most of the wreckage including the engines had been removed, enough remained to definitely identify the aircraft as a Lancaster M.K.X11 equiped with H 2 S (some remains of this were found.) There was also evidence of very fierce heat - saplings being charred for a radius of 60 feet. The only serial no which could be found was that of the wireless receiver unit :- Type R 3515. serial No.TO 11902.

Enquiry at all the above mentioned places and neighbouring villages has revealed no trace of a sixth body. The possibility that this was utterly cremated in the main section of the aircraft and subsequently removed with the wreckage remains,[see below].

Further investigations will be conducted in this area and a further report submitted if and when this sixth body is accounted for.

In the case of the five buried in Schwaebisch Hall exhumation is requested. (see later report dated 15/ 4/ 44, below.)

27th.March 1947 -
A.M. Cas. Enquiry No : G 562.   Aircraft type & number : Lancaster M.E. 848.
Date & Time : 9.30 P.M. 17/ 3/ 45.   Position of crash : 1 Km. N.E. Mittel Fischach.
Map Reference : S. 51. 5/ 56.
Crew :   Particulars of burial : Coffin grave in disused cemetery.
Cemetery & Map Reference : Mittel Fischach (old cemetery) S. 51/ 55.   Articles found : nil.
Any further action : exhumation requested.

RESULT OF INVESTIGATION AND FINDINGS :

Rumours of the crash of a four engined British aircraft in the district were eventually confirmed at Mittel Fischach, and it is probably confirmed that this aircraft was Lancaster M.E.848.

The crash was reported to the Rathaus at Mittal Fischach by Herr Collin, the local undertaker, as having occurred at 9.30 P.M. on the night 16/ 17 March 1945, one dead English flyer being found 20 metres from the wrecked fuselage.

The aircraft had been flying in a west easterly direction (toward Nuremberg) when it was shot down by a night fighter. It exploded on contact with the ground.

Five other english airmen apparently from the same crash were taken prisoner that night.

One being captured at Ob Fischach (3 Km. N.W. Mittel Fischach) and Hothen, at Buhlertann (3 Km. E of Mittel Fischach). All had made parachute descents. Questioning in these two other two villages failed to reveal any record of the names of these prisoners, but confirmed that they were English (from description of their uniform and flying kit).

The one dead man who was found was intact but very badly burnt on the hands and the face. Information obtained from the countrymen at Mittel Fischach indicated that he had worn blue battledress with three chevrons on one sleeve (of this they were quite sure).

He was buried in a wooden coffin on the 20th/ 3/ 45. There was no ceremony or pastor at the burial, but the villagers had apparently done their best.

The grave is situated in a disused cemetery that looks more like a back yard. It is cared for by Frau Collin, is in a very unkempt state. However there are no flowers at this time and the villagers are very poor.

A cross is now being erected to replace the two sticks which hitherto served that purpose.

The wreckage of the crash has been removed by the Wermacht. Slight traces merely confirmed that it had been an English aircraft and that it crashed with a bomb load and exploded.

Some five hundred metres away was found a complete Merlin engine embedded in the ground. (though it is most likely this may not necessarily belong to the crash as another Lancaster blew up in mid air 5 Kms to the West, whilst travelling in an East Westerly direction.

On this engine was found these numbers

    D.4480   > both on the
    T.P.C. 5884   > cyclinder block.
    P.P. 4838 A. 4809. on the exhaust cowling.

No serial numbers was visible, and owing to the nature of the terrain and the depth that this engine has penetrated, much labour and heavy machinery would be necessary to extricate it.

Exhumation will be necessay to determine whether the man buried in Nuttel Fischacvh is definitely Sgt. Fox.

5th.April 1944 -
A.M. Cas. Enquiry No : 978.   Aircraft type & number : Lancaster No 336. B.
Date & Time :22.00 hrs. 16/ 3/ 1945.   Map Reference : S. 5550.
Crew :- 131067 F/O.Liefooghe, R.J.   2206216 Sgt.Jonca, T.   1398604 F/Sgt.Higgins, A.E.   53446 F/O.Hughs, R.R.   1205745 F/Sgt.Davidson, V.C.   1526667 Sgt. Anthony, F.E.   1896760 Sgt.Self, F.E.
Particulars of burial : Mass grave. 5 coffins. 1 extra member of this crew in adjoining grave containing 6 unknown English flyers.
Cemetery & Map Reference: Schwaebisch Hall S.5946.   Articles found : Nil.
Any further action : Exhumation requested.

RESULT OF INVESTIGATION AND FINDINGS :-

With reference to the report submitted by this unit on A.M. cas enquiry no. G 370, on the 25th. of March 1944 a further report is rendered to account for the fate of the sixth missing member of this crew, referred to in the last few lines of the first report.

According to information received by Herr Spreng, the friedhofmeister at Schwaebisch Hall a sixth body was found fifty metres from the main fuselage wreckage of Lancaster N.G. 336 "B" at Michalbach three days after the other five dead airmen had been taken to Schwaebisch Hall for burial. (This information is confirmed by some of the woodmen at Michelbach).

This sixth body was dressed in R.A.F. battledress, and questioning revealed that he was the rank of Flight Sergeant. The body was intact unburnt and apparently uninjured except for one large flesh wound in the left thigh. He was taken to Schwaebisch Hall cemetery on the 20/ 3/ 45 and was not buried until the 3/ 4/ 45 when 8 other unknown allied airmen apparently were buried. He was buried with them for the sake of convenience and removed three of the eight airmen he was buried with, have since been found to be American, so the grave is now marked

" 6 ENGLISH FLIEGER."

The grave no. is XX 1-2 and is adjoining grave XX 3-4 where the other dead members of his crew are buried, on the eastern side of the southern section of Schwaebisch Hall cemetery.

10th.April 1947 -
A.M. File Reference : . . .   A.M. Cas. Enquiry No : . . .   Unit Reference : . . . .   Section Reference : X 328.
Aircraft type & number : 4 engined bomber.   Date & Time : 26/ 4/ 44 2 a.m.
Position of crash : 2 km.West Kirchensall.   Map Reference : S. 37.
Crew : Unknown.   Particulars of burial : One grave. Two coffins.
Cemetery & Map Reference : Kirchensall cemetery. S.37.   Articles found : nil.
Any further action : Information regarding the identity of this crew requested.

RESULT OF INVESTIGATION AND FINDINGS :

Investigations in the region of Kirchensall revealed that a four engined British aircraft had crashed at Goltenhoff a hamlet two kilometres West of Kirchensall on the night of 25/ 26th.

April 1944.

This aircraft had been flying in East Westerly direction after it had been attacked by a night fighter and set on fire. It crashed at 2 a.m. 26/ 4/ 44 in the farm of Herr Huegel.

According to the latter the aircraft exploded on contact with the ground and burnt fiercely.[sic] Two charred bodies were found some ten metres from the main fuselage wreckage.

All wreckage has since been removed by the Wehrmacht and the ground since ploughed over but Herr Huegel has recollection of at least three four bladed aircraft engines the description of which fitted that of inline Merlins. He was also quite sure of the red white and blue R.A.F. roundels which he saw on a section of the main plane.

Apart from the fact that they were wearing an uniform similar to R.A.F. battle dress, no further information as to badges of rank and aircrew category could be ascertained in regard of the two charred bodies from either Herr Huegel, or Herr Kuhler, the friedhofmeister at Kirchensall. These two dead airmen were buried at 11 a.m, without ceremony in one grave (two coffins). The grave is in the South-East corner of the cemetery and is excellently tended and cared for by Frau Kuhler. It is surmounted by a cross, and a wreath depicting christ [sic] crucified.

Further information regarding the fate of the survivors of this crew was obtained from the burgomaster's office at Neuenstein 4 km. South of Kirchensall, in the vicinity of which two English airmen had baled out on the night of the crash.

The grave at Kirchensall has apparently been visited within the last 15 days by a British registration [sic] unit. According to the burgomaster at Kirchensall the friedhofmaster has been informed of the names of the two dead airmen (these names however he has since lost, and they are not known by anyone else in the village). Nor is there any record at Neuenstein of the names of the captured airmen.

Information regarding the supposed identification of the two dead and the number of missing in this crew is requested.

A separate page from a notebook is attached which reads as follows :-

Investigations were made at Kirchensall since a grave at Schwaebisch Hall cemetery containing 5 Airmen, bore "Kirchensall" on the cross - date 1940 X330 - no trace of this X case was found at Kirchensall but another X328 case (1944) is reported on.

Since Kirchensall is outside this section's area, perhaps this report should be forwarded to the appropriate section, as they may have reported it already - with apologies for interference.

15th. April 1947 -
Section reference X.331.   Section Reference : X. 331.   Engine type & number : Four engined bomber.
Date & Time : 22.00 hrs. 16/ 3/ 45.   Position of crash : Rohrbach and Reitenau.
Crew : AC.(?) W.S.Keenleyside. A.C.(?) E.Finch. Tree(?) unknown dead.
Particulars of burial : Three members of crew buried in mass grave (no coffins).
Cemetery & Map Reference : Oppenweiler. S. 44. 5. 26.   Articles found : Nil.
Any further action : Exhumation requested for one unknown. Investigations proceeding on identities of the two other unknown.

RESULT OF INVESTIGATION AND FINDINGS :

Information received at the "Landratamat" Kreis Backnang, revealed that three English airmen were buried at the protestant cemetery in Oppenweiler, two of whom were identified as (1) AC2 Williams Keenleyside No.1826847. Born 8 / 6 / 1922, identification card no. - 1231326. (2) AC2 E. Finch No.1865655. Born 16 / 11 / 1924, identification card n. 1231340. The third was registered as unknown.

Investigations at the Rathaus Oppenweiler confirmed these details and the following information was ascertained from Herr Zehender, the town clerk.

At 10p.m. on the night 16/ 3/ 45 an aircraft flying from West to East exploded in mid-air 3 1/2 km's. W.N.W. of Oppenweiler (subsequent examination of the wreckage by the police showed the aircraft had been carrying its bomb load).

The main fuselage section landed in the woods 500 metres West of Rohrbach. The main spar, four engines and other wreckage, together with most of the bomb load crashed in the vicinity of Reitenau.

At 7.30 a.m. 17/ 3/ 45 three bodies were found in the main fuselage section at Rohrbach two of whom were identified as above (cause of death broken bones). The rank classification of AC2 was taken from their identity cards (it was often the case with N.C.O. aircrew not to get the rank altered on their identity cards after receiving their chevrons). Close questioning of Herr Zehender, who with the Friedhofmeister was the only civilian who had seen the bodies showed that all three airmen had been dressed in sidecott flying suits and blue R.A.F. battledress. He could remember nothing of the brevets or badges of rank and could not even assert that there was none.

The Friedhofmeister himself was 85 years old and quite unable to recall even the crash or burial.

The three men were buried in pine branches at Oppenweiler cemetery at 5 p.m. 17/ 3/ 45.

There was no ceremony. The grave is situated NE corner of the cemetery. Grave No's 822-4. It has not been registered by the British and has no cross of inscription. It is however well kept and has a stone surround.

Other items found near the fuselage section at Rohrbach included 3 observer type parachutes (unopened) and four machine guns. With the assistance of Herr Zehender further investigations were conducted at Reitenau. Neither at Rohrbach nor in Reitenau were any remaining traces of the crash apart from dents in the ground. One of the inhabitants however recalled that the German soldier guarding the wreckage had spoken of the aircraft as a "Manchester." (There were definitely four engines and he must have meant Lancaster). On the 19/ 3/ 45 several human remains - 3 arms, 2 feet, 1 hand and various other portions were found in the vicinity of Reitenau. 2 months later a foot (encased in R.A.F. flying boot) was found in Sulzbach 7 km. NNE. of Reitenau. All these remains were buried as a minimum of two English flyers at Reitenau cemetery. (It is quite possible that they may have represented more than two). These remains were exhumed and removed by the Americans on 4/ 6/ 46.

The Exhumation was performed by Pfc. Joseph F.Solak No. 31497826, Organisation 538 Q.M. Group American G.R.U. A.P.O, 154.

An effort is being made to trace the destination of these remains, and to ascertain the number of English airmen they represent and if possible their identities.

Exhumation is requested in the case of the unknown at Oppenweiler cemetery.

The Commonwealth War Graves Commission gives the following information -

Sergeant William Scott Keenleyside, RAFVR.,Service No.1826847, of No.153 Squadron, air gunner, killed 17th.March 1945 aged 22 years. Son of Ernest and Elizabeth Swan Keenleyside of Low Fell, Gateshead, Durham. He is commemorated at Durnbach War Cemetery, reference 11.A.16.

Sergeant Edward Finch RAFVR, Service No.1865655, of No.153 Squadron, air gunner, killed 17th. March 1945 aged 29 years. Son of Edward Higham Finch and Margaret Finch of Ashford, Middlesex. He is commemorated at Durnbach, reference 11.A.17.

9th.May 1947 -
Five unknown burials dated 15th.March 1940, (date thought unreliable), in a mass grave in the 1st. row "Auslaender" section Schwaebisch Hall Cemetery bearing the inscription

HIER RUHEN 5 ENGLISCHE FLIEGER   BAL. KIRCHENSHALL,
19 OCTOBER 1940.

Is the only information on this case. Investigations at and within a radius of 12 kms of Kirchenshall have revealed no trace of any aircraft shot down at that date. It has been impossible to trace any person who was present at, or who remembers the burial. (The Friedhofmeister being long since dead.) All documents etc. referring to English graves at Schwaebisch Hall were destroyed at the end of the war. Further, on account of inaccuracies and discrepancies on the other crosses in the Auslaender section, even the date, is deemed unreliable. Exhumation will be carried out as soon as possible in order to identify these remains.

9th.May 1947 -
MREU / X349.   Probably a Halifax, 23.40 hrs. 15 / 16 March 1944. 1 Km E. Gallenhof S / 335 / 40. Five unknown bodies, Sechselberg Cemetery S / 33 / 40.
Particulars of burial: 3 burnt bodies in one coffin. 2 other bodies in separate coffins. Mass grave. East end Sechselberg Cemetery.

Information received from Herr Gustav Elser confirmed that a four engined British aircraft had crashed one km east of Gallenhoff at 23.40 hrs on the night 15 / 16 March 1944.

The aircraft approached Gallenhoff, circling from the S.W., when it was shot down by a fighter and crashed near Gallenhoff. The target that night had been Stuttgart and the aircraft crashed without its bomb load. The forward section of the fuselage contained the charred remains of three bodies. Two other bodies - one minus two legs and one arm - the other intact, were found within 50 metres from the main wreckage. An unsuccessful attempt by one member (the one whose body was intact) was indicated by a half opened parachute.

All five bodies were buried at 11am. 17 /3 /44 in a mass grave at the eastern end of Sechselberg cemetery; the three burnt members of the crew in one coffin, the other in separate coffins. There was no ceremony. Interrogation of Herr A.Walter, the Friedhofmeister, and another man who had also seen the bodies revealed that two of the crew had been wearing Irving Jackets (in which they were allegedly buried), but no information as to marking or rank or aircrew category.

Identity discs and papers were taken to N[?]essental by the Luftwaffe and the main wreckage was removed within a week. The intact member of the crew was buried with a signet ring inscribed with his initials.

A visit to the scene of the crash indicated that the plane had made a powered approach apparently under some control. It completely cleared a straight strip of pine forest 170 metres long by 20 metres wide. Part of a roundel marking confirmed the aircraft as British and construction of fuselage wreckage closely resembled that of a Halifax. The plane had been equiped with "GEE" and had been carrying window.

The grave at Sechaelberg is moderately well kept and surmounted by shrubs. Instructions were given for the erection of a cross.

Exhumation will be carried out in the near future for the purpose of individual identification.

16th. May 1947 -
X 352......13 Section.   Unknown (including however 3 F/ Sgt's, 2 Sgt's).
Particulars of Burial : Mass Grave Schwaebisch Hall, Friedhof.

A grave containing 6 unknown English flyers is located in the first row of the foreigners section at Schwaebisch Hall cemetery. The cross bears the burial date 3/ 4/ 45 and gives the presumed position of the crash as Einkorn. Einkorn refers to a district South East of Schwaebisch Hall, in which three other British aircraft crashes occurred about the same time. An extensive search has been made of this area in connection with the above case, and with this three other cases and no definite information with regard to the crash date and position of this aircraft has yet come to light. All wreckage from all the crashes in this district has since been recovered, and the bodies connected with them were seen only by the Wehrmacht in most instances.

The following information regarding the contents and history of this grave was obtained from one of the grave diggers at Schwaebisch Hall. On 2/ 4/ 45 a Wehrmacht truck brought in eight bodies of allied airmen stating that they had been found in the Einkorn district and inferring that they were members of the same crew. These were buried at Schwaebisch Hall on the 3/ 4/ 45 together with another airman, who had been awaiting burial for 14 days (refer case G 978 second report). In June 1946 the grave was opened by the Americans and three of its members were removed as American, leaving the grave containing 6 bodies, one of whom is identified as belonging to a crew in a neighbouring grave. (AM Cas.G 978).

With regard to the appearance and clothing of these other five the grave digger was able to state that they were unburnt, dressed in RAF battledress, all wearing Sgt chevrons, three also having the crowns of F/ Sgt's. Since the information on the crosses in this cemetery has been found to be unreliable as to crash positions this grave will be exhumed as soon as possible. Should any further information regarding the fate of this crew some to light. Meanwhile, a further report will be submitted.

22nd.May 1947 -
A.M. Cas. Enquiry No : X   Aircraft type & number : 4 engined bomber   Date & Time : 27/8/ 43.
Position of crash : unknown.
Crew : Proston. Fitgerald. 5 unknown.
Particulars of burial : Mass grave containing 5 bodies, 2 individual graves.
Cemetery & Map Reference : Schwaebisch Hall.   Articles found : nil.

RESULT OF INVESTIGATION AND FINDINGS :

Information received from Herr Spreng the Friedhofmeister Schwaebisch Hall cemetery reveals that on the 1st Sept 1943 a Wehrmacht truck brought in 7 bodies taken from a British four engined bomber. It was they stated had crashed in the Einkorn district (S.W. Schwaebisch Hall) on 27/ 8/ 43.

Two of these bodies were identified as Proston and Fitgerald by their identity tags and were buried under separate crosses on either side of a mass grave containing the remaining five bodies.

An extensive search has been conducted throughout the Einkorn district in connection with this and other cases, and no grave has been found of this crash, nor is any other information of the fate of this crew available.

The bodies were buried on the 2nd/ 9/ 43. The five unidentified members were buried but Herr Sprey states that he has recollection of two members wearing Sgt chevrons.

The grave is situated in the second row of the auslander[sic, Auslaender] section of Schwaebisch Hall cemetery, and is neatly kept. Information is requested regarding the . . . the five unknown members of this crew, . . . exhumation will be conducted to ascertain their separate identities.
B.A.F.O British Air Forces of Occupation.
M.R.E.U Missing Research and Enquiry Unit.

Squadron Leader P.E.Laughton-Bramley
M.B.E., O.N.M., (Fr.)., G.C.M. (P)., F.R.G.S., R.A.F., (Retd.).

The man Flight Lieut.John Grimer worked under was Squadron Leader Philip Laughton-Bramley, the RAF *protege* of Bleriot, a war hero, former diplomat, and acquaintance of Stanley Baldwin the Prime Minister and British Royalty. He, together with his team tracked down the graves of thousands of missing airmen after WW2. John was one of a team, but he really knew nothing regarding the person, or his military history and WW2 achievements.

Laughton Bramley was aged 94 years when he died in September 1994. Apparently while being taken to hospital by ambulance he gave the ambulance men his name, rank and number, and then died from a heart attack.

He had been taught to fly by Louis Bleriot (who on July 15th.1909 became the first man to fly the English Channel in a three-cylinder mono-plane), and his flying certificate was signed by Bleriot himself. In 1938 he was arrested by the Gestapo in Ludwigshafen, Germany.He rejoined the RAF as an intelligence officer in Europe during WW2, from where he had escaped from behind enemy lines in France and Belgium.

After the bombing of Pearl Harbour he became Staff Officer to Admiral Halsey, Comander-in-Chief of the South Pacific Fleet, and fought a wireless war against Tokyo Rose with broadcasts on Radio Noumea.

Squadron Leader Philip.E.Laughton-Bramley was born in Norwich in 1900. During WW1 he joined the Royal Navy Air Service and in 1918 was a foundling member of the RAF before being demobbed in February 1919 from RAF Rendcomb near Cirencester. He learned to fly and served as a pilot during WW1. His flying certificate was signed by Blériot himself only fifteen years after the Wright brothers pioneered powered flight by crossing the English Channel in July 1909 in forty-three minutes.

"Bram" and Isobel his wife retired to Australia in 1969 where he was soon made president of the Royal Air Force Escaping Society (Australian Branch). During June 1993 he wrote to Grimer saying how recently he had been visited by Pat and Ernie who had been sent to him by Eric "Chic" Risdeal, who always kept in touch with him. In his letter of thanks he mentioned he had written to Eric Risdeal, John Gosling, and John. Moreover, "Bram" also kept in touch with "Rosie" Rosabie in Canada, and Angus MacLean who became a minister of some Canadian church.

Isobel returned to her homeland in 1969, but Bram, (although he had no other relatives in Britain) also returned and kept the Missing Research (M.R.E.S) group together for a total of twenty-one years, after they packed up the group in Germany, from where he left the European comforts.

Bram never forgot that John Grimer had a good sense of humour, and often commented on his use of his gift when John was serving under him in Unit 3 of the M.R.E.S in Karlsrake. Bram himself served in M.R.E.S Units 2, 3, and 4. The M.R.E.S was formed in 1945 to track down, dis-inter, and catalogue all missing crash victims of the RAF during WW2.

For two years previously he was in Holland, Belgium, North France, Germany, (North and South, and the Black Forest), Chekoslovakia, and by late 1945 back at Karlsrake where Grimer joined his team. After WW2 he served for a period in the South Pacific and visited Australia and New Zealand when on leave from the South Pacific.

Some sixty years later when someone wrote further letters to The Times condemning the severity of the destruction of medieval German towns, its civilian population, as well as children and babies by Bomber Command; Grimer wrote his answer (see p.116). "Bram" followed those accusations and following comments and voiced his agreement to Grimers' answer. He even wrote to "Johnny" Grimer and congratulated him on his spirited answer, saying "I am also of the same opinion, when I was doing the Hamburg district I covered plenty of traces of ruins and devastation."

"Bram" received newspaper cuttings from Paul Adoras on behalf of the Canadian branch of the RAF Escaping Society. Paul was with him in Chekoslovakia. Later, he married a Check girl he met in Prague and they removed to Montreal where she died from cancer many years ago. They had one son.

He had four M.R.E.S "types" living near to himself in Sgary ?? Australia. Vincent Macauley, Douglas Angus, John Robershaw, and a fellow called Woodward. Every October they had a get together over lunch. But he was always in touch with so many of the M.R.E.S "types that when he moved to Australia he was made president of the RAF Escaping Society. Another of his wartime compatriots from whom he occasionally received a letter was Moorcroft, who was headmaster somewhere in the south west of England. Also Mike Shaw and

Jaques Fusy who is of French parentage and who flew Spitfires in the RAF during the war.

His house was a shrine for all those aircrew who died over occupied land. The walls of his room were festooned with M.R.E.S stuff, accounts, newspaper cuttings, letters, everything appertaining to those thousands of aircrews missing, believed to be dead, but having no known grave. Often he would sit with his friends (all ex-servicemen) members of M.R.E.S when they would re-live their days.

Sadly his life in Australia was becoming "pretty grim;" by what be believed to be radical political thinking under a Socialist government, especially when he suspected the country will shortly become a republic : and on issues such as immigration of some two million non-English speaking people from various parts of the world.

He was sad when in 1993 his driving licence was taken away from him - because of his age. Without his car he found it difficult to do his shopping from the local village of Lane Cove.

Appendix Three
LETTERS

Regrettably, yet understandably, Jean destroyed all her letters she wrote to John during his time away, apart from a few brief examples shown in the main text which stand to illustrate what a loss her action was; because she wrote letters of prime interest and in a singular style, as well as using strict economy with words : often showing an excellent sense of humour.

Jean was an atheist and would tolerate no mention of our Christian Faith in her presence. Her father also was a firm atheist and would allow his children to have no access to any Christian, or other religious knowledge while at school. But Jean was a private individual, and as such she destroyed that which she wanted no one else to see; including her letters.

Letter written in pencil from John to ? dated Wednesday February 5th.

"Have not been able to put this to Post until arriving at Karbsrhur (which I did 3am. this morning after 8 days journey from London).

Frankly many things seem horrible. It is of course much too early for me to form a cut and dried opinion, but I have seen enough to confirm many of my views, and you know what they are. An awful sense of depression and anger is my main feeling, but that is not a general sentiment, although many feel the same - but then - what can be done ?

However I'm going right into the American Zone wherethings though bad, will I think be better. Although no one seems to know. Prices tho' should be higher and living not so cheap - but still I should think cheaper than England. Also I hope its warmer than this!

I detrain at Hanover for further instruction, and at this rate it will take me five days. Just coming into a most nightmarish tangle of wrecked factories and twisted girders which stretched for miles -- Hanover! Will finish this this afternoon when I can post it.

For Occupation Troops, fags, spirits, and drink are ridiculously cheap, (6d. and 1/- for all tots of spirits, liqueurs, etc. 9d. for 20 Players -- allowance 200 [cigarettes] per week). Plus as yet I have seen little of the bombing of the people. In this certainly, I should think the most bombed, overcrowded, and the poorest fed part of Germany, and on this job I may not get chance of doing so.

Incidentally, it is so bitterly cold (the North Sea was full of ice floes which held up the ship).

The only incident was in the Marshalling yards near Hambourg where no one expected the children begging for food and fags (the best currency to buy food). We were all told not to encourage this as the children run across the tracks and lately many have been knocked down by trains. I couldn't resist throwing a bag of ham rolls and some fags, but then I almost wished I hadn't. Something must be done - they looked cold, ill fed, pathetic, some poorly clad, others not. People don't look like Belsen, many have warm clothes, but they do all definitely look undernourished, ill and worst of all look hopeless. I shiver in my greatcoat in a supposedly heated train. . ."

Letter card from Jean

Addressed - P/O Grimer J.A. 138336., R.A.F. Station, Elvington, near York, Yorks.

Letter from Jean

[October 1943?]   "Trevanion. [Liskeard]

My dear darling husband, how I hope and pray everything was alright when you returned & that you haven't been sent to quod - just cos you married me !

Also I hope you are well. Wouldn't it be wonderful when this war is over & we can look after each other & - if you're sick I can nurse you.

Darling husband - I'm at Ruth's place - everyone surprised & pleased & wishes us happiness. Look after yourself sweetheart for my sake. I love you darling more than I ever thought possible.

I was terribly happy with you - but why, oh why was your leave so short ? How war breaks up our normal human "happinesses" - what must it be like in Europe today - we're lucky really. It's very funny now to speak of "my husband" one day I'll get used to it I suppose !

Love from your loving wife - Jean."

Letter card from Jean

Addressed - F/O Grimer J.A. 138336., Officers Mess, R.A.F. Station, Elvington, (near York), Yorkshire.

27th.November 1943.

"from Grimer, Trevanion, New Road, Liskeard.

Darling love, received your wonderful exciting long letter yesterday but no time to reply as it deserves for a day or two. Sweetheart if you knew how often in the past I'd cried myself to sleep about what WAS our biggest problem i.e. your outlook & my outlook upon "the morrow."

I think you've exaggerated (a) My influence. (b) Weekend here on Education because deep down in you, you've always had those vital interests in other people i.e. social problems. Darling, you & I of course can't do much & yet "every little counts." What music did you buy for the Mess ?

Am sending a few "education" books along just in case they're any use.

All my love & I hope you are safe & well dear. Jean."

letter from Jean -

"Until August 15th. C/O Major & Mrs. Underhill, "The Brake" Ewshott, Farnham, Surrey. Letter No.5 Aug 6th.

My darling John,

Its your birthday tomorrow dearest and I wish I could send you cigarettes, but am not able to send parcels to Dulag Luft. I love you so much and baby Frances and I send you all our love. She herself is looking so well and cuddlesome that I can't imagine a nicer birthday present for my husband ! Am hoping to have her photographed so that you'll be able to get used to her appearance and survive the shock of seeing what we have produced !

The Red Cross tell me that you are wounded and in a military hospital at Rheims - your letter tell me (the latest one I had dated July 2nd. - only a month to reach me) that you are almost better. Do take care of your health please 'cos I love you and don't want you back as a crock - there will be so much work to do.

Your spelling is still perfectly bloody. You might do worse than study phonetics & philology whilst you're a P.O.W ! I've sent the page of tripe on to your parents. They'll be pleased. Actually your mother has written several decent letters to me - rather overflowing with tips as to how to attain everlasting godliness but still she can't help that. My mother is well, bless her, and sends you heaps of love, so do all the kids who think you must be almost divine to have baled out ! Imagine the stories they must have told their cronies at school, about their brother- in-law !

My address from August 15th. onwards will be C/O Mrs Mann, St. Meva, Plymouth Road, Liskeard, Cornwall, in a much healthier place for babies these days. Anyway all you need ever worry about is yourself. Baby & I are safe, well & financially in clover ! Also from the way the wind is blowing you & I will be together very soon - after all, wars must end sometime.

So look after your health & let your mind rest in peace about Frances & me - I jolly well realise how you long to see her (& her mother !) & our taking care of our health & safety for your sake darling.

Dearest ole John - keep happy somehow - even though it must be hellishly difficult when you're a P.O.W with nothing to do. Won't it be simply wonderful to be together again after this palaver is over

I love you so much J . . . "[?]

~~~~~~~~~~~~~~~~~~~~~~~~~~~~~

<u>In a letter to The Times</u> dated May 22nd. 1993, Mr John A Grimer wrote :-

"Sir, When working with the RAF missing research and enquiry teams in Germany in 1947 and 1948, locating, exhuming and identifying the corpses of aircrews, I was appalled at the wanton and excessive destruction in most German cities - especially as I had, in part, been responsible for it.

But it ill behoves members of a nation which had perpetrated and permitted the camps and the Holocaust to regard such as the Dambuster crews as war criminals. At the time, theirs was a shinning example that gave many of us the courage to continue. The country was fighting for its life and there was little else we could do.

True, Nazi Germany reaped the whirlwind; but let us never forget who it was that sowed the wind.

John A Grimer,

(77 Squadron, Bomber Command 1943-4)
High Windmill, Bay View Road,
East Looe, Cornwall.   May 17."

A further letter to The Times, dated 22nd May 1993, by Mrs Gertrud Walton.

"Sir, Mr John A Grimer and Mr Stephen Lewis defend the Dambusters by the argument that the country was fighting for its life and that they were doing their best for their families, their squadron and their country. Such humility does the British honour. Allow me, a German, to point out that millions in other countries, Germany included, knew that their survival depended on the British. That there were so few of them, and that victory came too late for many, is, of course, sad; it does not detract from the achievement. It is symptomatic of delinquents to complain of wounds incurred in attempts to stop their murderous pursuits; Germans who love decency and freedom will not be found among those who today indulge in self-pity."

A letter to The Times. by James Hampton, Thame, Oxon.

"Disparaged. For a good many years it has been fashionable to disparage the achievements of Bomber Command. Your article, in giving great prominence to only one side of a very complex question, is treading a well-worn path.

For almost the whole of the second world war, Bomber Command was the only arm of the British Forces able to engage in offensive warfare against Germany itself. Almost half of its air-crew perished. Although they represented only about 2% of the armed forces, they accounted for 14.5% of the war dead.

At the end of it all, the commander-in-chief of Bomber Command was denied a peerage and his aircrew a campaign medal. It is doubtful if, in the recorded annals of war-fare, any body of men who achieved so much, fought so hard and suffered such losses was ever so badly treated by its political masters.

Perhaps one day those who denounce the activities of Bomber Command will tell us what the alternative to the bomber offensive was . . ."

Letter to The Times from Jack Arkinstall, Squadron Leader, RAF., retired, Chichester.

"Sir, Do articles like that by Roger Boyes ("Flood of bitterness," May 17th. 1993) disparaging the effects of the Mohne and Eder dam raid of 1943, achieve anything except cause anger to those who survived, and grief to the relatives of those who died in these and similar raids ? Some of us like to feel that our war efforts were not in vain.

I am sceptical of the German version of this raid, that the "production of weapons was not interrupted even for a day." It is also reported that the Germans consider the raid was an atrocity. All war is an atrocity, Mr.Boyes, as we who survived it know."

~~~~~~~~~~~~~~~~~~~~~~~~~~~~~

Extract from :-

Newsletter of No.77 Squadron, 'Nickle' Leaflet No.8 dated October 1992, editor - Mr. Harry Shrinkfield.

"The erection of a statue in honour of Butch Harris and the 55,000 dead of Bomber Command appears to have created some considerable furore among people who have much to be thankful for and yet remain uninformed. The Mayor of Cologne for instance deplored the fact that the statue was dedicated on the anniversary of the first 1000 bomber raid of the war when the target was that city. I wonder just how many anniversaries we could bring to mind should we so wish? The letter to Butch from Winston Churchill [below] sums it up nicely. Bomber Command can hold up its head with pride."

~~~~~~~~~~~~~~~~~~~~~~~~~~~~~

One must appreciate that there were sixty seven squadrons in Bomber Command, and 56,000 young aircrew of Bomber Command were lost in those five years of war, "when freedom was no certain thing, and each man risked all he had to fight for that freedom. For 500 of the squadron who never returned, their last home on earth was a now-deserted airfield in Elvington."

A Book of Remembrance, *Achievements of 77 Association,* **Ron Stewart, Hon.Secretary, (ND.), p.18.**

"What did they die for ? Those young airmen of more than fifty years ago flew night after hazardous night were demonstrating their technical skill and bravery, their loyalty to King and country, their love of family and comrades, their willingness to make, as they did, the most of their lives, for each man was a volunteer. Their motivation was the defeat of the enemy, to overcome not a nation, but a perverted and wicked philosophy which had somehow overtaken the German people. These young men of Bomber Command flew to achieve freedom from the oppression of this evil regime for the freedom of mankind worldwide. Loyalty, love and these lie at the very heart of Christianity. The cross of Jesus is our continuing reminder of the example He gave us. It was He who taught us self-giving love which has been reflected in the lives of these young men, for there is no greater love than that a man shall lay down his life for others so that they may enjoy freedom from want, freedom from fear, freedom of speech and freedom of religion. They are the four cornerstones of civilisation."

(An address given by the Chaplain-in-Chief of the RAF, the Ven.P.R.Turner, QIC, BA., AKC, on the 5th.October 1996, at the dedication of the York Air Museum Memorial Chapel.)

to "Air Chief Marshall Sir Arthur Harris,

I wish to express to you on behalf of the Government the deep sense of gratitude which is felt by all the nation for the glorious part which has been played by Bomber Command in forging the victory. The conduct of these operations demonstrated the fiery gallant spirit which animated your aircrews and the high sense of duty of all ranks under your command. I believe that the massive achievements of Bomber Command will long be remembered as an example of duty nobly done."

Winston Churchill.

~~~~~~~~~~~~~~~~~~~~~~~~~~~~~

In a letter from Alfred J. French of Spalding, Lincs,

dated 24th.May 1993, he writes the following.

"I write as one of your old comrades - Lancasters - 156 Squadron P.F.F. Upwood, navigator.

. . . On 24th. March 1943 - we were shot-up over Harpenerwerg in the Ruhr and when about to bale out I witnessed our mid-upper - Francis MacWilliams - leave the aircraft on the shoulders of the wireless operator because his own parachute was burnt. It was a brave reflex action and he was never seen again.

Can you tell me please if there is a special department I can write to and perhaps find out if Mac has a grave ? . . ."

~~~~~~~~~~~~~~~~~~~~~~~~~~~~~

Letter to John Grimer from Victor F.Gammon, newsletter Editor for the

Royal Air Forces Ex-P.O.W. Association.   Dated 24th. May 1993.

"Thank you for your spirited letter in the 'Times' in defence of the 'Dambusters'. Gibson and his men were indeed a 'shining example'. Another angle of the 'Flood of Bitterness' article was that the raid did little to hinder the German war effort and that is perhaps partly true but the effect on German morale was tremendous. Prisoners in Germany will well remember the down-cast eyes of the guards and interpreters when they realised that the men of the RAF were determined and that their country was so vulnerable to that kind of determination. The fuss made about the raid in the black bordered newspapers, particularly the Volkischer Beobachter, convinced POW's that Germany was sorely hurt . . .

Thank you again for your letter in the 'Times' John, it will be appreciated by the relatives and all RAF men who took part in the Second World War."

~~~~~~~~~~~~~~~~~~~~~~~~~~~~~

Letter to The Times dated 13th.February 1995.

"To Flight Sergeant Don Bennett, the briefing at 5pm on the chilly afternoon of February 13, 1945, at RAF Balderton was no different from any that had preceeded his 15 previous missions. The target was just another German city: Dresden.

"We thought, 'Oh Christ, another long one; ten hours there and back.' We were to bomb an important railway and communications centre; they never mentioned that the place was full of refugees. The good news was that the intelligence people told us not to expect too much opposition in the air that night."

With the life expectancy of a rear gunner little more than two weeks, to survive seven missions was thought lucky. Flight Sergeant Bennett, a mid-upper gunner with Squadron 9J of 5 Group, Bomber Command, was posted in a greenhouse atop a Lancaster's fuselage. He had had far more than his quota of luck, and went to fly seven further missions before the war's end. He was aged 19.

They took off at 6pm. under a lowering, moonless sky and flew south to rendezvous with the rest of the first wave, a swarm of 244 bombers heading east in a formation two miles wide and a 1,000 feet deep, the growl of their Rolls-Royce engines playing an accompaniment of menace. They crossed the Continent untroubled by the Luftwaffe, and only very occasional light flax. Their enemy, at 18,000ft. was the cold. "Icicles grew on my oxygen mask; my electrically heated flying suit frequently failed.

By the time the undefended city was within sight of Flight Sergeant Bennett's seven-man Lancaster crew just before 11pm, the action had begun. "On the ground I could see the sparkling lights of the first incendiaries, and the first markers, brilliant red and green like a giant display of Roman candles. I could see the very first fires starting - lots of individual fires that were clearly going to spread and join up." Ten miles from its target Flight Sergeant Bennett's Lancaster began its level run above broken cloud. As the bomb doors opened to release 4,000lb of incendiaries, cold air rushed in. "After the bombs had gone we had to continue on the same course for a bit longer, while the camera photographed our hit; those seconds were always a lifetime. You just wanted to get the hell out of there."

By the time the second wave of 529 bombers approached at 1.30am. an inferno was raging; crews reported seeing the firestorm when they were still 200 miles from the city. As they reached their target, navigators left their seats to gaze aghast on a spectacle the like of which they had never seen. Dresden was a city whose every street was etched with fire.

The sky blazed scarlet and white. Crewmen filled in their log sheets by the eerie light that filled their cockpits; their bodies felt the hot breath rising from the furnace. "It was the first time I ever felt sorry for the Germans," a bomb-aimer recalled. "But my sorrow lasted only for a few seconds; the job was to hit the enemy and to hit him very hard."

Mr Bennett now lives in retirement in Hertfordshire. "I never gave Dresden another thought until years later, when the controversy began to emerge. Dresden is not on my conscience of war is that people get killed. A great many were killed in Dresden, but you must remember that we were fighting, and risking our adolescent lives to defeat, a greater evil."

Appendix Four
POEMS
by John Grimer

(Written after WW2 - probably in Germany when working with the M.R.E.S - 1947)

      VERY awkward to reach the perspex nose of the Halifax,
with sextant, maps and parachute,
And Mae West grotesquely strapped by heavy harness,
The floor slopes steeply, oddly.

      But when you get there you can relax
Compose your thoughts and watch the evening clouds.
Now you can show your maps and check your sights
Fidget with your harness - jerkily chew your gum.
You've come a long way - you've had a very costly training :
Only make sure to leave yourself behind
        In the lavatory,
        Behind the dispersal,
        Where you prayed to the God you did'nt believe in,

      It made you feel better to pray - for the women and children.
It gave you a chance to pray for your crew too - for yourself -
        Ah - for yourself !

      Peering vacantly into space stupidly waiting.
Not knowing their immense disgrace,
Their self betrayal.
No Glory - no vindictiveness.
Only cold and individual loneliness
On the flight out.

      "There's the target - that glow to port.
That's Hamburg burning. Right - right - steady - steady."
"Bombs away skipper." Thank Christ, no fighters ready.

      The glow a little brighter now sinks to stern.
Three days now the people have seen the fire burn.
Eating the heart out of their city.
"Must'nt let it go out boys - you can't miss it."

      "Is there any water in the streets to help the firemen ?
Where are the firemen ?
      Two lie crumpled on the hot pavement the air sucked out of their lungs.
To feed the inferno above the street.
      Is there any water in the Elbe tunnel ?
      Only the thick black heavy water of the river
      And the bodies of eighteen hundred people.

      Her body had been white and sweet until she had embraced
The eternity of the four thousand pound bomb.
She was buried beneath three different city blocks.
Three days later - her separate limbs were green and filthy.

Three weeks later - some SS men sprayed the rubble with lime and liquid fire
To purge the putrid stench.

You can hear the eight o'clock news on the flight back.
It'll tell you, that you've just bombed Hamburg.
You're nearly safe now.
You've done a good job helping to win the war.
It's a pity you don't think so.
But then, you're only thinking that you're cold
And want your breakfast.

P.S.   "Was'nt on Hamburg raids - but experiences with M.R.E.S
probably sparked me to write this.
Hamburg raids were during August 43
I joined Squadron 97 in Sept. 43."

~~~~~~~~~~~~~~~~~~~~~~~~~~~~

Factual reminiscence of an exhumation
by John Grimer
unfinished   (Written some time in 1947)

WE got to Grosse Oppenweiler in the heat of the day.
The village was lazily deserted, and only a few hens scuttled from the roadway into the dung heaps and woodpiles.
Twice up and down the street the heavy Humber lurched - but nowhere
Could we see the usual Cypress trees and massive memorials that mark so many
German cemeteries.

"Nach Friedhof" roared Jock - my driver, in a lusty Scots accent.
After very many "Nach Friedhofs" which always received the attention of the very
Deaf and toothless ancients, or the youngest of the children -
Who seemed to think we were going to bury them.
We eventually found our way up a ploughed hill through an orchard -
To a quaint little church and cemetery perched right on top of the hill -
Very very old.

It was one of the most beautiful little cemeteries I have ever seen.
For once there was no Cypress or privet - no sombre Wagnerian angels - no granite skulls.
Just bright sunlight on the daisy speckled mounds.

"Nach eine stunde " said the friedhofmeister - very dignified in his official uniform.
We settled down beneath the shade of the church wall to eat our sandwiches
And drink some "bauer must."
"Christ it's hot," said Jock.
I grunted assent. "They'll stink like a sewer today, how many are there ?"
"Seven" I replied. "A whole crew then, as far as we knew."

"Och ! why can't they let the poor bastards lie -
If they know it's the whole crew -
What the hell's the use of separating the fucking mess in seven piles of shit -
Just to say that pile's Peter - that lump's Paul.
All this petrol - seven good army blankets - and even so you don't always get it right."

"And the kids freeze for want of a blanket this winter."
I added - "Wish it was freezing now."
We could begin to smell our work. "Let's walk out into the orchard" he finished.
Which we did - and helped ourselves to some apples under the glowering gaze of a fierce
Peasant.
"Ferdick" yelled the old friedhofmeister - running out of the cemetery gates - mopping
his brow and looking as if he'd had enough.

       We made our way to the fetid hole - gashed in the corner of the cemetery.
Three brawny young peasants rested on their spades and shovels -
Waiting for the packet of 'Lucky Strike' which Jack split between them.
"Will ye want my help ?" he asked me as I drew on my gum boots and rubber gloves.
"Not yet" I replied. "They're all mangled up - no coffins - there wont be room for two
      Of us until the top ones are out."

       I jumped onto the squelchy contents of the pit -
"Shove a lighted fag in my mouth" I asked as it hit me.

       It was hot - very hot.
These rubber gloves never seemed to be cleaned out inside properly -
with the muck left at the tips of the fingers   . . .

unfinished 1941.

~~~~~~~~~~~~~~~~~~~~~~~~~~~~

"A touch of nostalgia"

I wish I could write a poem
- about the subservience of a 'traveller'
Waiting in a shop.
Shopkeepers are diffident, courteous and attentive
But a 'rep' is doubly diffident
as he waits between the polos and the groceries
never interrupting the serving of a customer
with his patient pad and pencil
hovering in his hand.
Can these quiet neat men
Ever have been ebullient raucous boys
Cheeking teachers
Chasing playground girls
At School ?

This one I see today was such a boy
At Menheniot School some thirty years ago
Oh the sadness of growing up !

March 2009.
Title mine - ed.

Appendix Five

"je suis blesse - aidez mol !"
by John Grimer

from NO TIME FOR FEAR, *True Accounts of RAF Airmen taken prisoner 1939 - 1945*,
Victor Gammon, 1998, p.173ff.

"Bomb aimer Flight Lieutenant John Grimer and his fellow crew members felt better at being taken off German targets and credited with only one-third of an operation for attacking French targets. The night of 23 April 1944 was the 77 Squadron Halifaxes third French trip. It was one of nearly 200 Bomber Command aircraft that were to attack the railway yards at Laon, an important marshalling centre and through-route to the French coast. Grimer was happy when able to call "bombs away" and observe a 'bang-on' bombing of the marshalling yards. Immediately after releasing the bomb load, however, he saw a 'roman candle' tracer dead ahead. He clicked up his microphone switch to warn the pilot just as the Halifax went straight through it. The intercom went dead but the navigator's shielded light still shone.

As Grimer saw a Junkers 88 beneath them breaking away, the bombsight before him shattered. He felt a sharp pain near his right eye as a splinter opened a superficial wound. Wiping the blood away, he watched with wonder as navigator Charlie Hobgen carefully folded his maps and raised his table and the collapsible seat to clear the escape hatch. Table and seat were both riddled with bullet holes but Hobgen was unscathed and cool. The wireless operator, though, had a foot almost severed. Grimer and Hobgen clipped his parachute pack to his harness and pushed him through the hatch. Flames were now roaring through the plane. Quickly Hobgen dived into the darkness, but Grimer's parachute pack had been hit and he was unable to secure it properly. He jumped with one clip holding, but his fears were allayed when the canopy snapped open and checked his headlong fall.

The blazing Halifax crashed with a bright orange flash and an enduring glow. John Grimer's descent was smooth until his canopy snagged on a tree. Swaying gently in his harness, he peered below and could see stars reflected in water. Thinking that he must be hanging over a canal, Grimer turned the harness quick-release button, thumped it firmly, and fell. The unexpected hurtling into a shallow puddle winded him and wretched his back. After gathering his breath, Grimer decided to stand and look around him. Then he saw that below the knee his right leg was a shattered, bloody mess. Until that moment he had felt nothing.

Pulling himself together, he took his Benzedrine tablets, applied a tourniquet to his right thigh, and began an agonising crawl through a small wood and across several fields, until he reached a small village. Grimer had learned French from his Belgian mother and as he neared the houses, he called loudly, 'Je suis aviateur Anglais - je suis blesse - aidez moi !'

The responses were curses from windows thrown open angrily and shouts of 'Taisez vous !'

Grimer was surprised and discouraged, but he crawled on through the village until he reached a small farmhouse. There he banged repeatedly on the door until it opened. An elderly couple, seeing his plight, took him in and treated him with the utmost kindness, giving him brandy, hot soup and a bowl of raw eggs to sustain him. They sat him on a chair, proping his wounded leg on a stool. During his long crawl Grimer had loosened the tourniquet every half-hour and, as he did so again, blood dropped on to the stone floor. He was sickened as a farm dog lapped the blood.

The couple sent for a doctor, who bandaged and splinted Grimer's leg, telling him that he might be able to be moved or even walk with crutches in about six weeks. The elderly pair courageously offered to hide him in their barn until he could be moved to a safer place.

Despite their care, Grimer was soon running a high temperature and was racked with bouts of delirium. He asked his hosts to send for the Germans and tell them that they had just found him in one of the fields. They reluctantly agreed. A few hours later, two German soldiers arrived to collect him on a motor-cycle and sidecar. Grimer's hopes of being taken to a hospital were dashed. After a jolting and painful journey, he was carried into a prison and locked into a small cell furnished with a wooden board and a bucket. A shuttered judas-hole in the door was opened periodically, but for John Grimer, passing in and out of consciousness, time began to lose its meaning. During lucid moments he heard French patriotic songs being sung and once a volley of gunshots as if a firing squad was at work. He reached the utter depths of despair.

Grimer had a vague recollection of being on a stretcher, driven in an ambulance, and laid on an operating table where the man leaning over him and working on his leg was referred to as 'Hauptmann Doktor.' The German surgeon saved Flt.Lt.Grimer's leg and very likely his life."

Addendum

The Happy Liberators

"The German guards at the American Military Hospital at Rheims were First World War veterans. They were strict but not unkind, although they told Flight Lieutenant John Grimer with satisfaction that London was being destroyed by V1 flying bombs. The news of the Normandy invasion did not reach the RAF men in hospital until the end of June.

In the late summer of 1944 the Americans were about to capture Rheims and the hospital. John Grimer was still in great pain from his leg wounds, although the German doctor had worked unceasingly for him and the wounded. The doctor's care was limited by the lack of drugs and bandages. Only once did Grimer know this dedicated man to lose his temper. During a daylight raid the hospital had been bombed and three nurses killed. The doctor was furious and threatened 'to cut off all your arms and legs.' Such a threat was but a momentary lapse from his professional ethics. When Grimer begged him to amputate a leg that was badly infected with gas gangrene the doctor declined, telling him that if the hospital was liberated by the Americans they would have adequate drugs with which to save his leg.

One morning at the end of August the doctor walked round the ward saying 'Goodbye' and shaking hands with the wounded RAF men. The Americans were near, he told them, then left with the guards. The prison ward remained unlocked and those of the eight prisoners who could walk pushed the others, in wheelchairs or trolleys, to the *Kommandant's* suite of rooms. The setting was sumptuous but the only nourishment the near-starving prisoners could find was a supply of Champagne and tomatoes which immediately upset their shrunken stomachs.

Several hours of distant gunfire was followed by uncanny silence. Suddenly the door was thrown open and framed in the doorway stood a huge black US Army master-sergeant levelling a sub-machine gun at the startled prisoners. Hysterically the RAF men identified themselves. The master-sergeant was drunk when he arrived and the plentiful supply of Champagne increased his intoxication. He regaled the prisoners with tales of wild exploits, punctuating his story with repeated jabs into the highly polished rosewood table with a great Bowie knife. As his wine consumption increased so did his extravagant flourishes with the knife. The prisoners became alarmed for their safety and were relieved when a small American major arrived. At last, thank heavens, they thought, discipline will be restored. But the Americans were old buddies and soon the small major was the more sodden of the two.

An ambulance ride followed through corpse strewn lanes. The stench of death was overpowering. Sometimes bodies and parts of bodies were neatly piled along the hedgerows. As they passed through villages, laughing and cheering girls threw flowers and offered wine. Grimer was filled with admiration for the American troops and their complete informality and compassion. In their stripped hospital pyjamas the ex-prisoners were often mistaken for Germans. German prisoners lined up with American GIs for 'chow.' Grimer saw precedence for a flight to England given to a badly wounded German private over that of an American general. The German's medical needs were greater It was a remarkable lesson in humanity.

Because of their emaciated condition the prisoners were soon aboard a Dakota and then quickly comfortable in the American hospital at Taunton, Somerset. Proper drugs, good food and a quart of Guinness daily put Flight Lieutenant John Grimer on the road to recovery. Despite Grimer's protests the Americans gave him a GI uniform, crutches when he could walk, and awarded him a Purple Heart. Two months later the RAF claimed him back and he went to the RAF hospital at Locking near Weston-super-Mare.".

Appendix Six
by
Victor Clare

Per Advas ad Avra and Switzerland.

"My story begins at 23-25 hours on the 22nd April 1944, when we bombed our target, which, incidentally was LAON, we were flying about 7000 feet when the pilot said, - "Bomb doors closed", as always I was very relieved, its strange perhaps but whenever I was over a target area, I had an empty feeling in my stomach, probably nerves keyed up, but when we were clear of it, my nerves seemed to relax a little.

As I left the target the speed of our "Halifax" was increased to 1851, A.S., to do this, we lost a little height, but it didn't matter, as we weren't far from the French coast. Everything seemed alright, so about 5 minutes later I told the pilot I was going back to check if all our bombs had gone from the fuselage bomb-bay. Having making certain I had my torch, screw-driver and goggles with me I took my inter-com plug out and went back. I started off from the rear and worked forward, after checking 6 out of the 9 panels and lying down full length to inspect the next one, flames suddenly burst up in front of me which was the port side. I noticed a fraction of a second later the flames were all around me. What happened after I've only a faint recollection, but I know I went down to the flare shute to get a fire extinguisher, to have a try at putting the fire out. As I wasn't on inter-com I didn't say anything to the rest of the crew, nor do I know for certain whether the pilot gave the order to "bale out". As I turned the extinguisher on, it spurted right in my face, this all seemed to take hours, but really I suppose a few seconds, then one fire that I was concentrating one seemed to be going out. At the same time I saw the mid-upper gunner drop out of his turret and grab his chute, the significance didn't occur to me for a few seconds, I believe I was too busy with the fires. When it did, I can only describe my feelings as wanting to get away quick, my other feeling seemed to be numbed, probably if I'd heard the pilot order us to bale out, I'd have been as scared as hell, but I wasn't.

The front spar I took in one leap at the same time I was busy tearing my helmut off, my chute was laying on top of the 'window', so as I passed by I picked it up and took it to my position as the flames were more protected there, and not so much fumes. I knelt down and clipped it on, but one side was only on the elastic, but I noticed it, otherwise it would have fallen off when I jumped, it took a few more precious seconds to rectify this, then I hurried for-ward to the escape hatch. As I passed the pilot I noticed he was just getting back into his seat, he saw me and stepped back to the floor[sic] and by his gestures and what little I could make out of his shouting, I gathered his parachute was burnt and that he was going to try to crash land, at this time we were only approximately 3,000 feet, and as we had lost two engines were going down pretty fast, I tried to tell him that I'd stay and help as it needed two people to land a "Halifax," let alone crash land it.[!] This seemed very brave I know, but at the time I didn't realise the danger, he pointed to me and then downwards, so finally I jumped, not forgetting to have one hand on the rip cord and the other wrapped around the chute. As I jumped I've a faint recollection that I saw our aircraft pass over before I pulled the cord, no sooner had I done it I felt a terrific jerk, mostly from the straps in between my legs, and then came deadly quietness and I was floating down, I heard another of our aircraft pass over and I thought what lucky devils they were, as I passed out of earshot I heard a terrific crash, I couldn't see what it was as the straps of the chute were touching my ear and as one ear was burnt it hurt, but I took it to be our aircraft and that the pilot had failed to land it properly, I was too busy wondering what was my future, so I looked down wondering how long it would be before I hit the 'deck'. I wasn't too sure of the landing as a lot of people sprain their ankles or worst, it looked some way yet as the moon was coming up and I could make out the ground, so I contented myself with at least 5 minutes more of freedom. All this occurred to me as I hit 'it' very lightly but it knocked me on my back, more my instinct than through practice I turned my quick release lock and banged it with my fist. I could then stand up, shaken but truly thankful to be alive.

All our intelligence lectures came back to me about M.I.9. so I picked up my chute and harness, rolled it up and tucked it somehow under my arm as best I could. I looked around to find that I [was] in a fairly large field with cows in it, they were just looking at me and chewing. I didn't wait to say any "good byes" to them, but just got walking, not knowing what way I was going or caring much, a barbed wire fence loomed up so I had to walk along to find a decent place to climb over, just on the other side was a lane so I turned right when I climbed the fence, and half ran along the lane for half a mile before I realised that it was a private road, so I turned back and covered the half mile quicker, I passed a river on my way again, and I realised I was still carrying my chute etc., so I threw them all in and watched them float along, then I carried on. Before I got to my first village my mind was going a bit funny as I thought I was in a peaceful south English Country, it took me a full minute to make up my mind that I was in an enemy occupied country . . .

The dogs in the village was the only welcome I got at the village, there seemed to be hundreds of them. I noticed a window that showed a streak of light, so I knocked as I wanted help, I wasn't feeling so good, and didn't think it worth going on as I had sickly spells every few minutes, I expect it was shock and the fumes from the fire in my lungs. A woman of about 40 years old opened the door and after a slight hesitation and without saying a word pulled me inside, much to my surprise I found a sort of party going on, there were at least 25 people there, men and woman of all ages were drinking wine, naturally I stopped what fun they were having. I must have giving them something to talk about, so they took it in turn to come and goggle at me. Four were trying to question me in French, but I couldn't understand so we had to use signs and what little German I knew. I had to prove that I was English and not a German spying on them, after I had done that by showing everything in my pockets, they gave me a big glass of wine, which I drank thankfully and after such argument two of the younger men took me out. When I got out I was sick again and too weak to walk properly, so they linked arms with me, one each side, we went well outside the village to a hay loft, they dug a hollow out of the hay and when I'd laid down they piled it over me to keep me warm

    I understood they would come to me in the morning, so they left me to try to sleep, this was impossible, (not because of the rats), but everything kept on coming back to me, I was worried, but I did doze off, but the cold woke me up again. I tried thinking of my home and the girl I was going to marry, Joyce.

    It seemed very hard to realise that we'd been shot down and that I'd baled out . . . In the morning I was about early but didn't leave the hay loft, as I was expecting the two men back. As too many people saw me the previous night, [would I be safer if I went on my way?] Finally at about 07.00hrs, I made up my mind to get moving on my own, so I cut the top of my flying boots off with the razor blade that I had in my pocket, this made them, to all outward appearances look like ordinary black shoes. The next job was to distribute my "escape aids" in various pockets. I had 2000 French francs, these I split up into four lots of 500 each so that if I had to take it out people wouldn't think I had much... My stripes etc., had to be taken off as well, after all this I had to brush myself as best I could...A farmer passed by the hay loft with his wagon that was drawn by oxen, I'm sure he saw me, so I left my hiding place to find out where I was. I had the maps of the district and compass in my pocket, so I had a chance, even though it did seem small. I started by taking the smallest and lesser used roads I could find, although it was Sunday I had to pass a few people, they looked at me, I'm sure they knew who I was as they even turned around to have another look some of them even said "Bona Soir" as they passed. I was heading in a southerly direction as I was NE of Paris, and Spain was south. I knew that if only I could get to Spain I'd be alright for getting back to England.

    That day was very hot which didn't help my thirst at all, but I was not hungry, too scared probably, so when about 12 o'clock I came across a cafe I made up my mind to try to get a drink of beer if that was possible, so in I went. The only occupant of the room was a middle aged working man, so I sat down next to him and took my "phase card" out and pointed to "I'm thirsty", he ordered a bottle of beer and when that was gone, a couple more. The land-lady fried me two eggs which I ate with bread that tasted very similar to saw-dust and butter or margarine that looked like lard. Luckily I had about 25 cigarettes in a tin on me when I landed, these in the past few hours steadied my nerves a lot. I had another of my precious cigarettes there, they were precious as I had no idea when I'd be able to buy any more. When I'd finished eating and drinking I was going to pay, but NO, they refused the money although they were poor. Here I found a good chance to know if my French money was any good, I was pretty doubtful of it, but it was, which relieved me a lot.

    Turning to the right outside I carried on walking, still in a southerly direction, nothing exciting happened except for curious French people, I met no Germans, nor did I see any signs of them. At 13.30 hours I was getting near a village that seemed too big to go through, so I thought it best if I went around it there would be less danger. Not far ahead a road led to the right which suited very well, at this time just behind me were four cyclists, young men and believe me I was getting quite worried, as they kept coming nearer and then stopped to talk to one another, all the time staring at me, so I knew it was me they were discussing, they passed me and stopped at the corner where I was going to turn off to circuit the village, so I put on a brave front and strolled around the corner, one said "Sprecken sie Deutch"? I took no notice and carried on walking, they came up on their cycles and asked in one word "English"? I took a chance and stopped, no sooner than I'd said "Yes" than I was sitting on a cross bar and tearing along the road I intended to take. Some way along we stopped and went into a disused hut, they called "shack", they asked tons of questions in French and I couldn't understand, so they told me to wait for ten minutes while they went for food. They gave me a decent compass pen-knife and maps, they were trying to explain which was the best route to take. While they were explaining I fetched out my "phrase card", they almost pounced on it and pointed to the bit that said "Can you hide me"? One of the chaps had a lame leg, it was him that pointed to himself and nodded his head, so it was decided that I should hide locally until 21.00 hours then I was to go back to the "shack", they were to have civilian clothes waiting for me to change into. Before he left he sent his friend away for a bottle of wine for me to drink between then and 9 o'clock, he also gave me 20 cigarettes and a box of matches to help to pass the time away.

I hid quite near the hut in a sort of grass that was at least 5 feet high, rolling my blouse so that it could be used as a pillow, and as I was going to lay down it wouldn't look quite so much as a uniform, also I could always pretend to sleep. I did try to sleep as waiting 6 1/2 hours with nothing to do isn't much fun especially if ones mind keeps on running wild, as mine was, but I didn't succeed very well. The cigarettes were comforting, I smoked a lot during those hours. I had my own watch which was undamaged so I refused the Frenchman's watch, it was much better than mine as well. It was necessary that I had the right time as I had to be there at dead on 9 o'clock.

I was relieved when the time came to meet them, they both turned up dead on time, after shaking hands warmly I took my blouse off and put on a jacket, the other chap who since this time had done much for me put my blouse under his own. His was navy blue one with a zip-fastener on it, it covered mine completely. When we got outside I went with the chap with the lame leg. The other chap went on his own, he was to meet us later on, it was too dangerous to walk about in more than pairs. He didn't say much except when we passed odd people on the way to his home, when he spoke in French so that they happened to hear us, they would take me for a Frenchman as well as him. It succeeded pretty well, no one took more than a glance. It was just getting dark so that helped as well.

At his home his wife and boy were waiting dinner for us which I enjoyed. His wife was very nice. Her age? I'm not at all sure but somewhere around thirty seems more probable. She was kind, good natured and homely as well as being pro-British. After we had eaten we waited for George, that is the other man who helped me. When he came we spread maps on the table and the four of us had a conference; his wife as well. Strange to say we covered quite a lot of ground with the help of a French-English dictionary. About midnight we had a final drink of wine and I was taken into my bedroom. It was nice and clean and the bed was comfortable. Before I went to sleep "our" aircraft were out again over France bombing somewhere not very far away, as I could see the glow of fires and hear the bombs going off from my window.

The next morning I awoke to find a neat pile of civilian clothes on the chair by the bed. All my uniform had gone so I dressed in these and went to breakfast. They told me that they would keep all my uniform until after the war, then I should have it all back. The only part that I was allowed to keep was my singlet: as this was dirty the lady had washed it for me.

During the next few days I was staying with these kind people quite a lot of people called. Whenever there was a knock on the door I had to go into the room I was sleeping in. The room seemed very cold so to keep warm I had to move about. It was a good there wasn't a house to house search, as there wasn't any good hiding place that I could get to. When the lady went shopping the door was locked and I had strict instructions not to open the door. When she came back the following day after I had got there she told that the "Gerries" were looking for me in the village, someone had also told her that an RAF Officer had asked the way to Belgium the previous night at a farm house. I took this to be F/O John Grimer our bomb-aimer who had relations there.

The food was entirely different to what I'd been used to. As it happened I couldn't eat much as my tongue was still swollen, nothing could be done about it, they gave me first-aid for the burns I had on my right ear and a little on the side of my face. Many people came with baskets of food and to meet me; eggs, bread and butter was general, they helped out the strict rations of the people I stayed with. One woman fetched me three books to read as I had nothing else to do, I did read them but they were very old fashioned, printed sometime in the eighteen something. It was rather funny now I look back, every word I wanted to say to them had to be looked up in the dictionary. So, although it only cost about 2/6d. it was precious.

On the Monday a young man came in to see me. He gave me his identification card, the photo had been taken off and one of my escape photos put on and re-stamped with the German stamp. Although it was a lovely piece of work, the only doubtful bit was that if it was looked into very thoroughly it would be noticed that my eyes were 'blue' whereas on the card it had 'brown'. We couldn't change the name on the card, so I had to have an alias, it was "Rene Charmadin".

The next day I was told that Georges, that is the other chap whom I met on my first day was coming right the way through with me. We had to do the final planning so we decided to leave on Thursday morning. We had quite a lot of preparing, the route, food, money, change of clothes and tons of other little things. When he came around to the house on Wednesday evening he had a suitcase, two overcoats and a ? with him. He had a dozen or more things we didn't need, the lighter we travelled the better it would be. So we got busy sorting it out, to look at it all as though he was going on a months holiday.

When everything was planned we went to bed, Georges was to sleep with me in a single bed. After trying it always, we found it best one at the top, and the other at the bottom. We had to have an early start so we both tried to sleep quickly, I went straight away.

We were woken up at 4 o'clock. I got very cheerfully up and dressed, today I was to start my escape, whether or not I was captured didn't occur to me; not then anyway! The long wait had made me feel very 'fed-up' and now we were to start I suppose I was excited. Our breakfast was in silence. I think all our thoughts had gone on to more important things. Leopold went outside to see if it was light enough to move on, but it was still dark. We were all disappointed at waiting about another hour, we dare not go out until it was lighter, as if we were spotted it would look as if we were on our way to work. Finally the time came to thank Leopold and his wife for their kindness and to say "goodbye". It was the usual French way, kissing on both cheeks and on the mouth, they were truly sorry to see us go, tears were streaming down both cheeks on both of them. Why, I didn't really know, but I had an idea that they were afraid what would happen if we were caught. For Georges it meant death as thats the punishment for helping RAF airmen. For me, Prison camp at the least, that's after the Gestapo were finished with me. "What had I done with my uniform ?" "Who gave me civilian clothes ?"

Leopold came as far as the gate with us. I had the suitcase while Georges pushed the cycle, we hoped to make better time with the cycle as one could ride on the crossbar. We set off at a brisk walk and by 7 o'clock we were well away from the village, although we could still see the church spire in the distance. At first we took it in turns to carry the case or ride the cycle, but this was too much like work, so we tied the case onto the back of the cycle. It was easier and quicker afterwards. At 9 o'clock we had some bread and sausage. We were just outside a village so we got some coffee.

Whenever we were in villages buying a drink, or even staying all night in a hotel, as long as people were about I didn't speak, as I couldn't speak French. If we were stopped Georges was to do the talking while I played silly. It was tough going sometimes when we were having a drink in a cafe where a few people were, as I had to follow their voices around just in case they laughed, I had to laugh when they did. Carrying on until about 15.30 hours we were hungry again so we had lunch in a hotel at the next village. Villages seemed to be flying past, thank goodness we had made good time, it was cheerful to look back and count the kilometers that we had covered. Any big village we had gone around it, this made the distance much longer but the cycle helped, riding two on it when the road was downhill or level.

In the afternoon I came across my first German in uniform. We had to cross a river by punt. They had their boat right next to the punt. You can imagine how I felt, scared stiff. But we pushed the cycle on to the punt and we were towed across. They seemed suspicious, but as they didn't speak, it must have been my imagination. Whenever we were thirsty we called at a cafe for wine, this gave us a little rest. By 9 o'clock that night I was pretty tired so we decided to call it a day and get a room at the next hotel. So we had dinner and booked a room between us. The landlord knew I was an airman and was very pleased. Before going to sleep we made plans for the following day, and somehow or other we both understood each other: the plan was to get to Milan the following day. It wasn't very far. From there we could get a train south-wards that would take us nearer Spain. With this in mind, and feeling much surer of myself, I went to sleep not caring if all the Germans in France were after me.

In the morning my not caring mood had gone, and once more I was feeling shaky. They fetched breakfast to us in our room at 8 o'clock, so we got on our way directly afterwards. In our plans we hadn't counted on the RAF, as when we stopped at a cafe for a drink we learned that Milan had been bombed while we were asleep, and that no trains were running. We altered Milan to Montereau which was further south, it didn't need changing much. The weather was very hot during the time I was in France, and this day was about the hottest : we were calling in practically every cafe we came across. The same morning as we were getting a drink Georges asked the best way to Spain from the landlady. He went behind the bar to the room to find out with her. I was left waiting on my own wondering if he was being careless in his talking. He seemed to have got some of the "gen" from them so we left. Before we had a chance to go far the woman came out running and calling us back. This time we both went into the other room. I found five people in it three men and two women. Georges must have told them who I was as they had sent for a teacher who spoke English. The teacher was fairly young and quite pretty, she wanted me to stay the night there, in the morning she would phone the gendarmes, they would take me to prison were an American was supposed to be. By what she told me that if I did I'd not be sent to a POW camp as it was unoccupied France. I believe I was rude to her, but she didn't understand, so we left them all. Just in case they reported us we altered our route as they knew the original. I'd love to know if they did. Once again I was shaken.

For lunch we stopped at a fairly small cafe about 16 kilos east of Montereau. The chap who owned it was pro-allied, he knew who I was and helped a lot by phoning the times of the trains. He wouldn't hear of our paying for the food we ate. Perhaps the most important help he gave us was an address to go to in Montereau. He also patched my sandals as they were worn through on the sole. My identification disc was slid in between the leather right down under the arch of my left foot before it was tied around my left ankle.

Once again luck was with us as right outside of his shop we got a lift into Montereau in a van, there aren't very many cars or lorries of any sort. I was in for a shock as the town was full of German soldiers and airmen, quite a few Gestapo as well. I was even more scared of the French Gendarmes, as these people you couldn't "flannel," still what I'd been told helped a lot. If you happened to to catch a German looking at you, turn your head the other way, its surprising how it works. We found the address alright with the help of a passing Frenchman, it turned out to be a green-grocers shop. I stood outside while Georges went in. He was only a few minutes. He and I this time went in through the side entrance. Once again we were very well treated, food and wine. It was very nice to have a wash and shave. Then we got down to the job of catching a train to Spain. First of all the lady asked if I had any papers, so I gave them to her to study. When after about five minutes she told me I'd not get past the Station Gestapo, as anyone going South had these papers scrutinised by them. As the colour of my eyes were not the same she seemed certain I'd be caught.

Naturally my hopes of getting away went down. At the same time my imagination went on to being captured and from there to a prisoner of war camp. Then I had an inspiration, how about Switzerland: so I suggested it, they seemed very pleased as it was easier, also I'd be able to get back to England from there within a few days of crossing the frontier. We all had a few more drinks on the strength of this, including a brandy which was strong enough to fetch tears into my eyes. I might add that my spirits had risen again. At 22.15 that night we went off to the station, the woman as well. She didn't come all the way so we had to say goodbye in the usual French manner on the way. Nearer the station we ran into a bunch of German soldiers at least eight of them. Georges asked one of them the way to the station.

We had over an hour to wait in the platform after we had got the tickets. A crowd of about 1,500 or more Germans with kit were on the same platform waiting for a train. They were singing in typical mass German, their own type of songs and to me they seemed to be kicking up a devil of a row.

Exactly one hour and ten minutes after it was scheduled at the train came in. Everybody panicked to get on, me not knowing anything about these sort of things didn't hurry. All I knew was that the carriage I had to get in was marked "Francois", only there were a few on each train "for Germans only". When I did actually get in, or on the footstand when it started, I was left there for five minutes while people inside tried to make room for me. As I stepped in who should I see but a great big "Jerry" standing up with his rifle at his side. Nobody spoke a word to him during his journey, he didn't seem to expect it. For six hours I was sitting next to him, now I can see the joke, I couldn't then. In catching that train we were told to change at Dijon, but it wasn't necessary we carried right on to Besancon.

By the time I arrived I was dead tired. It was 10 o'clock on the 29th April and I hadn't been to sleep for over 30 hours. Also standing up in a cold railway corridor doesn't help much. I can't try to describe my feelings in the train properly, but if I brought to your mind that every minute we were going I was saving myself miles of walking that I'd thought I had to do. That ten hour trip by train probably saved me weeks of hard walking.

When getting the tickets we had booked right through to Mortau, and not to Besancon. But when we arrived at Besancon we found that the next train was over ten hours wait. I couldn't imagine myself waiting on a station that was swarming with enemy troops, so we decided to go out and try to find some other means of getting there. Georges cycle had been sent by rail to Mortau, so we couldn't use that, by bus was our only hope. So after a cup of coffee we enquired when the next one was leaving; that was 5 1/2 hours wait, it wasn't advisable to hang around the town as it was a big one with hundreds of German soldiers in it, practically every other person was a German. So after a beer we decided to move on in the direction of Mortau and if we could get a lift all the better. On the way out we passed a barracks, guards were marching about in pairs. The average age I should say of those that I saw was about 35, because all of them were either younger than 19, or older than 45, its the queerest bunch of soldiers I've ever seen.

It was hard going as the roads were so bad. Also we were so tired. we had a case and a small haversack of goods, we kept on changing over as it was pretty tough on one person to carry the case all the time. Mortau was 58 kilos away, and after a few kilos we laid down for a rest hoping a car came along so that we could get a lift. None came; so we carried on for a while then laid down for another rest. This went on for 18 kilometers, and it had taken hours. The next cafe we came to we stopped there until the bus came along. Much to our disgust it was crowded and didn't stop. Then another the same. The third one stopped, why I don't know as there were 22 standing up already. Still we got on thankful for the ride. it wasn't very long before practically everyone had got off as it didn't go right into Mortau. Georges asked him if there was any decent hotels, it only went to within

15 kilometers of the town. The driver was a good chap as he gave us the address of a hotel at the last village, also a little "gon" on the frontier. The hotel was good, once more no questions asked. We both slept very well that night. As the next day was Sunday we decided to have a lay in until 8 o'clock. So we had a lovely sleep, blissfully unaware that there was a war on.

When I awoke next morning, it was to hear men shouting outside of our window. Georges must have woken up the same time as we both jumped out of bed in a flash and were looking out of the window. It was a false alarm as it turned out to be the village fire brigade practice. We had a wash and shave in peace. While we were downstairs having breakfast the whole brigade came in to have a drink of wine. That caused me some anxiety as the local gendarme had come in with them. Once more my luck held good, he didn't speak to us but sat with the firemen, but when Georges went to pay the bill I was left alone, so I had no morale support. He glanced suspiciously over at me but nothing happened. The landlady helped a lot by waving "Good bye" to us as though we were good friends, this was to distract the gendarme I was told afterwards.

From the hotel to Mortau only took two hours, we went out across the fields, and as there were no one about my mind was at rest for the first time, even if it was for only a short while, it was nice while it lasted. We were coming up for the most dangerous part of the journey, the crossing of the frontier, and I didn't want to be too confident. Once we got into Mortau Georges knew his way around as he'd lived there a long time only a short while ago, so we had no bother in finding his friends place, which turned out to be a hotel.

This kind person turned out to be a woman of about 50 years old, she welcomed us with joy, even knowing I was an airman. She hated the Germans and showed it in many ways. After we had both eaten she asked us to help with the room we were to sleep in. For our room she cleared the attic out and we took a bed upstairs. In the attic there was only a small window, and if it was necessary, all we had to do was to jump out of bed, throw the clothes back to cool the bed and get out the window. There was a ledge that was wide enough to stand on, and if we edged round the corner we wouldn't be seen from the window. A chap called Pierre was to give us time to get out if we were raided. He had been in a German Camp for 3 years, so he had no love for them. It looked as if I was in with a bunch of decent friends, they certainly were.

The next day was Monday the 1st.of May. I was told a girl would be coming to see me who spoke English. I was looking forward to it. I'd not heard English spoken, the last time being was asking me to give myself up. Just to speak to someone who could speak my mother tongue would be a joy that many people wouldn't understand unless they hadn't spoken or heard it for days.

In the afternoon I went up into Pierre's room to listen to the radio. It was good to hear the dance tunes that I'd danced to not so very many days ago. I was jealous to think that some lucky people were probably even then dancing in England to the tunes I was listening to, all the time wondering how long it would be before I could do the same. The announcer was a woman, she said something about Forces Favourites and hoped the Forces wherever they were would enjoy it. I thought at the time, I wonder if she realises that they listen "in" in all sorts of queer places in war.

He fetched out his hidden brandy so that I could have a 'tot,' it gave me the feeling then that only the best was good enough for me, not because it was me, but because I was British and in the RAF. They all seemed very patriotic. When a patriotic tune came over the radio from London to the French they turned their radios up to full volume, not caring who was listening, it seemed the regular thing to do.

At last five o'clock came.I was to have a talk with the Doctor's daughter who spoke English. The landlady took me to a private room adjoining the dining hall, the girl in it I saw was fairly tall and nice looking. What I liked first of all about her was that she came forward with her hand out and said "I'm pleased to meet you", in good English with just a little accent. I think I could have fallen in love with her then if I wasn't too full of love for someone else. Anyway, I shall always be thankful for her speaking to me. Her main job was to act as an interpreter for me, to make sure I knew what was to happen, also to make sure I was English. After she was sure she told me a story of a few weeks before me. Someone had asked her to call at their house to speak to an Airforce chap. After a while she doubted whether he was really English, or, if he was in the RAF at all. She couldn't understand his English very well. She was frightened he may be a German spy, so she told the people who was looking after him. When she had gone away she was sorry as it came to her that he might be Canadian, Australian, Polish, etc., by the way she spoke she seemed very sorry. I was told that we were to cross the frontier the next day and that I was to be ready to leave at 16.00 hours, she would come just after dinner to see me again just before I left.

Naturally I went to bed early that night not knowing what I was to come in contact with the following night, and expecting to get no sleep for two days. I awoke the next morning feeling fit and almost ready for anything, but rather nervous. Strange to say the morning seemed to pass quickly. After dinner the young lady called again. She gave me the final "gen." She was to get our bus tickets to a small village 15 kilometres south and meet us at the bus stop. At the village we were to go to a cafe and wait for a man to come for us. He was an electrician by trade who was going to show us the best part to cross, or take us himself. He was a friend of Pierre's. As I had no cigarettes left I asked if she could get me a packet through the black market. Normally they cost 10 francs, but black market 110 francs, so I made her take 100 francs.

The next hour we spent filling our little haversack with what we needed; 2 bars of chocolate (incidentally the first I'd seen in France) 2 packets of biscuits; cheese and pepper to sprinkle behind us to put dogs off our scent. The guards on the frontier had dogs with them. We took shaving kit with us as well, besides a few odds and ends, We had our last meal in France, it wasn't much but we weren't hungry. I left my home address with the lady so that when the war was over she could get in touch with me. Also two photographs that Leopold gave me, they were of his baby.

At 15.45 hours it was time we left so we said our "good byes" to the landlady, who was pretty cut up at our leaving. She only said "bon voyage" as tears were streaming down from her eyes; we also had to say "Good bye" to Pierre and the lady who helped run the hotel, although she was coming to see us off. So tucking one arm in each others we went out. When any Germans passed us she gave my arm a reassuring squeeze, it helped a lot; although she was neither young nor pretty.

Georges went on ahead just before we reached the bus stop, so he could meet the English speaking girl. The other woman and I had to look in shop windows so as not to attract attention. The shop we looked in has vases in the window, I remember that she pointed at one and we both laughed, why I don't know. I did it to seem more natural because two Germans were standing a few yards away. Georges and the other girl came across just before we got into the bus, so we kissed both "good bye" in turn before we finally got in. The one who spoke English went off, the other woman from the hotel started to talk. When the bus started we saw her waiting further up the road and as we passed she gave us a wave and just smiled, then she was gone.

Georges gave me an envelope that she had given him for me, inside was 20 cigarettes also the hundred franc back, also a flower with a piece of paper around it, on the paper in English was "For Good Luck". I put the flower in my wallet and had a much needed cigarette, with the light I burnt the paper with the English on it.

The village was only a tiny one, with only one cafe. So we couldn't go wrong by going to the wrong one. Inside we ordered a wine that tasted to me very much like pomegranate juice. He was due at 18.00 hours and when 18.45 came I thought he wasn't coming. There was no point in going on our own, so we waited, he came at last at 19.30 hours and after another beer we all left together.

The village was only 3 kilometres from the frontier so from where we were to the frontier was a prohibited area which was patrolled. No one without a special pass was allowed in. First of all we had to climb the barbed wire, from there we began to go up, it was a fairly steep mountain. He led the way. Before we started he told us to roll our overcoats up and tuck them under our arm, I didn't realise why, but I do now. The upward part was really tough, he didn't go slow, practically running up, I needed both hands free to hold on to weeds or trees to stop me going backwards. It was about the most strenuous hour I've ever had. At times I though about letting him go on alone, but somehow or other I kept up with him. When we got to the top we turned right along a narrow path, more a track than a path, this was level walking and it gave me time to get my breath back. I had lost my tommy hat somewhere, I can't remember losing it. At exactly 21.00 hours we came to the frontier stone, it was very similar to an English milestone. It was here we gave him our French papers for him to burn, shaking hands and he was off. I got a bearing on my compass so that we wouldn't lose ourselves, even on the frontier we weren't out of trouble, as a "No Mans Land" was in between, this was patrolled. We had been very lucky in not seeing any of the Germans, although we had heard them a few times. But as there was still a good chance we tried to be careful, but going downwards wasn't at all easy to keep quiet. Stone after stone rolled from under our feet made a terrible row, after this happened we stopped to listen, as all was quiet we carried on. It was still twilight so we could see fairly well, it wasn't far down, from there up and up again, this time not so steep, but higher than the last one by a long way. We tried to keep to the shadows as much as possible, just in case anyone was watching. Often stopping to sprinkle pepper behind us, and to listen. As we got higher the level of the ground became more normal, so we guessed we were in Switzerland. Still we didn't want to get caught as our idea was to get to the British Consul at Bern.

The countryside was all fir trees, very thick, but in between there were lanes. It was down these that we went, after a few minutes we came across snow. It seemed all around us, so we had to go through it, always trying to get down. I only had loose sandals on, so not only did my feet get wet, but right through up to my knees. Walking along we ate a couple of biscuits with cheese. Somewhere about 40 minutes later we found a path leading downward, travelling was much easier and faster then going through woods, when we thought we were safe we heard footsteps coming upwards, so we dived into the side of the path where there were plenty of shadow and laid down. It turned out to be a gendarme, he passed us barely 5 yards away.

When he'd gone out of earshot we cautiously got on our way again, and as all was alright we had a cigarette walking along. At 80 minutes after midnight we came across our first village, and as we weren't at all sure of our luck, that it was really Switzerland, we made sure by the number plate of a lorry, also by the yellow post box, with the horn and cross on it.

In France we had been given an address at La Loche to go to, to change our French money into Swiss. These people would help us on our way to Bern. As the town was only 4 kilo- meters from the frontier (Le Loche) we had to walk parallel with the frontier as we were some way south of it. The first house that had a light showing we knocked to ask where we were. After telling her who we were and where we had come from she invited us both in to have something to eat and drink. While we were having this I noticed her clock which said it was 23.20 hours. Mine was one hour fast by hers. So I pointed it out, but in Switzerland the time was different to France, so we put our watches right by Swiss time. The lady of the house told us that it was 20 kilometres to Le Loche. She also pointed out the best way.

We started out hoping to get there by morning, but we were very tired. So we looked about for somewhere to sleep for a couple of hours, eventually, which was about an hour later, we found a disused farm with plenty of straw in it; not clean, but that didn't matter. Burying ourselves deep in this we tried to sleep, but it was too cold. About an hour later we were up again feeling very cold. Dawn was just breaking when we set off again. Before going many yards I saw a light in a farm house. We knocked on the door hoping to get a cup of coffee. Inside were four men, one of them must have been a vet, a horse was giving birth to a foal, so we watched. Afterwards the dairymaid made us coffee, and once again we had bread and cheese. The farmer gave us five Swiss francs to pay the fare to Le Loche and told us a bus was due. He also showed us where to catch it. We had to borrow a brush from him to take the dirty straw off our clothes.

The first thing I saw in the bus was a gendarme. He looked at both of us very suspiciously, and I could see he was asking a girl who got on the bus at the same place as us, whether she had ever seen us before. She must have said "No", only he came up to ask for papers. I didn't even know we were supposed to have them. Anyway Georges told him that he was a French Canadian and that I was English, and that we were both in the RAF. He moved us back to the back seat of the bus where a Russian and a Swiss soldier were. It turned out that the Swiss soldier was caught trying to cross the frontier, he was a deserter. The Russian, he came from France and had crossed over the frontier about the same time as we did. He spoke English as well. The gendarme took us all to the police station at Le Loche where he asked for particulars. The Russian acted as interpreter for me. The type of questions I was asked were, number, rank, name, date shot down, type of aircraft, group and squadron. I wasn't allowed to say which squadron and group, or whereabouts it was. He got mad when I told him I wasn't going to tell him, so I told a pack of lies. As he didn't know he was pleased, as Georges was pretending to be in my crew, my answers did for both of us. They then gave us breakfast and locked us up in a cell. A guard came and woke us up at 12 o'clock with lunch and told us to be ready to move in an hour. Another gendarme took us to the station and put us on a train, not in an ordinary carriage but in a type of cell that was in the guards van. He was very apologetic and said it was orders. But once the train started the guard opened the door to see we were OK and gave us cigarettes, cigars too! Also a different stop two or three men who worked on the station passed in more cigarettes.

Our destination was Neuchatel, at the station another gendarme was waiting, he spoke a little English. He took us to a Captain of the gendarmes for interrogation. As I couldn't speak French I didn't say much, it was Georges who did all the talking, and I learned afterwards that the Captain had asked him how he came through France with his Canadian accent. When we had finished we were taken to another prison, it was too late to get us a room in a hotel. On the way to the prison the guard took us the long way around to show us the town. Practically everyone whom we passed stopped to stare at us. Everybody seemed to know who we were, probably because we were so untidy. In Switzerland the people are all well dressed in the towns.

In prison it was horribly dirty and cold. The food wasn't so good either. Our cells had two big doors, it seemed impossible to break out even if one wanted. In the passage every few yards there was another door. We were lucky as they left our door open most of the day; the other cells were only opened at meal times for 10 minutes. We had a few biscuits and a little chocolate left so we ate that to help out our prison rations.

The following day we were taken to Bern for interrogation by the Swiss Air Force. I got on well with him as he was the first person whom I came across in Switzerland who spoke good English. I enquired from him how French civilians got on who crossed the frontier. He gave a satisfactory answer so I told him about Georges. He didn't ask many questions, and very few were not ones I need not answer. He told me not to tell Georges that he knew he was French, as if he got it out of him himself he could find out the truth and as he came out to fetch Georges into his room I didn't have the chance, after waiting 20 minutes outside, the Swiss officer called to me to tell him that all was OK. So I explained to Georges that he knew everything and all went through quickly.

From here we were taken again by train to Olten for our quarantine. That same night we were given a couple of blankets and told to sleep on straw. One thing it was clean. Next morning we were sent into the town for what they called 'cleaning'. It consisted of first having all your hair cut off. As these were a couple of English lads as well as a couple of Americans among Italian, Germans, French and every other nationality, we stood together and refused. There was a terrific row between us and the Swiss Colonel. He told us he'd send us back across the frontier and various other things. In the end we won. Although we had our hair cut, not too close, while the chap was doing one the others stood around to make sure it wasn't too close.

In the afternoon we were moved to Lostorf which is an hour and a half walk from Olten. When we had lined up outside the camp at Lostorf . . . . . popped out of the window just above us. It was those chaps that . . . . started a few days ago. I saw a face I knew well, it was Peter O'Brian, you can imagine how pleased I was to see him. So as soon as we were free we got together to exchange stories of the past, and as he had a couple of francs had a beer for old times.

We were here three weeks. I won't go into details of life in the camp, all I'll say is that if the three weeks had any comparison with the rest of our stay in Switzerland, give me Germany. It couldn't be worst. We had an armed guard all the time watching over us.

When we left we went to Bern to call on the Legation. Here I was warmly greeted by the Officer in Charge, and he told us from then onwards Switzerland would be better. I stayed in a decent hotel with good food,.I went shopping with a civil servant, I got a new suit, shirt, tie, shoes, hanks, cuff-links etc. At the Legation they gave me tons of other things.

On the 5th.June we went on to where the rest of the RAF boys were, in a decent hotel. Looking back now (in another day or so we are leaving) its not been so bad. The hotel has been pretty good, even to my putting my shoes outside the door at night for cleaning. On the whole there is a decent lot of officers and NCO's here. Although at times I have felt bored, I've made it up other times.

Now to close. All I can say, without looking at the duty side of affairs, although it was my duty to evade capture by the enemy, from a purely personal comfort side of things I'm glad I didn't. But believe me I'd not trust luck too far as to say I'd do it again.

Our one thought now is "When will it be ? " or I should say I wonder if its true, only we've been told the day we are leaving here, and I at least am hoping to be back in "Blighty" in a weeks time.

Victor Clare (Sergeant).
2nd. October 1944.

When I returned I found that the rest of the crews conditions officially are as follows, dated 1st.May 1945:-

Pilot	Still missing.
Navigator	Prisoner of War (fit).
Bomb-Aimer	Repatriated POW calf of his leg off.
Wireless Operator	Repatriated POW right leg off.
Rear Gunner	Evaded capture and now in England.
Mid-Upper gunner	Repatriated POW foot off.
Engineer (Myself).	Evaded. "

Many years afterwards John Grimer was asked if he could give a description of the crew. This was his reply:-

"S/L Bond - ex Indian Air Force. Much older than rest of us - late 30's. Conversion to 4 engine bombers not easy after flying bi-planes. Very much the regular RAF officer - cared for his crew - but not close or informal - (brother Derek Bond the actor.)"

"Sgt (later Group Captain) Hobgen - my closest friend - super chap - excellent and meticulous navigator."

"Sgt Johnson - Wireless / Operator. Very friendly with Charles and me, engaged to Helen - WAAF M.T. driver."

"F/O.Mason - Mid.Upper Gunner - again older 30's ? Very affable Scot. I shared prison hospital cell with Johnson & Mason - (both amputees)."

"Sgt.Clare - nice chap - very efficient and thorough."

"Self - then P/O started training as pilot - then air gunner / observer / navigator / air bomber. Navigation poor - bomb aiming & air gunnery good."

"F / O Jacks, - replacement stand in rear gunner on night of 22 / 23rd April 44."

"The 'Halibag' - Just over half as many as the Lancs operating. Not so fast - not so high - smaller bomb load - heavier losses. One big advantage - easier to get out of !!"

"My job as Air Bomber. Assist pilot on take off & landing. Then lie in the nose - map read - especially coastal pin points - look for fighters & operate nose machine gun. Go to astro dome to take star shot fixes when requested by navigator. Lie in nose on bombing run & give instructions to pilot - fuse & release bombs on aiming point - ditto on home run."

"All crew have bacon and eggs on return - debriefing."

Appendix Seven

The navigator Charles Hobgen, spent the remainder of his life writing a series of books for his family, particularly his war experiences. I here include Chapter 7, from

" WITH PREJUDICE AND PRIDE "
(book 4 - PT3)

> "There are three stages to the hawk's demise ; the instant when an arrow breaks its wing, those long moments as it flutters earthwards and that interminable time as it scrabbles for an earthy place to hide."
>
> "My transition from predator to prey was quick and merciless. For five seconds, cannon-fire tore 'plane and crew apart. Then for (what seemed to Ray Silver) a dozen minutes I had dropped through the silent sky feeling detached and omniscient as the gods. Now the earth reclaimed me, clutched my feet and held me vulnerable."

Warrant Officer, later Flying Officer, (his commission was announced by the German camp adjutant, Hauptmann Hans Pieber, during the course of a morning Appell) L.R. Silver, R.C.A.F., a navigator with 10 Squadron, RAF Leeming, shot down over Germany 30th. May, 1942 and a POW in Stalag Luft 3, Sagan. Extract from his book *"Last of the Gladiators"* A World War 2 Bomber Navigator's story.

"1944 came in like a lion, with two operations to Berlin, the first in January followed by another in February. Throughout both of them we were forced to fight our way out, having attacked the target, to fight our way back. From those two raids alone seven of our squadron aircraft did not return. Of the forty nine men involved, forty two were killed and seven were taken prisoner. Of those killed, nineteen are now recorded as having no known grave and because of this they are commemorated on the Runnymede Memorial.

As I recall, it was then, for the first time in my life, I became aware that exhaustion could originate in the over expenditure of both physical and mental effort. In my experience, first came the hollow-eyed weariness derived from the lack of normal sleeping pattern, to which was soon added the burnt out emptiness every bomber crewman experienced after hours of concentrating on his task and expending the effort required to put out of mind the understandable but seldom acknowledged fear that travelled as the "Eighth Passenger" in each of our aircraft. In my own case this was made the more debilitating by the doubts and uncertainties, ever present in my mind, born of the inexactitude of aerial dead-reckoning navigation. When fear of what might be visited on one's self and one's crew by a ruthless and determined enemy was augmented by all of those other stresses and strains, the ensuing bone-weariness became an inevitable part of our every day lives.

Once back on the ground after the Berlin raids, neither one of us in our crew had a shred of energy left with which to respond, with any degree of ease, to the interrogating debriefing officer. In this we were not alone, one had but to glance around the room and note the deadpan, ashen faces devoid of any animation despite the urgent questions directed by the intelligence officers at the men behind them . . .

Little wonder that at this time our C in C removed the Halifax squadrons from the Battle of Berlin. The terrible losses were no longer sustainable and it was left to the Lancaster squadrons to continue the bloody battle.

Four days after returning from our last trip to Berlin we undertook a lengthy flog to Leipzig. During the return flight, realising our hydraulics had suffered some flak damage and, as in addition, we were unsure of just how much fuel we had left. Ken Bond decided to land at Coltishall. We made a good landing and was doubtless thankful he had allowed the aircraft to drift lazily onto the runway with a minimum use of the engines. A touch on the brakes revealed little or no residual hydraulic pressure and we counted ourselves lucky to have been able to get the under- carriage down without mishap, thanks to some skilful help from our flight engineer, Vic Clare.

Thereafter Bond allowed the aircraft to roll to a standstill at the extreme end of the runway where we awaited the ministrations of a tractor to tow us to flying control. By the time we had breakfasted the ground crews had rectified the problem and we trundled back to Elvington, there to sleep deeply before leaving the station late that afternoon for some previously planned leave.

We went minelaying on 22/23 March and would have gone again on 30/31 March had it not been for the unfortunate incident described in Chapter 5 of this book. However, we participated in some more 'gardening' (minelaying) [or "planting mines" - John Grimer] on 12/13 April.

All in all I was not much taken with this type of operation, it lacked the electrifying urgency and the cataclysmic culmination of a normal bombing raid. One flew off into the night across the unfriendly North Sea, heading for the distant coastal waters of Norway and Denmark relying, if the skies were clear, on being able to put to good use one's skill in astro navigation. Alternatively, there was the hope, springing eternal, that the winds forecast by the met. would bear some relation to reality and that my dead reckoning plot keeping would do the rest. At times it was possible, if the fates were kind to us and John Grimer was on the ball, to pounce on a pinpoint formed by an obliging enemy coastline. With it I would be able to bring my plot up to date and thereby speed us on our way home towards the blessings of radar help from the Gee chain.

It was about this time that what was to become known as the Transportation Plan came into being. The plan was part of the proposed bombing policy for Operation Overlord aimed at the German armies' known dependance on rail transport. It was hoped a 'railway desert' between western Germany and the French coast could be brought about by attacking a large number of railway centres where locomotives and wagons were maintained and repaired. Such depots had multiple tracks and marshalling yards which could also be heavily damaged thus bringing about a German military transport paralysis.

Initially, our C in C, Air Marshall Harris, was not enamoured of the plan and in this he had the tentative support of the Prime Minister, Winston Churchill, and the War Cabinet, whose members were apprehensive of the harm the ensuing casualties amongst French and Belgian civilians would do to the Allied cause. Eventually, and to assist in arriving at a decision, Harris was ordered to carry out some trial attacks.

Much to the surprise of all concerned the trial attacks resulted not only in an absolute minimum of civilian casualties but served also to demonstrate the accuracy achievable by the Halifax crews if they were provided with accurate target marking by the Pathfinder Mosquito aircraft and the direction and control of a Master Bomber or, as we referred to him, a Master of Ceremonies. Harris was converted to the concept of the plan as were the others who had initially expressed doubts about it.

These attacks on western European targets were assessed by some amongst whom were not numbered the operational bomber crews, as being an easier option than, say, targets in Germany. As a result of this assessment, the decision was taken somewhere in the Command hierarchy that they would be scored as half an operation when it came to calculating a tour's length - usually seen as being represented by thirty operations. There was a good deal of muttering amongst the aircraft rank and file along the lines that one could as easily be killed on half a trip as one could on a whole one and, sadly, it was not long before this irrefutable estimate was proved to be devastatingly correct. On 15 March 44 during a raid on the yards at Amiens in France the squadron lost two aircraft with thirteen out of fourteen crew-men killed.

On 23/24 March we were amongst those despatched to bomb the marshalling yards at Laon in France but, for the one and only time during our tour of operational duty, we were forced to return without completing our mission. This was due to the severe icing we experienced which prevented poor old 'S' - Sugar from clawing its way above 5,500 feet and which eventually caused me to warn Bond that, apart from anything else, we would not be able to make our concentration point on time. We therefore jettisoned our bomb load off the French coast and returned home.

As we encountered warmer air, the noise made by the lumps of ice breaking off the wings and the resulting battering the aircraft took from this form of 'friendly fire' was. to say the least, impressive and Bond decided he would make a precautionary landing at RAF Wing and return to base later. Despite all the pre=operation tension and a three hour flight fighting the elements we had not achieved even half a trip. More seriously, yet another of our squadron aircraft did not return from the operation. All of the seven man crew were killed.

During 29/30 March 1944 we were sent to the marshalling yards at Vaires and on 9/10 April 1944 to those at Lille and on 12/13 April 1944 we once again went minelaying. During the latter trip we made six sightings of enemy night fighters but thankfully no attacks developed.

At this stage we had completed thirteen operations successfully. Additionally we had made one early return and failed to take off on another operation for which we had been briefed; a memorable occasion, in more ways than one. It was generally held by those experienced in such matters, that at this point in an operation tour crews tended to become over confident. The half way point in our tour's length was approaching and we were still buoyed up by the shibboleth that if anyone was going to 'get the chop' it would be the other chaps, not us. I don't think we were over confident, in fact I'm sure we weren't, Ken Bond would not have permitted us to become so. He still insisted on regularly rehearsing our emergency drills on the ground and during air tests and the daily checking of our aircraft and equipment was something we took very seriously indeed - we knew it could mean the difference between living and dying. It could, I suppose, be said we were confident but careful.

By this time the exciting news had filtered through that the squadron was not only to convert to the Mark 111 Halifax, a much improved marque of the type, but was also to move to RAF Full Sutton some five miles NNE of Elvington. Two squadrons of the French Air Force were scheduled to take our place at Elvington. On Sunday 16th April 1944, once he had learnt the squadron had been stood down and with the projected move in mind, Ken Bond announced his attention of driving across to Full Sutton to spy out the land and whilst so doing to mark down his office. John Grimer and I went with him.

It was strange to stand on an airfield where everything was new and as yet untouched The hangers were vastly empty and the dispersal pans still free from oil stains that would eventually bear witness to the day to day servicing of the aircraft parked on them. The domestic site, with its messes and NAAFI canteen, was much like the one at Elvington although, if anything, a little more spacious and incorporating some improvements. We were pleased with what we saw and excited when Bond told us he would be among the first of the pilots to be converted on to the Mark 111.

With the promise of a vastly improved aircraft in which to continue our tour, a bright new station to welcome us and summer not far away, things could not have looked rosier - or so we thought at the time.

Saturday 22nd.April 1944 dawned bright and Spring fresh. As I walked down the Wheldrake road towards the mess and a leisurely breakfast, there seemed little wrong with the world. There was a burgeoning warmth in the air giving encouragement to the primrose clumps unfolding beneath the hedgerows and a plodding herd of cows moving towards their milking sheds gave an added touch to the feeling that there was a great deal that was called right with the world.

At a more mundane level I was very much looking forward to another driving lesson at the hands of Doug Thorn, a RCAF fellow navigator. The car was a small runabout owned jointly by Ken Bond and myself which he used to commute daily between the airfield and his flat in York but which was to be mine whenever I wanted it and when Bond thought I was competent enough to drive it ! There was of course no such thing as a driving test during the war.

Breakfast over, together with a clutch of other navigators, I strolled down to the Navigation Section there to await with them an announcement as to what the day or, more importantly, the coming night, held in store for us. We were not kept waiting for long. Soon after mid-morning the Battle Order list appeared on the back of Paul Jousse's office door. Following its display and as though a whip had been cracked calling us to order, the horseplay and gossiping ceased as we moved in anticipatory silence toward the small piece of acetate covered white board.

The list revealed a requirement for fourteen crews, including our own, to undertake an operation that night. An ingrained habit led me to raise my eyes to the name at the top of the list and only thereafter did I allow them to slide down the alphabetically arranged schedule. In so doing I was following a mental quirk - a compulsion neurosis - which demanded I should play it that way rather than go straight to the bottom of the list where I knew 'S' - Sugar together with Ken Bond's name would be found if we were required to fly that night. The list read as follows.

'B' - Baker	Pilot Officer Wickham-Jones
'D' - Dog	Flight Lieutenant Welch
'E' - Easy	Flight Lieutenant Pritchard
'G'- George	Flight Serjeant Sykes
'J' - Jig	Flight Lieutenant Wodehouse
'L' - Love	Pilot Officer Pearce
'N'- Nun	Pilot Officer Robertson
'Q'- Queen	Flight Lieutenant Thompson
'R' - Roger	Warrant Officer Jakeman
'S' - Sugar	Squadron Leader Bond
'T' - Tare	Pilot Officer Judd
'V' - Victor	Flying Officer Hale
'W'- William	Pilot Officer Hunter
'Y' - Yoke	Pilot Officer Smith

Navigator's briefing was scheduled for late afternoon with crew briefing detailed for 18.15 hours. That was the sum total of the information immediately available to us. It was time to start the preparatory drills leading inexorably to a take-off into the night skies and a flight eastwards to - we knew not where.

Having cadged a lift from the WAAF driver of a crew bus several of us went to our individual aircraft to ensure all was in order and, hopefully, to extract information from the ground crew senior NCO's as to bomb and fuel loads. The bomb load, we learnt, was to consist of 5 X 1,000lb (medium capacity) and 10 X 500lb (medium capacity) bombs whilst the fuel load was commensurate with a flight of medium length. From this information the possibility of another French target sprang at once to mind.

16.00 hours found we navigators of the raiding aircraft at our plotting tables in the navigation section, pencil poised ready to start compiling our flight plans. The room was quiet, the spirits of the morning having given way to the more sombre mood that always preceeded the disclosure of the target for the night. Paul Jousse, as outwardly unruffled as ever, stepped up onto the dais at one end of the room where, quite deliberately, he proceeded to remove the sheet of white paper covering the topographical map of Great Britain and Western Europe. A glance told us the target was in France.

The red, track-marking tape stretched southwards from Elvington to Beachy Head via Reading and thence across the Channel to a point a few miles north of Dieppe. Once past the French coast the tape indicated we required to turn onto a track of 110 degrees and fly directly to the target - Laon. The route home was planned to start with a short south easterly leg out of the target area, covering some 10-15 nautical miles, followed by a turn to starboard to bring us onto a track of 280 degrees leading to Fécamp on the French coast. Thereafter the red tape headed across the Channel to Selsey Bill and then towards base via Reading. The estimated flying time was calculated to be in the region of 5 hours, with take-off scheduled for 21.00hrs.

As we set to work on our flight plans there was a noticeable easement of tension among us. No one was foolish enough to tempt fate by dismissing the operation as, 'a piece of cake' but the thought passed through my mind, that as French targets went this one appeared to be relatively unspectacular. Providentially, as far as the met. forecast was concerned there was nothing about the weather to make us contemplate the possibility of any problems arising from that quarter. Visibility was good, the winds were light to moderate westerlies and only broken cloud at a medium height was forecast at base on our return. All in all, if not exactly a gift, the operation was not cast in the same mould as targets such as Berlin and Leipzig.

After his initial briefing, Paul Jousse, as usual, returned to his office leaving us to translate his directions into our flight plans. A few minutes later he reappeared having, as he told us, received orders concerning a special requirement for the night's operation. As an experiment and with the purpose in mind of increasing the concentration of the attack, one navigator from each of the participating squadrons, having calculated the best possible wind velocity within thirty nautical miles of the target, was required to report the result back to Group HQ by W/T. The group Navigational Officer, we were told, would average out the wind speeds and directions radioed to him and immediately thereafter broadcast the result to the 4 Group aircraft. This was to be the 'wind' to be used by all bomb aimers in their bombing run-up to the target. It of course meant breaking the strict radio silence normally imposed on the bombing force, the thought of which departure from the norm was not immediately attractive to any of us.

"Of course," said Paul with tongue in cheek, "This is a task for one of the most reliable amongst you, we can't afford to have the squadron let down by incompetence. Any volunteers ?" Dead silence and much assiduous contemplation of maps and staring anywhere but in Paul's direction. For it was not, when all is said and done, a task to be undertaken lightly. "Right Hobgen, your my choice, you've got the job." His words were greeted with muted cheers, along the lines of my being an unlikely potential choice for Pathfinding duties ! For my part I was quite pleased to have been chosen but, at the same time, more than a shade apprehensive.

Ken Bond and John Grimer arrived as I was putting the finishing touches to my flight plan and together we discussed the planned route, marking on the plotting chart potential trouble spots and reviewing the location of suitable airfields on which to make an emergency landing. There- upon, with the feeling that we had everything well in hand we made our way to the main briefing room near the road at the bottom of the field where we met up with Vic Clare, Bob Johnson and Mathew Mason. Jack Waddilove, our rear gunner, was also there but brought with him the news that our medical officer had grounded him because of a heavy cold. His place was to be taken by a Flying Officer Bill Jacks, one of the squadron commanders gunners who was not known to me.

The briefing followed the usual pattern but with considerable emphasis placed on the need for accurate bombing. The marshalling yard complex, located on the northern outskirts of the city, we were told, had attracted a considerable amount of housing provided for the railway workers and their families and the paramount need in this connection was the avoidance of casualties among them.

The force consisting of 181 aircraft, a mixture of Halifaxes, Lancasters, Stirlings and Mosquitoes, would bomb in two waves, 77 Squadron aircraft were to be part of the first wave. We were pleased to learn, the raid would be orchestrated by a master bomber whose presence, we were assured, would go a long way towards guaranteeing a telling concentration of bombs confined to the railway complex itself. Many years after the war ended I learnt that the aircraft in which the master bomber, Wing Commander A.G.S. Cousens, DSO, DFC., of 635 Squadron was flying, had been shot down during the course of the raid. Of the eight men in the aircraft all but one of them was killed. Amongst those who lost their lives was the Wing Commander.

It looked as though it was going to be a busy night for the enemy defences. 596 aircraft were to bomb Dusseldorf and 238 aircraft were briefed to bomb Brunswick. As usual we derived some comfort from the thought that these two heavy raids might attract at least some, if not the major portion, of the attention of the German night fighters which in other circumstances might well have been directed at us.

For very obvious reasons Bob Johnson was warned by the Signals Leader not to spend any more 'time on the key' than was absolutely necessary for him to send his callsign and the wind velocity provided by me, the Germans, both the night fighter pilots already in the air and their controllers on the ground, were always on the look out for any aircraft breaking radio silence rule.

Once we had collected our escape kits and the perspex encased pieces of rice paper on which were printed such things as the identifying colours of the day and other sensitive inform- ation we left to prepare ourselves for the flight and, thereafter, to eat our flying meal. There was a noticeable lightheartedness amongst the crews as we dispersed, even perhaps some misplaced confidence. After all, we told ourselves, it was only a French target and someone at HQ Bomber Command in High Wycombe must be convinced it presented a lesser threat to life and limb when they decided to count attacks on such targets as representing only half an operation.

Back in my room I dressed carefully with warmth and comfort in mind donning clean 'long johns' and my thick white, roll-topped pullover beneath my battle dress blouse. I made certain my whistle, for signalling if we had to ditch, was attached to my blouse collar. I had already emptied my pockets of everything but a handkerchief and cigarettes immediately after briefing. My flying boots and sea-boot stockings were in my flying clothing locker down at the airfield, as was Mary's scarf. These I would change into at the last minute before going out to the aircraft.

There remained only my usual moment of private contemplation during which I knelt by my bed to say, as I did before every operational flight, Sir Jacob Astley's prayer which he used to say before the Battle of Edgehill in 1642.

"O Lord thou knowest how busy I must be this day :
if I forget thee, do not thou forget me."

Feeling much more relaxed I gave a last glance round the room little knowing I was never again to set foot in it, although at the time the possibility of a catastrophe overtaking us was furthermost from my mind. Belief in one's own inviolability as opposed to the other chap's vulnerability was, like a child's favourite teddy bear, a comfort not to be denied. It was time to make my way to the mess there to face the laboured humour, always prevalent, as we munched our way through the traditional pre-flight meal of bacon and eggs.

Later there was the habitual hurly burly in the parachute section with people reaching over the shoulders of those in front of them as pigeonhole numbers were shouted out even though the faces and the whereabouts of the parachutes of all but the very new boys were well known to the WAAF parachute packers. As usual, and much to my continuing delight, the pretty little blonde-haired girl, Dot, touched my hand as she handed me mine. "See you tomorrow Charlie," she smiled. And I had no cause to think it would not be so.

Fortunately there were always far too many last minute preparatory chores to be performed to permit of any prolonged and, therefore, unnerving consideration of what lay ahead of us. But the routine hour's wait out at the aircraft after the engines had been subjected to a test run up and then shut down was a prolonged soul searching time for all of us. It was then that conversation became stilted and final cigarettes were dragged on as though our very lives depended on taking into our lungs as much nicotine as possible. But eventually we found ourselves ensconced within the chilly cocoon that was 'S' - Sugar, lumbered round the perimeter track in an orderly gaggle with the other thirteen aircraft heading for the lead-in to the runway in use.

As we groped our way forward I was stationed in the nose cone of the aircraft directing the beam of the Aldis lamp in such a way as to help Ken Bond avoid the soggy grass verge of the airfield lying on our starboard side. To allow the aircraft to become bogged down was frowned upon, to do so when preparing to take-off on an operation was just about the deadliest of the seven deadly sins. In this connection I recall a flight safety poster in the crew room which put it in a nutshell. "Have a taxiing accident and try as an AC2 !"

As we passed flying control I was able to wave back to the usual crowd of officers, airmen and airwomen, aircrew and ground crew alike, standing there with thumbs up to wish us God speed. It was yet another simple but sincere manifestation of the squadron's pride in the bonds of brotherhood that held us together and one that gave a final lift to our spirits. The absence of that little valedictory band to see us off was unthinkable.

As we paused before turning onto the runway the green light from the airfield caravan giving us the all clear to line up for take-off flashed our way. Round went the aircraft until it was pointing directly down the centre line of the 2000-ft of tarmacadam stretched out before us. The brakes were forcefully applied and Ken Bond's voice came over the intercom with his customary query followed by his equally familiar calm announcement. "All OK chaps ? Here we go then !" Without more ado he gradually opened up the engines, at the same time holding the aircraft against the brakes until 1,000 revs were indicated. As he released the brakes the aircraft accelerated ahead until at about a quarter of the way down the runway he pushed forward the four throttle levers to their fullest extent at which point John Grimer, who was performing his second pilot duties, put the lock on but continued to hold them firmly in place. I felt the tail come up as Bond eased the control column forward with the aircraft steadily gaining speed - 80-90-100 knots. She was now airborne and as the speed increased still further she started a gentle climb into the darkness. We were on our way.

Once we were at our crew stations Ken went through his check to ensure all was well with us. "Rear Gunner, OK ?" "Fine Skipper, guns cocked and ready to fire." Bill Jack's soft-spoken Scottish accent softened the harshness of the inherent threat to any potential marauder contained in his words. "Mid Upper, all set?" "All set Skipper. Guns cocked and ready to fire." Mathew's quiet reply always had a settling effect on me, although he was unaware of this. "Engineer, all OK ?" "Everything in order Skipper." Vic's voice had a youthful quality about it, almost the sound of a schoolboy answering the roll call at the day's first assembly. Listening to him my thoughts went back to Hastings Grammer School, where the first thing we learnt as new boys was to answer the roll call of our names with "Adsum" - I am here. "Wireless Op., tuned in ?" "All in order Skipper. Listening out." I could see Bob from my seat and he grinned at me reassuringly as he dropped the oxygen mask from his face and switched off his microphone. "Bomb Aimer, all right up front ?" "Fine thank you Skipper." John was already reclining full length on his pad ready to map read and help me in any other way open to him. "Navigator, ready to take us there and back ?" His question to me never varied. "All ready Skipper." There was little more I could say. "Overhead base. First course please navigator." "Steer 175 degrees."

The routine of setting course over base at precisely the briefed time was now a well rehearsed procedure known to Ken Bond and myself. Almost inevitably we had to waste a few minutes but, as I had foreseen the probable need for this whilst putting together my flight plan, I had the first course to steer well in mind before we took off and was able to pass it to the pilot as we continued to climb away from the airfield. All appeared to be going well and the crew quickly settled to their various tasks as we headed south towards Reading. The Gee set was functioning like a thing possessed allowing me to maintain an accurate plot and thus keep a running check on the wind velocity which, happily, differed very little from that given to us by 'Inky' the met. officer.

I have always felt grateful for having, as a navigator, so much to keep me busy and mentally occupied, with scant chance to worry over what might happen to us. It was not a case of being unafraid or over casual I simply did not have time to spare for such apprehensions, my essential task was to check and re-check our progress by every means available to me.

As we thundered past Sheffield, Nottingham and Leicester to our starboard John appeared at my elbow, map in hand, to give me a pinpoint of the L.M.S railway line crossing the river Ouse near Newport Pagnell. I found we were dead on track.

The Thames soon marked our steady progress southwards and London could be seen as a slumbering dark mass to port. Overhead Reading. "Navigator to pilot, turn to port on new course 135 degrees."

We crossed the coast near Beachy Head, making a barely discernible turn to starboard onto a course of 135 degrees. What with its own blunt protrusion into the Channel and the inward sweeping coastline on either side, to starboard Brighton, Hove and Worthing, to port Eastbourne, Bexhill and Hastings, on a clear night Beachy Head was a gift of a pinpoint to any worthwhile map reader. By now we were nearing our operating height of 18,000-ft and would certainly reach it before crossing the enemy coast near to Dieppe. A few minutes later Ken called up the gunners. "OK gunners you can test your guns, but don't waste ammunition we might need it later." There was a brief pause and then the reassuring clatter of our eight .303in Browning machine guns could be heard followed by the smell of cordite. John Grimer, not to be outdone, joined in with his Vickers pop-gun fitted in the nose. All in all, I thought, we ought to be able to give a reasonable account of ourselves if attacked by enemy fighters.

According to my calculations we were on track and on time and as our ETA Dieppe drew closer I pulled aside the curtains separating John Grimer and myself in time to see what sort of reception was to be ours as we crossed into France. Initially there was nothing to see although occasionally we could feel the reassuring turbulence caused by the backwash from another aircraft's engines - I say reassuring only because it gave us a comfortable feeling of not being alone. Suddenly, immediately in front of us, up came some light flax, presumably from a flak ship stationed just off the coast, hosing ineffectually into the sky to a height of some 15,000-ft, well below our operating height. Undeterred, on we flew, whereupon John Grimer, not to be denied his opportunity of uttering the well worn phase so loved of film makers and writers alike, spoke up. "Enemy coast ahead." To hear it never failed to cause me to feel a frisson of excitement. John always managed, I am sure quite unwittingly, to turn what was, after all, a pretty mundane piece of information into a "Once more into the breach dear friends" exhortation. It was like something out of the Boy's Own Paper, a touch of Death or Glory.

No great alteration of course was necessary as we turned to port to fly on a heading of 110 degrees. We were now flying directly towards Laon and in the process of descending to 7.000-ft, the height at which we had briefed to bomb. It was time for me to make my final wind checks before passing the result to Bob Johnson for transmission to HQ No.4 Group at Heslington Hall. The luck of the devil was with us for the ground was clearly visible making the acquisition of good pinpoints comparatively straight forward. Having averaged out the latest of the several wind velocities I had calculated I passed the result to Bob Johnson and listened whilst he tapped out the information to Heslington Hall. He had a first rate wireless operator's 'fist' and was on the air for barely five seconds.

Whilst in the vicinity of Amiens a certain amount of activity on our port side was visible. It looked very much as though an exchange of fire was taking place between a bomber and an enemy night fighter. Again it wasn't a case of being callous, but in such circumstances one was grateful it was not we who were at the receiving end of the attack. As we flew on towards Laon the likelihood of night fighter activity increased and I was reminded of this possibility when I noted I had marked on my plotting chart the existence of three enemy airfields lying not far off our planned track - Tergnier, Athies ? Laon and Juvincourt. Little did I know then that within a matter of a few days I was to make the closer acquaintance of one or other of them. As it was I reminded Bond of their nearness and he in turn warned the rest of the crew to be vigilant.

Bob Johnson handed me the averaged out wind velocity he had received from HQ $ Group and as I drew aside the curtains to pass the chit to John Grimer to feed into his bomb-sight I could see in the near distance the green target indicating flares already cascading dead ahead in front of us. It was good to have our well timed arrival in the target area confirmed and it was not long before John began intoning his bombing run spiel. "At this rate Skipper a change of course won't be necessary, we can run straight in." Flak was now beginning to become intense and above the pounding of our engines the occasional burst could be heard and, for that matter, seen. Shrapnel rattled on the fuselage in a quite disturbing way and I hoped none of it would hit any vital part of the aircraft or its crew.

Through the crackling static of the air waves I could hear the voice of the Master Bomber. There was about it a slightly strained quality as though the speaker was experiencing some difficulty in directing the efforts of the bomber force beneath him. "Come on you Halifax's, bomb the centre of the green markers, they've been well placed . . . . Keep it coming . . . . No edging back now. We don't want any fringe merchants . . . . Bomb the greens . . . . Well done . . . . Well done . . . . That's the stuff, but keep well up to the centre of the greens." John Grimer started his bombing run. "Bomb doors open please Skipper . . . . Bombs selected and fused . . . . Hold it steady . . . . Steady as you go . . . . Right, right a little . . . . right a shade more . . . . steady . . . . steady . . . . steady."

It was at this stage in any operation when we all held our breath, for it was essential, in the case of accurate bombing, for the aircraft to be held steadily on the line of flight being called for by the bomb aimer and thus both it and its crew were placed in an unenviable vulnerable position. The one thought common to each of us was, for God's sake John get it right first time, don't let's have to go round again as we did on the previous occasion.

The intensity of my own physical excitement was as though I had been dosed with a powerful stimulant, whilst at the same time the level of my fear reached an almost unbearable pitch. For those few minutes, that seemed like hours, I felt a clammy sweat momentarily covering my whole body. There was nothing I could do to relieve the sensation, I had perforce to wait for a release from it. A release that lay in the lap of the gods and in the hands of the bomb aimer. Meanwhile my eyes remained glued to the thumb on John's right hand poised unwaveringly above the bomb release 'tit.' Suddenly it flashed downwards and I heard the welcoming words giving at least a semi-release from my tension. "Bombs gone . . . . jettison bar across . . . . hold it steady for the flash." As the aircraft was released from the weight of bombs it rose upwards but was otherwise held steady for a further thirty seconds to allow the photo flash to explode on the ground and for the camera to turn over to record the accuracy or otherwise of our bombing. "Flash gone . . . . Close bomb doors." Ken Bond needed no second bidding. As he closed the bomb doors he put the aircraft into a dive to clear the target area. Once clear he pulled back on the control column in a stomach wrenching manoeuvre to regain some of the height he had lost. Without asking to be asked for it I called out the change of course to take us south on the short leg before turning for home. In the minutes immediately following a successful bombing run a sense of relief momentarily engulfed me, a feeling I knew was common to each of us. Bond would sometimes crystallise my thoughts by saying something like, "Well done, bomb aimer. On the button. Let's get out of here and go home." And John would roll to one side of his couch whereupon, by the light of what was taking place around us I could see on his pale face sweat brought about by the concentration he had given to his task.

On we ploughed into the night on the short leg out of the target area. Within minutes it would be necessary for me to pass a further change of course to the pilot to take us to Fécamp on the French coast and that much nearer to the comparative safety of the English Channel and home.

Suddenly, the soporific drone of the engines was shattered as all hell was let loose within the aircraft. I was just about aware of a shouted warning, "Fighter. Fighter. Cork-screw . . . . " from one or other of the gunners but it was cut short by several other happenings which, in retrospect, seemed to occur simultaneously.

There was the clatter of attacking gunfire that swept through the aircraft from the rear to the front and through the small window facing me as I sat at my desk I caught a glimpse of flames engulfing the port inner engine. Undoubtedly we were on fire with the aircraft already showing signs of falling out of control, suggesting Ken Bond might well have been wounded. As the attacking night fighter raked the length of 'S' - Sugar, my desk disintegrated before my eyes as a hail of cannon shells sliced through it with explosive precision. Within micro-seconds my knees and feet were entangled in a pile of debris and I realised the intercom was no longer functioning.

Vaguely I became aware of Victor Clare peering down from the second pilot position where he stood outlined against the glare of the flames behind him. With one hand he gesticu- lated wildly in a way that could only mean the order to 'bale out' had been given. Many years later I read his account of what took place during those few seconds. He wrote it soon after he returned to England having evaded the enemy and reached Switzerland where he was interned. *(see Appendix 6, p.99.)*

This must have been the moment when I saw Vic standing at the top of the steps leading down to my position in the aircraft when his gestures left me in no doubt we were to get out of the aircraft immediately. John Grimer was already on his feet and standing near me but Bob Johnson was still sitting in his seat looking dazed and uncomprehending. I leant towards him shouting. "Bale out ! Bale out !", at the same time pointing downwards. He raised the thumb of his right hand signifying he understood what I was about to do.

Having, with John Grimer's help, already pushed to one side the debris that had been my plotting desk I ripped off my helmet and grabbed my parachute from its stowage position behind me. Using both hands, with a single movement I rammed the pack onto the two 'G' clips of the harness which, as a matter of standard practice, I was wearing and turned my attention to the escape hatch.

The navigators seat in a Halifax was located atop the forward escape hatch. It therefore simply remained for me to fold my seat back against the starboard side of the aircraft and to seize the ring catch securing the hatch in position. I gave the ring an almighty twist and pull whereupon, much to my surprise, because I had never operated the catch before, the whole of the door came away in my hand. For a brief second I gawped at it and then realising this was exactly what was supposed to happen I dropped the door through the gaping hole whence lay my way of escape.

Looking up I noticed Bob Johnson dragging himself towards me. He was obviously in considerable pain. he had removed his helmet and I could see below his tousled hair that his face had taken on an ashen almost death-like appearance. Each of his flying boots was covered in blood as were the legs of his battledress trousers. Somehow he had managed to clip on his parachute. John Grimer, who was already standing at my side, helped me pull him to the hatch where, together, we helped him jump out. Not a word passed between us. Thereafter, in short order, I followed him. John Grimer, whose own severe wounds were not obvious to me at the time, and Vic Clare must have been hard on my heels.

As I hurtled into the night with my hands clasped protectively over the metal ring on the front of the parachute pack I counted a measured, One, Two, Three, then pulled the ring hard, at the same time uttering a hurried supplication to any deity within hearing distance that the wretched thing would deploy and gently lower me to mother earth. There was a momentary pause before the canopy, with its attendant webbing and shrouds, swept upwards past my face and ballooned into its life-saving position. As it did so I felt the painful wrench of the harness straps between my legs indicating that I should have tightened it even further as I had constantly been advised to do by our station Physical Training Instructor who not only doubled as our parachuting guru but was also of a biblical turn of mind.

> " For what shall it profit a man, if he shall save his life - courtesy of Mr.Leslie Leroy Irvin founder of the Irvin Air Chute Company - and lose his manhood because he failed to tighten his harness straps properly."

As I floated downwards I was able to see 'S' - Sugar, by then engulfed in flames, and in a shallow glide. Before I reached the ground I heard the crash and saw the flash of fire that lit up the sky which, together, heralded her end. [Together with the pilot Ken Bond].

Momentarily my attention was diverted from what was happening to myself and all too suddenly, ill prepared as I was, I saw the ground rushing up towards me. For some reason or another I drew up my legs into what I can best describe as a sitting position thereby ensuring that when I did touch down I did so heavily and painfully on the base of my spine. The jarring shock from the jolt travelled up my back to my head and for a moment I thought I was about to lose consciousness. I have carried the residual with me from that day to this.

I twisted and banged the lock designed to release me speedily from the parachute harness and watched the canopy deflate into a pile of flattened silk [silk or nylon, this was in 1944 ?] An almost tangible silence followed. There I sat in the middle of a ploughed field in France, so near yet so far from England, home and beauty, thankful to be alive but bitterly regretting my sudden change of circumstances. I did however remember to give brief thanks to him who, a bare three hours beforehand, I asked not to forget me.

It was now I tried to recall the substance of the squadron lectures designed to prepare us for the kind of predicament in which I now found myself. My hand went immediately to the inside of my battledress blouse where I expected to find my 'escape kit' only to realise it was no longer there. It could only have dropped out when I jumped from the aircraft. Oh well, I thought, I would have to make do with out it. I still had my two compasses, one disguised as a rear collar stud the other to be made up from two of the fly buttons on my battledress trousers - they were designed that one balanced on a minute spike which formed part of the other.

Bury your parachute we had been advised. Well, I don't know how many of my lecturers had ever tried to bury an outsize armful of canvas, silk and yards of rope in a ploughed field from which the frosts of winter had not fully departed, but my frantic efforts to do so and without benefit of something like an entrenching tool came to naught. I therefore made for the nearest hedge and managed to hide it. As quickly as possible put as much distance as you can between yourself and the area in which you have landed, our lecturers had advised. With the purpose in mind of doing just that it took me but a minute or two to find a barred gate, once over the gate I set out at a smart pace down the lane. I must have walked for some thirty minutes, partly through a wooded area, before coming to the first signs of human habitation. I discovered I had reached what turned out to be a hamlet consisting of little more than thirty cottages and farmhouses and a church. On my immediate left stood one such dwelling from which a light was shining through a partially curtained window. I stood for a while contemplating my next move and having concluded there was little likelihood of a German presence in the village, bearing in mind the flagrant breach of the blackout regulations, I decided to try my luck with the occupants of the house I had been watching.

As a point of interest it was to be some years later before I learnt that we had been shot down at a position some 5 kilometres east of Soissons and some 25 kilometres south-east of Laon. This would have placed me, at the time, near to the villages of Villeneuve-St-Germain, Missy-sur-Aisne and Bucy-le-Long.

Arriving at the front door of the house I was watching I knocked with some circumspec- tion having no wish to arouse the whole neighbourhood. There was a pause before the door was opened by a young man who had used one hand to raise the door-latch whilst with the other he was attempting to pull up his trousers which, judging from the japing flies, unfastened belt and protruding shirt front, he had but very recently drawn on. Behind him I could make out a brightly lit living room where, at the far end, a pretty girl was lying in a state of near nudity on a couch. It occurred to me as I stood forlornly on the doorstep that I had not only interrupted a rustic courtship but had done so, it seemed, as it was about to reach, its inevitable climax.

It was obvious the next move was up to me and having dug deep into my recollections of 'Neuter' Pearce's French lessons at Hastings Grammar School for Boys I managed to cobble together, "Bon soir, monsieur. Je m'excuse mais je suis un aviateur Anglais de Royal Air Force. Aidez moi, s'il vous plait." my attempt at explaining myself in his own language must have impressed the young man, for with a torrent of words that meant little or nothing to me he seized me by the shoulder, dragged me into the room and sat me on the couch in close proximity to his girl friend who was busily engaged in adjusting her clothes. Having done so she got up, extended to me a brief bob of a curtsey and disappeared through another door into the back regions of the house.

The young man meanwhile, continued the struggle to hitch up his trousers. This done, he turned from me to run up a flight of stairs, which I presumed gave access to bedrooms above. I was able to hear his urgent hammering on a door followed by the sleepy response of male and female voices. A few minutes later I was once confronted by the young man who now introduced to me, as his father and mother, the middle-aged couple accompanying him.

The remarkable thing about all of this was the coolness with which the trio received me. It was as though they found nothing unusual in being dragged from their beds in the middle of the night to be confronted by a complete stranger, who had fallen out of the sky and who was now seeking shelter with them. The woman fussed around me in a motherly fashion, plucking at my uniform blouse, patting my shoulder and, as far as I was able to understand her heavily accented French, commiserating with me over the situation into which I had been pitched. "Pauvre garcon, Comme il est jeune. Es tu blessé ?" I did my best during the next half hour, during which I was plied with coffee and cake, to explain my presence whilst they, for their part, asked me time and again when they could expect the arrival of a liberating army of 'Les Tommies.' They appeared to have more knowledge of Mr.Churchill's intentions in the matter then I had, nevertheless, in an attempt to improve their morale and at the same time enlist their sympathies I assured them their day of liberation could not be far off.

I tried to make them understand I must not fall into the hands of the Germans and was given some reassurance by the man when he told me there were none in the village and in the morning he would see what could be done to help me on my way. Eventually conversation slackened and the woman suggested, "Tu doit fatigué. Viens avec moi." Taking me by the hand she led me to a small bedroom situated to one side of the front door. It was plainly furnished with a large double bed covered by a patchwork counterpane, a chest of drawers and a vast wardrobe. On the wooden floor a small rug lay alongside the bed. On the walls were one or two devotional pictures, propped up on the chest were what I took to be family photographs. The room's solitary window looked out onto the village street. She bid me sleep well but as she turned to leave me she must have noticed the tears in the seat of my trousers caused by the barbed wire. "Donne moi votre pantalon et je vais les réparer pour toi." The fact that I was tired and the bed looked inviting combined to overcome my youthful modesty and possible embarrassment at undressing in front of a strange woman. Having taken off my blouse and shoes I removed my trousers without further ado and handed them to her.

As she disappeared through the door she bid me *"Dormez bein mon garcon.Dormez tres bien."* I climbed into bed and was soon asleep, deep in the folds of the feather mattress. Not, however, before the thought crossed my mind that it was barely four hours since we had taken off from Elvington and here I was in the depths of the French countryside where, having gained access to a farmhouse whose owners were complete strangers to me, I was now in a warm bed having been told to sleep well by a woman who, without turning a hair, had relieved me of my torn trousers with a promise to mend them.

I was woken up by the sun shining through the bedroom curtains. For a moment or two I lay there wondering where the devil I could be. Through no great feat of memory the happenings of the previous night came flooding back and with them a sense of depression over the situation in which i now found myself. I noticed my trousers, neatly folded, had been mended and placed on the chair beside the bed.

I got up and made my way through the living room into the farmhouse kitchen where I found my three benefactors of the previous evening seated round a table. In the centre of the table was a bowl of coffee into which they were dipping their bread rolls. The younger man, whose name I learnt was Lucien, took me out into the farmyard where he showed me the earth closet and the pump under which he invited me to wash myself. Back in the kitchen he lent me a razor and soap and under the eyes of all three I completed my toilet at the kitchen sink before being urged to join them at the kitchen table.

The farmer and his wife, whose names I never learnt, had started to tell me how they planned to help me when the front door opened to reveal a man dressed in the uniform of an agent de ville - in later years, when I was stationed at Fontainebleau, I was to learn they were not Gendarmes but unarmed village policemen. It soon became clear my presence in the farmhouse was already known to him, presumably the farmer had been out and about early setting in motion the help I so urgently needed if I was to evade capture by the Germans. After handshakes all round, that included myself, the visitor began, with some excitement, to speak of the previous night's raid on Laon and of the aircraft that had crashed nearby. Our aircraft, I presumed.

What with the almost impenetrable local accent and the speed with which they conversed, I found it difficult to follow the conversation, nevertheless it became apparent the agent was speaking about a fellow airman who had been discovered lying wounded in a field not far from where we were then sitting. By the description he gave I decided the man could only be Bob Johnson. To my surprise I was asked to accompany the agent who was on his way back to Bob to await the arrival of an ambulance that had been sent for.

I could hear a solitary church bell ringing and realised it was Sunday morning. On the one hand it depressed me bringing back as it did memories of home. On the other hand it surprised me, church bells had been banned in England since September 1939 their pealing being reserved for warning of an impending invasion. I thought a similar ban existed in France, but apparently not. Everyone appeared to be wearing their 'Sunday best,' black dresses for the women and dark suits and some top hats for the men. The children were less sombrely dressed. Lucien told me the villagers were on their way to church and had lingered out of curiosity and to give me what support they could, which was little enough in the circumstances.

Seated as I was beside Lucien's father and still in uniform although I had followed the advice given us on the squadron and cut off the tops of my flying boots to make that part of me less conspicuous, I felt horribly exposed to the gaze of the world at large. My fears were in no way calmed, indeed they were heightened, by the number of people surrounding the cart who were laughing and chattering for all the world as though they were off to a football match. Several of them, shouted up to me as I sat above them, attempting to seek my assurance that their liberation from the Germans by the 'Tommies' would soon come about.

I remained ill at ease in the midst of all this attention, constantly wondering whether I was doing the right thing by accompanying the noisy posse of people. It was, I reminded myself for the umpteenth time, my duty to evade capture if I could possibly do so and in an attempt to ease my conscience on this score I decided that once I had made certain Bob was cared for I would disappear as quickly and as surreptitiously as circumstances permitted. Such was the undisguised dislike of the French crowd for the Germans, I had no misgivings as to the help I could get from them if and when my chance to escape materialised.

After some ten or fifteen minutes the cavalcade turned through a gate into a grassy field where we found Bob lying on a slight rise in the ground. He was in a pitiful condition. Although he was still wearing his flying boots I could see he was wounded in both feet. His face was drained of blood and at first I though his injuries were such that he was not long for this world. He was shivering uncontrollably partly, I am sure, with sustained shock and partly because he had spent the night in the unsheltered open. I felt guilty at having passed the night unhurt and in the warmth of the farmhouse.

On seeing me his eyes lit up and he attempted to raise his shoulders from the ground only to fall back again through exhaustion. I knelt beside him giving him what verbal comfort I could whilst assuring him that medical help was on its way and that he would soon be properly looked after. I told him of my plan to disappear quietly once I had seen him taken care of. All he could bring himself to mutter was, "Good to see you Charlie. My God it's good to see you Charlie," and to ask me not to leave him until he was in medical care. He would not have been in any way reassured had he known the torment of self guilt that threatened to overwhelm me. Whilst I was devastated by his suffering it was all I could do to stem the urge I had to get away from the turmoil surrounding us which, I foresaw, would only invite unwanted attention.

Many years later, in the 1980's, after I had re-established contact with Bob I asked him to write his account of what happened to him. Here I will include the first few paragraphs.

> "On that fateful night in April 1944 I became aware that we had been hit as both my legs shot up with such force they hit the underside of my table. I tried to contact the Skipper but the intercom was dead. By this time my area was filled with smoke. Someone poked their head up from the front and motioned that he was going to bale out, I assumed it was Charles, and I put up my thumb to show I understood. I was disconnecting my electric's when I felt the cool stream of air and i knew that Charles, and probably John, were baling out. The cool fresh air was a Godsend.
>
> I got to my feet to follow and I found I could not stand. The force of self preservation, or whatever, was very strong and I crawled to the escape hatch on my knees. The plane was burning fiercely when I reached the hatch so I wasted no time in baling out. * Counting five, whether quickly or slowly, I don't know, I pulled the ripcord. I was immediately aware of a rush of air and the burning plane vanishing from sight and then a fantastic stillness and I realised my parachute had opened. I blessed the girls in the parachute section.
>
> I knew both my feet had been hit and reached down to my boots and felt the warm sticky blood and became concerned about landing on them. Suddenly there was a terrific thud which almost knocked me out and I knew I had landed. I gathered in my parachute so that it would be inconspicuous. Looking round I could see I had landed on a wooded hillside, I was fortunate not to have been caught up in the trees. I tried to get to the top of the hill in order to get my bearing but the effort was too much for me and I knew I had to stay where

I was and hope that I could be found before daylight came.

Dawn came and after a while I saw a dog. It came over to me followed by a Frenchman. He could see I was in no state to move without help and motioning me to stay where I was, he made me understand he would return with help. I indicated I did not want the Germans to find me and he nodded to show me he understood.

Some time elapsed before I noticed a lot of people began to arrive and it seemed as though the whole village had turned out to see the poor wounded airman in the woods! I was told I would be taken to a farm by horse and cart where I would be seen by a doctor, when who should turn up but Charles - It was certainly great to see him.

He told me he had sought help in the village and they had cared for him overnight. When he heard of my plight he came out to see if it was one of his crew. I was about to be loaded onto the cart when Charles cursed and said some German soldiers were making their way towards us, presumably they had been told of the fuss and had come to see why so many people were streaming out of the village. Charles wondered whether he should make a dash for it, but they were armed and he though better of it.

We were both taken in a German staff car to a place called Soissons . . . "

* Bob's memory played him false here. When he reached the hatch John and I, realising he was badly hurt, helped him out and then followed him. (CWH).

Whilst still trying to give Bob what supporting comfort I could I became aware of a movement in the crowd and of a sudden silence amongst them. I heard a shouted order and watched as the French onlookers drew apart to leave an open path for what I thought might be the arrival of medical help. To my bitter disappointment there appeared, striding towards us, two German soldiers in their unmistakable grey/green uniforms, complete with jack boots and metal helmets. Around the neck of each of them, suspended by a chain, was a metal gorget indicating they were members of the Feldjager whilst on the left tunic sleeve they wore a red arm band bearing the inscription, 'Oberkommando der Wehrmacht - Feldjager.'

It was not until 1960, when I was serving in HQ Allied Air Forces Central Europe, Fontainebleau, that I was to learn of the origins and duties of the *Feldjager*. It would seem that by the late summer of 1943 events all along the Eastern Front were definitely turning in favour of the red Army. The need to stiffen crumbling German resistance in the face of the enemy brought about desperate measures. One of these measures was the establishment on 9 January 194?, of *Feldjager* units.

Consisting of experienced combat soldiers, NCO's and officers, these units, who were answerable only to the *Oberkommando der Wehrmacht* (OKW), the High Command of the German Armed Forces, were charged with the task of hunting down deserters, arresting insubordinates, looters, and general malingerers, combing through echelon areas for troops who were fit enough for front line duty and, through the use of fear, generally stiffening up the will of the German soldier to stand and fight the enemy.

Those units were empowered to arrest and fling back into the front line any one they caught who could not account for their absence from active service. Unit Commanders had the power to conduct drum-head courts-martial and when necessary have the defendants executed on the spot. The power of the *Feldjager* units most definitely came out of the barrel of a gun, backed up by the authority of the OKW.

Members of *Feldjager* units wore two items which distinguished them from ordinary Army and *Waffen*-SS troops. When on duty they wore a special *Feldjager* duty gorget and a red arm band.

Perhaps it was just as well I did not know, that morning in April 1944, the nature and powers of the two men who were about to arrest me. The face of the elder of the two, whose rank I was later to learn was that of *oberfeldwebel*, or flight sergeant, showed all the signs of a thousand beery nights spent in a thousand different bierkellers. It was a square, unsmiling, face giving forewarning of a man not to be trifled with. His companion was much younger, barely eighteen or nineteen, an *obergefreiter* or lance corporal, whose fair skin and blue eyes marked him down as a specimen of Hitler's *Herrenvolk* or master race. Each of them was armed with a short-barrelled automatic weapon carried, in this instance, at the ready.

As they halted in front of us the senior of the two jerked his weapon upwards, indicating I should get to my feet. "*Steh auf. Hande hoch.*" There was no mistaking the meaning of the first two words, I was to get to my feet. *Hande hock* on the other hand was one of the few German expressions with which I was familiar having heard it used, and indeed had used it myself, in many a piece of schoolboyish tomfoolery back in the squadron's crew room. Accordingly I wasted no time in raising my arms above my head at the same time feeling a little foolish whilst doing so. It was like something out of a Hollywood production except in this instance it was for real. *"Mach ihre jacke auf."* My face must have betrayed my inability to understand what was being said to me and quite gratuitously a young Frenchman standing nearby volunteered his services as a translator. "He says to open your jacket." Then turning to the policeman he added, *"Er spricht kein Deutsch."* And to me, "I've told them you don't speak German and they say they don't speak English. Mais, prenez garde" he added, behind his hand.

The younger of the two Germans came closer, to stand immediately in front of me, his eyes glaring into mine, his face creased in a grin of contempt. With scant ceremony he ran his hands over me lifting up my heavy pullover to get at the shirt beneath, presumably to see if I was armed. *"Dreh sich um."* "Turn round." said my interpreter. For some reason best known to himself the young German gave me a firm push in the back as I turned causing me to stumble forward almost to the point of falling down, whereupon a growl of disapproval came from the crowd followed immediately by some shouting and arm waving from the *oberfeldwebel*. As my searcher continued his hunt for my non-existent weapons he hissed in my ear,*"Der Krieg is fur sie zu ende, Terrorflieger."* There was no need for an explanation. I was already familiar with the phase. It was one I had often heard in jest back at Elvington. Terroflieger' or 'Terror Flyer' was one of the expressions used by the English traitor William Joyce (Lord Haw-Haw, the nick-name originally given to him by Jonah Barrington of the Daily Express, it was an allusion to his accent) who broadcast anti-British propaganda in English from Germany. After the war he was arrested, tried for treason and hanged in 1946.

The search ended, two of the French spectators were told to assist Bob into the vehicle in which the Germans had arrived. "Steig in wagon ein." This accompanied by yet another shove in the back as I made my way towards the military police vehicle. The crowd remained silent as I passed Lucien and his father and mother, who now in tears, their whispered encouragement came to me *"Courage! Bon chance!"* Words that were taken up by some of the other spectators.

I was pushed into the rear of the vehicle where in an effort to relieve Bob of at least some of the pain I lifted his legs to rest in my lap, and thus we set off to waves of farewell from the crowd. We had travelled no further than three or four miles when we stopped at a small building in yet another hamlet. The *oberfeldwebel* disappeared inside and a few minutes later reappeared with two men half carrying none other than John Grimer whose trouser legs were stained with blood. He too had sustained a severe wound. He managed a grin and with raised forefinger to lips bade us remain silent. Many years later he wrote a description for me of the last few minutes before he parachuted from our aircraft and what happened to him when he landed. see Appendix 11

No attempt was made to handle John with care knowing he was wounded, he was pushed into the vehicle where he occupied the other rear corner seat. This done we once again took to the road. Much to my surprise the young *obergefreiter* began to address us in halting English and it was then I called to mind the Frenchman's advice to me to, *"prenez garde."* Recalling our constantly repeated intelligence briefings to give only our number, rank and name in response to any questioning from the enemy we remained silent, much to the young man's annoyance. Thereafter the journey continued in silence.

There was yet another stop when Mathew Mason, the mid-upper gunner was fetched from a house where he had been given shelter. He looked dreadful, the blood stain on his trouser legs telling their own story. At the best of times he was a man of few words, I was not therefore over surprised when he said nothing as he was pushed into the vehicle. I felt desperately sorry for him looking as he most certainly did as though he might succumb to his wounds. How the *feldjager* NCO's managed to fit him into the rear of the vehicle along with John, Bob and myself I shall never know, but get him in they did.

We soon reached the outskirts of a sizeable town which I was later to learn was Soissons. There were only a few people about as we drew near to and were waved through a guarded gate to come face to face with a dreary looking building which could only be a prison. On the orders of the *oberfeldwebel* I was the first to leave the vehicle, whereupon his young companion grabbed one of my arms possessively and frog marched me into a reception area, where an aged, pencil sucking army NCO seated behind a desk signed for my body. Having done so he indicated to my guard that he should take me to a cell accompanied by one of his own men who wore a nondescript uniform of non-military cut. It was a lengthy march to our destination, down endless corridors with forbidding looking doors in either side. Eventually we stopped outside one such door and with a great rattling of keys and shooting of bolts I was ushered into a cell.

The cell was barely large enough to accommodate a narrow wooden bunk bed. There was nothing else by way of furniture. High up on the wall opposite the door was a single, barred window through which I could see the sky. Once all three of us were in the cell the warder slammed the door shut and shouted to me *"Zieh alle ihre kleider aus."* I stared at him incomprehendingly and was glad when the feldjager came to rescue with, "Er spricht kein Deutsch" and to me, "Get your clothes off."

The two of them stood watching me as I undressed as far as my underwear. The warder took each article from me as I removed it and diligently went through pockets and felt along the seams of my jacket and trousers and looked with some envy at my cut-down flying boots. He did not notice the compass in my back collar stud or the two fly buttons which together made up yet another rudimentary compass. This done he gesticulated towards me and the *feldjager* obliged with, "Get the rest off." I did as I was told and received a kick from a jackboot on my ankle making it plain I should stand with my legs wide apart. If I had felt vulnerable before I now experienced in addition a mxture of shame and anger at being treated in this fashion, a feeling that was heightened as I felt the warder's hands move over my body whilst laughing and chattering to his partner in my degredation. "Dreh sich um und hande hoch." "Turn round and get your hands up." I now found the warders face barely inches from my own. He reeked of garlic causing me to jerk back ny head involuntarily. Whether he was annoyed by my reaction I know not, his further examination of me was rough and personally demeaning. Eventually I was allowed to dress and the two men left me alone in the cell.

From outside in the passage way I could hear raised voices as the other three were brought in and, as I was later to learn, placed in three separate cells next to mine. Thereafter the day was broken only by the sudden opening of the cell door to reveal the warder who tossed me a couple of blankets and a small pillow. He returned after an hour or so bearing a tin tray which he thrust at me "Mittagessen."

My lunch consisted of a bowl of cabbage soup, a hunk of black bread and a mug of what I supposed was coffee. Hunger alone made the food edible. The rest of the day passed slowly. As the sky outside darkened an electric light in the ceiling was switched on until daylight once again brightened the window. I saw my warder only once more that day when he appeared with what he announced as "Abendessen."

Before turning in the inevitable bowl of soup I managed by sign language to tell him I wish to go to the lavatory and in so doing increased my limited German by yet another word, "abort', which in it's guttural, descriptive, brevity seemed to sum up all that I detested in my captors. He took me to an ablution area near to my cell and there I performed under his watchful eye. When I indicated I would like to wash he ordered me back to my cell where once I had undressed I clambered onto the wooden bed and drew the blankets over me. A bit different, I thought, from the comfort and warmth of the feather bed in which I spent the previous night in the farmhouse, but at least the firmness of my wooden pallet granted me some relief from the nagging pain in my back. Eventually I slept, a sleep punctuated throughout the night by the metallic rattle of the Judas hole in the cell door as a guard checked on my well being.

Breakfast, or Fruhstuck proved to be little more than a hunk of bread covered in a thin, sickly sweet jam-like substance and a mug of eratz coffee, said to be made from acorns. Later I was allowed to the lavatory but was again denied the chance to wash myself. On returning to my cell there was nothing to do other than to perch on the wooden bed and turn over in my mind the events of the immediate past forty eight hours. If only I had done this, if only I had done that. The regrets came thick and fast only adding to my despair at being behind bars when I could have been making my way south to freedom.

I was not left to my solitary thoughts for long. To my surprise not one of my captors had so far attempted to interrogate me. I had not even been asked for my name let alone for information which, in my case, I was forbidden to provide them with. Theoretically at least there were sound reasons for leaving newly captured prisoners to their own devices for a while, not the least of which was the psychological undermining of their strength of purpose by the dejection and recriminations that were bound to beset them following capture and incarceration. Fortunately RAF aircrew were constantly reminded of the need to keep their mouths shut when faced by interrogating officers and NCO's. The provision of number, rank and name was the extent to which we were permitted to identify ourselves to our captors.

Thus it was that when later the door of my cell opened to reveal an elderly, balding oberlieutenant of the infantry I felt I was ready to deal with any questions he was likely to put to me. He introduced himself with a click of his heels accompanied by a quick nod of his head and as there was nowhere else to sit perched himself alongside me on the wooden bunk. He spoke faultless English with a southern counties accent first asking me for my number, rank and name to which I replied. "Number 171703, Pilot Officer Charles William Hobgen." I see from your brevet you are a navigator. What squadron did you fly with ?" "I'm sorry " I replied, "I can only tell you my number, rank and name." "Oh come on. Be reasonable. We need the information to enable us notify the Red Cross of your survival." "I can only tell you my number, rank and name." "You were brought here with three other airmen. Are they members of your crew?"

I remained silent but nodded my head. After all I had been arrested when I was with Bob Johnson and the other two had been picked up in the same area as myself it therefore seemed futile to pretend they were strangers to me. On the other hand we had been advised to say as little as possible, silence we were told tended to discourage further questions. Thereafter I continued to keep my mouth shut.

He asked me whether I would like to write a note to my next of kin to let them know I was safe and had been taken prisoner. I could see no harm in doing this and happily scribbled a line or two on the scrap of note paper he handed to me. I still have the original note.

P/O Hobgen
R.A.F

Dear Helena,

I am quite safe and well as are three of crew. Keep chin up.

Lots of love,
Charlie

Mrs J Davey
3, Park Grove
Cardiff
England.

Gepruft 22

As my interrogator seemed inclined to be reasonably disposed towards me. I asked him whether I might see the other three chaps. With a jerk of his head he indicated I should follow him out of my cell into the corridor where he told the waiting guard to unlock the other three cells, one after the other. I had no idea what to expect.

I was devastated when I realised neither John, Bob nor Mathew had received any form of medical treatment despite their severe wounds. They were still wearing their uniforms, leading me to believe they had been entirely left to themselves since they had been brought into prison. But, I had but to look at their faces, creased in agony, to realise the intensity of their pain and suffering and could but admire them for their show of courage in the face of it all. The stench in their cells was overpowering, so much was this so the thought of gangrene came to my medically untutored mind and with it a determination to do something about obtaining treatment for them. It was the only way they would survive. I gave them what comfort I could and said I would attempt to see the commandant of the prison. My own discomforts, irritations paled into insignificance when compared with what was happening to them.

Once back in the corridor my fears for the future well-being of my friends got the better of any sense of caution I had entertained in my dealings with the German officer. I told him it was scandalous that wounded airmen should be denied medical treatment and that the disgusting condition in which my three comrades were existing was a disgrace to the German army. When I followed this up with a demand for an interview with his superior officer he said nothing other than to tell the guard to return me to my cell.

Within the hour I was escorted into the office of the person in charge of the prison and there I found my interrogating officer waiting for me. Expecting to find myself taken in front of a senior military officer I was disconcerted to find myself face to face with a man dressed in nondescript civilian clothes who revealed no signs of military bearing. I didn't know whether he was an army officer or a senior civilian member of the prison service. Up until then my anger over the plight of my three crew members had served to give me courage enough to speak my mind, now I found myself facing a man who's appearance and demeanour was enough in itself to quell my indignation.

Squat, broad-shouldered, bald and pale of face with protruding blue eyes, he looked for all the world like a double of Erin von Stroheim an Austrian-born US film director and actor. As an actor I remembered him for his portrayal of sadistic Prussian officers. He glared at me in silence. At last he spoke *"Was vollen sie, terror flieger?"* His tone of voice was unmistakingly hostile. *"Er spricht kein Deutsch."* explained the *oberleutenant*.

I pulled myself together and told him I was angry because of the lack of medical treatment being given to my fellow prisoners. I used the word disgraceful several times adding, with all the conviction I could muster despite my ignorance in the matter, that the Geneva Convention stipulated wounded prisoners of war should receive the best medical care at the hands of their captors. How I managed to keep the nervousness I was experiencing from revealing itself in my voice I do not know, but I did.

The oberlieutenant translated my words while the other man, who continued to glare at me, sat silently twisting a pencil between his fingers. When he spoke his anger was obvious as he shouted. *"Habien sie keine angst, terrorflieger, wegen der genfer Konvention. Ich werde mich entscheiden,was mit denwunden ihres kamerades machen werden soll."* The oberleutenant obliged with a word for word translation. "Don't worry you about the Geneva Convention, *terrorflieger*. I'll decide what to do about your comrades wounds." He waved a hand in dismissal and my guard returned me to my cell.

Several days passed during which time I was still not allowed to wash or shave. Such was my increasingly filthy conditions I began to loathe myself and readily came to understand how easily men can loose their self respect when denied the means of, for what of a better phrase, "to keep up appearances." There has always been good sense in the insistence within the British military forces that no matter the conditions under which men are called on to function, washing, shaving, maintaining uniforms in as clean and smart a condition as circumstances allow are of the essences if morale, pride in service and fighting ability are to be maintained. There is, therefore, perhaps more than simple bloody-mindedness in the denial to me of the means of keeping myself clean, although so far there had been no further attempts to question me in depth.

I was not allowed to see the other three again, but judged by the comings and goings in the passage way outside my cell I thought it sounded as though they were receiving some form of medical attention or, at the very least, some form of rough nursing, Meantime the days passed slowly and I was reduced to counting the rivet heads in the cell door and the number of bricks making up the four walls.

I suppose I must have spent six or seven days in Soissons gaol longing for something to happen. Its said that all good things come to those who wait, and presumably this must also apply to a proportion of things not so attractive. Be that as it may, the day arrived when an hour or so after the midday meal the door of my cell was flung open to reveal two hefty looking feldwebel dressed in the blue-grey uniform of the *Luftwaffe*. They were accompanied by a warder who would barely wait until he was in the cell before shouting, *"Wir ubergeben sie der Luftwaffe."* It didn't take much for me to understand from this announcement and the presence of the two jolly giants that I was about to be handed over to the *Luftwaffe*. Had I been in any doubt of what was intended it would have quickly disappeared as soon as one of the NCO's said in almost faultless English, "That's right, pilot officer, the *Luftwaffe* will look after you now."

There was nothing I could do other than to ask whether I might first say goodbye to John, Bob and Mathew. After a few words to the warder from one of the NCO's I was allowed into each of their cells. They were still in great pain but at least some attempt had been made to clean them up. John told me there was talk of them being taken to a hospital that day. I have never been much good at saying farewell to either family or friends - my upper lip is not particularly stiff - and in this case my feeling of dejection was heightened by the circumstance I felt from revealing itself in my voice but managed to do so by mouthing a banality such as, "See you back in England after the war. Don't let the bastards get you down." I don't know whether the two Luftwaffe NCO's had been specially selected as my escorts so as to present to the outside world an invidious comparison between them, the jolly, rubicund giants in their well pressed uniforms, and the pale-faced, unshaven, unwashed, sunken-checked *terrorflieger* in his bedraggled clothes that was me, of whom, let it be said, the two examples of German manhood could have made mincemeat had they been so inclined. At all events, it certainly looked as though that was what had been staged.

My morale went up a notch or two however when I saw the vehicle in which I was taken away. It was a 15 cwt. type truck with what appeared to be a gas-bag on its roof. At least, I thought, the RAF has not yet been reduced to fuelling its transport with other than petrol - courtesy of our Merchant Marine. "Up you go," said the English speaking feldwebel, who thereupon climbed into the back of the vehicle with me where we sat on benches facing each other. For the first time I noticed he appeared to be unarmed, not that this would have counted for much had I attempted to escape.

For one reason or another on the night we set out from Elvington to attack Laon I had departed from my usual habit of keeping my Longine navigator's watch on my wrist and had, instead, suspended it from the anglepoise lamp over my plotting table, the more easily to read it. It had gone down with the aircraft. It seemed but a short time after leaving Soissons that we stopped in a wayside village and a sergeant flight engineer was helped into the back of the vehicle where he sat next to me. I had never set eyes on him before. We said not a word to each other.

Recollection of warnings given to us during intelligence briefings of the possibility of Germans dressed as fellow RAF airmen being introduced into our midst, once we were captured, with the intention of first obtaining our confidence and thereafter extracting from us information of value to German intelligence, came speedily to mind. They probably came to the mind of my new companion as well as we sat there, side by side, in suspicious silence.

Our destination turned out to be a Luftwaffe airfield which at the time I was unable to identify but which I now estimate to have been one or other of the night-fighter airfields I had marked on my plotting chart whilst completing my flight plan. Based entirely on the comparatively short distance from Soissons it must have been either Tergnier, Athies, Laon, or Juvincourt : my choice being the later. Like military airfields it was in the middle of nowhere and gave the impression of being a temporary establishment, entirely functional, thoroughly uncomfortable and cheerless. Having negotiated a manned barrier we stopped almost immediately outside a wooden building, possibly a picket post or guardroom where our two guards handed us over to the senior NCO in charge of a party of some ten men who, formed a station guard.

At first we were the object of some curiosity and although none of the German airmen could speak English we were able to communicate with them and they with us by means of sign language. On the whole they were reasonably friendly and it wasn't long before the NCO in charge produced a bucket of hot water, a razor and some soap and bid us wash and shave. Together they may not have represented the last word in bathroom facilities, but half and hour later I felt like a new man.

Sleeping arrangements took the form of two mattresses, each with a couple of blankets, placed on the floor of the main room in the guard post which also housed the NCO's desk. Our meals, which appeared to be identical to those provided for the German airmen, were brought to us and we ate the food where we sat on our mattresses. We were also given some cigarettes. They burnt as would a piece of fuse cord. Within twenty four hours of using them I developed a churchyard cough of large proportions. No attempt was made to question us.

During the next forty eight hours the flight engineer and I treated each other with well mannered suspicion. We spoke of this and that, avoiding all mention of service matters. Gradually, it became obvious to us both that we were the genuine article and were not German stool-pidgeons. We still avoided any talk of flying and locations in England and amused ourselves with endless games of noughts and crosses and battleships, eventually we were loaned a pack of cards.

One morning we heard the screech of brakes outside the guard post followed by car doors being slammed shut and bursts of laughter. The door was thrust open to reveal three or four young Luftwaffe officers each wearing a flying badge. On seeing them enter our senior NCO sprang to attention at the same time shouting out his name and rank as though he was about to make some kind of report. One of the visitors waved him aside whilst together with his companions strolled across the floor to speak to us. His greeting, made in heavily accented English, was affable enough as was the conversation that followed. No attempt was made to obtain any information of intelligence value from us and after a while, with wishes of good luck, they took their leave after presenting us with several packets of Turkish cigarettes.

Had they been dressed in different uniforms their light-hearted display of general bonhomie could have encouraged the belief that they were in fact RAF officers. As it was, what with their breeches and top boots, the exaggerated uplift of the peak and crown of their caps, the close fitting cut of their badge bedecked tunics with their yellow lapel flashes, there was much about them that was gaudy and foppish, suggesting they might be better suited as characters in Hope's 'The Prisoner of Zenda' rather than as Luftwaffe pilots flying one of Willy Messerschmitt's fighter aircraft.

I was not so foolish as to under estimate their ability to give a good account of themselves in the air as tended to be confirmed by the neck decoration one of them was wearing which I was later to learn was the Knight's Cross to the Iron Cross (the much coveted Ritter- kreuz). So coveted was it that anyone who was over ambitious in their efforts to be awarded one was said to have "ein halsschmerzen" - a sore throat !

We were beginning to wonder whether it was planned we should spend the rest of the war in the picket post when one morning the two jolly giants unexpectedly turned up, this time wearing holstered side-arms and carrying haversacks. The one who spoke English broke the news of our departure to us. "You're off on a train journey. Were taking you to Frankfurt but before we leave I must give you a very serious warning. Should you be foolish enough to attempt an escape our orders are to shoot you," he said, patting his holster. "What is more, if you were to be so silly as to attempt to escape when we reach Germany the Luftwaffe cannot answer for the consequences were you to fall into the hands of some of the people whose homes and families you have destroyed. You'll be better off sticking with us."

The train journey that followed was long and tedious. It began in a French train in which a compartment had been reserved for us. The wooden seats were excruciatingly bottom numbing and the unscheduled stoppages were frequent and lengthy. At one such our guards told us it was due to damage caused by our bombers. At night we slept fitfully as the train made its uncertain way across France and Belgium towards Germany.

Some twenty four hours later the train drew into a mainline station to shouts of "Kohn - Kohm." It was here we were to change trains for the final part of our journey to Frankfurt. Our guards, rather surprisingly I thought, took us into the station cafeteria where our appearance was met by a host of staring eyes and some open hostility. One man in particular was not much taken by our appearance in the cafe and advanced on us waving fists and shouting I know not what, save that it was obviously to our detriment. Our guards shooed him away and off he went muttering under his breath.

Equally discomforting was the attitude towards us of the waitress who brought our bowls of cabbage soup to the table. She was young, tall, heavily built and had blonde hair and blue eyes. Almost a text book Brunhild or at least an enthusiastic product of the Hitler *Madchen* organisation. She slammed the bowls down onto the table spilling some of the contents in so doing but not before she had addressed herself to our *Luftwaffe* guards using an unmistakably hostile tone of voice whilst at the time pointing her fingers at myself and the sergeant engineer. He was unwise to laugh at her antics which brought forth a torrent of words undoubtedly offensive and probably calling into question our parentage. I was glad when it was time to board the train.

As if the whole business of the past weeks was not depressing enough we arrived in Frankfurt under overcast skies and intermittent rain. Here there was yet another change of train, a local connection to Oberursel, a small town some ten miles NW of Frankfurt. From there it was but a short ride in a tram to Dulag Luft (*Durchgangslager der Luftwaffe* - transit camp of the air force).

During the course of the next two weeks I was to learn just how helpful and comprehensive had been a talk given to us by Flight Lieutenant Oliver Philpot, MC., DFC one morning after our daily crew conference back at Elvington and only a few days before he was shot down. Philpot was one of the three officers who had made good their legendary escape from Stalag Luft 3 by means of a wooden vaulting horse and a tunnel they managed to dig using the horse as a subterfuge for their underground activities. The other two were Captain Michael Codner, MC and Flight Lieutenant Eric Williams, MC. Such had been the breadth of detail given us by Philpot that it was almost as though I had been to Dulag Luft before and knew the place well. There were to be numerous occasions when I was able to say to myself, "That's exactly how Philpot said it would be." In all his words proved to be a great morale booster.

On arrival we joined a party of some thirty other men who were waiting to be processed through the arrival procedure. There was about them a general air of what I took to be despondency as though nature had dealt them a cruelly unfair blow. This sort of thing was supposed to happen to the other chap not to me. The unthinkable had happened, I must grin and bear it.

You were first shown into a reception area there to be subjected to some typically ponderous German humour at the hands of a self opinionated *oberfeldwebel*. It was the kind of laboured facetiousness one would expect to hear from any drill corporal the world over. In the circumstances it produced not a vestige of a laugh not even a sycophantic one.

"Good morning gentlemen, welcome to hotel Dulag Luft where every comfort will be yours. But first there is the small matter of ensuring you have not hidden anything you wish to conceal from us. So, please gentlemen, may we have all your compasses, maps and escape kits. For you the war is over, you are now guests of the Third Reich. You are *Kriegsgefangenen* or, as your friends will tell you are the Kriegies and we are the Goons."

In 'Kriegie Speak' a Goon was any German officer or soldier, but especially one who was a member of a prison camp staff. What is more the guard towers on the barbed-wire perimeters of POW camps became "Goon-boxes' and any act of provoking the Germans was labelled 'goon-baiting.' It was said the Germans never really understood the implications of the word, in reality it was well known to any reader of the Daily Mirror which carried a comic strip depicting 'goons' as low-browed, primitive apemen of great strength and stupidity.

I suppose the use of the word enabled us to give vent to our feelings of frustration and irritation over the enemy's lack-lustre manner and what we contended was his hide-bound adherence to the letter of any order given to him. Its use also appealed to our brand of schoolboy humour and sense of the ridiculous.

But to return to our arrival at Dulag Luft. The welcoming speech was followed by a through personal search. We were required to remove every stitch of clothing which was then methodically examined in a one to one confrontation with a guard. Not content with this, and before we were allowed to dress again, we were subjected to an even more intimate examination during the course of which every bodily orifice and crevice was subjected to the none too gentle probing of the guards fingers. It was an embarrassing, anger provoking experience.

Having been photographed and fingerprinted I was escorted to the 'cooler,' a building containing upwards of two hundred solitary confinement cells. The small cell was ten and one-half feet long, five and one-half feet wide and had an eight-foot ceiling. The airman sat alone with his thoughts. There was nothing to divert his attention. The furnishings consisted usually of a bed, and one stool, and two blankets. No reading or writing materials were available, and the one light was turned on and off at random from somewhere outside the cell. Outside switches also controlled the temperature of the heaters, a source of much suffering for the prisoners. Frequently the temperature in the room became almost unbearable, rising high enough at times to singe a towel laid on the radiator and making the bed and all metal surfaces hot enough to scorch bare flesh. The thick cement walls retained the heat like a sauna, and the one window in the room was painted over.

Once the guard had left me to my own devices there was nothing to do but to await the next move from my captors. It was not long in coming. The cell door opened and in came a dishevelled looking oberfeldwebel carrying a clipboard. His uniform hung on him like an ill fitting and grubby sack and his jack boots were badly in need of the services of brush and polish. He sat down on the bed alongside me with a sigh of resignation and thrust under my nose a printed form carrying a red cross at the top together with a pencil. This was something we had been warned would almost certainly appear early on in our stay at Dulag Luft as an opening gambit to subsequent interrogation. "Please fill this in." I obliged him by answering the first three questions, but stopped at the next question which required me to reveal the number of my squadron. "I'm sorry but can only give you my number, rank and name. " There was another deep sigh of a kind that inferred he had heard it all before.

"I had hoped you were not going to be difficult about this. We must have more information about you if we are going to be certain you are who you say you are. How do we know you are a *bona fide* flier and not a spy? You realise the Gestapo will have an interest in establishing your *bona fides* and I am sure you do not want to become involved with them.

'I'm sorry, I've told you all I am allowed to tell you." With an even more profound sigh he gathered up my form and without another word unlocked the cell door and disappeared. I did not see him again. I was not impressed by the ease with which he gave up any attempt to extract information from me.

I heard nothing more for forty eight hours during which time I was not allowed to wash or shave. When I wanted to use the lavatory it was a case of pulling the lever by the door and then waiting for the guard to appear. Invariably he took his time in doing so and I soon learnt to give plenty of warning of my wish to relieve myself. There were three meals a day. Those provided in the morning and evening consisted of one slice of heavy black bread with a thin coating of margarine and ersatz jam and a mug of so-called tea which I now know to have been made of a mixture of hay, carrots and grain. For the midday meal there was a sizeable bowl of potato soup. At least it was filling and reasonably palatable.

On the third day of my confinement two young Luftwaffe officers visited me. They were immaculately dressed in uniform and were of a similar age to myself. Their manner was relaxed and friendly but in my dishevelled unwashed condition I felt at a distinct disadvantage to them, which of course was all part of setting the scene for my interrogation. They both spoke excellent English and told me they were resting having completed a considerable number of operational flying hours. They proffered American cigarettes which I willingly accepted at the same time making a mental note not to allow their largesse to be the means of loosening my tongue. Their undisguised ploy, in an attempt to gain my confidence, was my insistence that they were in the same line of business as myself and it would be of help to them were I to be a little more forthcoming about my background.

"You know what it is old boy, we're not really intelligence types (they actually used this piece of RAF jargon) but they do tend to expect us to get you to co-operate. Come on, just tell us your squadron number and the name of your squadron commander and we'll leave you alone." They were so pleasant and their manner so cajoling I felt sorry about telling them I could provide them my number rank and name. They smiled and left.

Nothing further happened for a day or two during which time I gradually learnt at first hand the morale sapping effect of solitary confinement wherein I had nothing to do other than to stare at the wall opposite me as I sat on the bed. I found myself counting the bricks as I sat there. I counted the courses and the number of bricks in each course. I did the same for the other three walls and then attempted by mental calculation to arrive at the total number. Irritatingly enough I arrived at a different answer every time.

It was also a time when, again and again, I went over what had happened to me since the night we had been shot down. Repeatedly the same self-doubts came to mind to tax the credibility I was looking for in my actions. Had I done everything I should have done? Had I been right to go back to Bob Johnson or should I have hardened my heart and tried to evade capture? Could I at any time have made good an escape from my captors? What had happened to John, Bob and Mathew since I left them at Soissons gaol ? What had happened to the other members of my crew - Ken Bond, Victor Clare and Bill Jacks?

I suppose two or three days must have elapsed when one night after I had rolled myself into my blankets and fallen asleep the door of my cell crashed open to reveal a guard standing in the corridor. "Raus. Raus," he shouted, at the same time advancing pointing his pistol menacingly. I wasted no time in getting off the bed and stepping out of the cell into the brilliantly lit corridor. *"Schnell, schnell,"* he shouted. *"Aber noch schneller."* I was already travelling at a fast trot and in attempting to quicken my pace tripped and fell on the ground. The toe of his jack boot only served to bring on the agonising soreness in my back which, until then, had been quiescent. With a meaningful jerk of his pistol, he urged me on until we reached an area given over to offices. Responding to his knock on one office door a voice from within bid us enter. The change from the stark decor of my cell to the tasteful aspect of the room in which I found myself was little short of staggering. Gone was the glaring whiteness of the lighting in the corridor to be replaced by the diffused light from a standard lamp in one corner and a green shaded lamp placed on the leather-topped desk. There were rugs on the floor and chintzy curtains at the windows complimenting the colouring of the walls on which hung pictures. The overall effect was one of warmth and simple comfort.

My escort's final push had propelled me to within a foot of the desk behind which sat a Luftwaffe officer whose red collar patches with their single pair of miniature wings surrounded by embroidered silver oak leaves signified his membership of the Anti-Aircraft Artillery or *Flakcorps* I was near enough to him to be able to note the meticulous cut and fit of his uniform, the crispness of his personal linen and the not unpleasant smell of *Eau de Cologne* that surrounded him. A large, expensive looking cigar burned lazily as it rested in an ash tray in front of him. In all, I found his well groomed appearance intimidating when compared with what I knew to be my own dirty and dishevelled persona. In the field of interrogation it was a well arranged piece of stage management.

Having, with a flick of his hand, dismissed the guard he turned his attention to me. "My dear chap, do take a seat." His English and his accent were both perfect and, I was taken aback. So much so my surprise must have shown itself on my face, for with another smile he further disarmed me by saying, "Yes, I've spent quite a lot of time in your country. It's almost a second home for me. Now," he continued, "What's all this about you refusing to fill out our Red Cross form ?" He said this as though my reaction to being asked to complete the form had been the exception rather than the rule amongst my fellow prisoners. I managed, however, to keep calm and once again trotted out the words that now came readily to my lips. "I'm sorry I can only tell you my number rank and name." "O dear what a nuisance. We must be sure you are who you say you are and if you wont help us by giving us the information we need then there are others whose methods of extracting information are, shall we say, a little more forceful than those we chose to use."

I said nothing and the silence that persisted began to stimulate a sense of embarrassment within me. It was a question of who was going to speak first. "Look at this way," said my interrogator, "We already know a great deal about you and anything you say will merely confirm or contradict the information we have so what can be the harm in you speaking out ?" Again there was a pause that left me wondering just what information he had. "Let's see what we've got. Your aircraft was shot down shortly after you had bombed the marshalling yards at Laon. The aircraft was a Halifax V, Serial No. LE7 10, Squadron Code KN-S-'Sugar.' Your pilot was Squadron Leader Kenneth Bond and I have to tell you he is now dead."

This was the first word I had received of Bond's fate and the news of his death given to me so dispassionately affected me greatly. I could see no reason for him to have misinformed me, he had nothing to gain from doing so. It was a bitter blow. Many years later later I was sent a copy of a report forwarded to the Yorkshire Air Museum by the Gendarmerie Nationale based in Clichy, Paris.

    GENDARMERIE NATIONALE   Clichy 14th.March, 1992.
    Brigade Territoriale
    Clichy la Garenne

I have received your letter of 13th.February 1992. Here is the information I have been able to obtain. "BOND, Squadron Leader Kenneth Franck (sic) Pennington Bond is indeed buried in the British Military Cemetery at Clichy under the following reference

> "Bond, Squadron Leader (pilot) Kenneth Franck (sic) Pennington. 40666 RAF., 77 Squadron., 22nd.April, 1944. Plot 16, Row 10, Grave 19."

> The unit to which this officer belonged was a unit responsible for gathering intelligence for the RAF. The aircraft was shot down between Laon and Senlis, exact spot not known. After the pilot baled out he was captured by the Germans. He was injured. He was taken to Beaujon Hospital in Clichy (92) where he died. The only eye-witnesses of this incident have died in the meanwhile. There are no photographs of the crash or the pilot. The

circumstances surrounding the capture of the pilot are somewhat unclear.

Gendarme Sauvaget.

When I had time to regain my composure my interrogation continued. "Of course we already know the names of your Bomb Aimer, your Wireless Operator and one of your Gunners because they were captured with you. What are the names of your Flight Engineer and your other Gunner? I continued to remain silent hoping against hope that Victor Clare and Bill Jacks had been able to evade capture.

What followed was indeed an unnerving revelation. For the next five minutes the major revealed the extent of his knowledge of 77 Squadron, its personalities, decorations awarded to individuals, the details of Ken Bond's service and personal background (including the information that he had served in India, that his first marriage had ended in divorce and that he had recently re-married in York). With a particular look of triumph he mentioned the planned move of the squadron from Elvington to Full Sutton. In all it represented a masterly achievement in the field of intelligence gathering and one that left me deflated. How the devil did they know all that. "You see Pilot Officer Hobgen, we know a little about what goes on back in England. Now please confirm you served with 77 Squadron and let me have the names of your flight engineer and your other gunner." I simply gaped at him and said not a word.

The interview was quickly ended and I was returned to my cell where I sat alone with my thoughts for what remained of the night. It had been an experience for which I was completely unprepared and my initial reaction was one of anger that during all our intelligence briefings no one had ever warned us we could expect to be bombarded with an arsenal of facts concerning our squadrons and its personalities. The major had even told me of the departure of, as he put it, 'Lofty Lowe' and his replacement as squadron commander by Wing Commander Roncoroni.

How had they gained this detailed information? I knew we used to laugh about the amount of information one could pick up during a night out in York. Most of it we classed as 'duff gen.' but there were times, when it seemed almost as though the target for the night was known to others before we ourselves learnt of it. Naively I thought in terms of the country being rotten with spies when the answer, as I was to discover later, lay with the German obsession with gathering snippets of information from a mass of sources and thereafter carefully collating and assessing it against the day when it might prove to be of use to them.

Arthur A.Durand of the USAF, in his book *Stalag Luft 111*, gives a graphic description of this acquisition by the Germans of information of intelligence value and how they put it to good use in the interrogation of prisoners.

> "An estimated 80 percent of the information the Germans obtained was produced by the Document Section, the most efficient and productive division in the interrogation centre. The staff secured newspapers, books, and periodicals, the pockets of captured personnel, and material from aeroplanes that came down in their territory. No item was too small or insignificant, and every scrap was scrutinised with extreme care.
>
> The results were startling. A one-way railroad ticket between two English villages gave the Germans an important clue about the impending transfer of airmen attached to a British Wellington bomber group. The Luftwaffe subsequently learnt that the RAF was shifting a number of these planes to anti-submarine patrol duty.
>
> The Document Section's experts became so resourceful and methodical they could identify a flier's unit by the manner in which his ration card was marked. At one base for instance, the clerk always used a heavy black pencil, and since the PX (the Post Exchange, an American military canteen facility) counter was constructed of rough board, all the cards from that group showed its distinctive grain in the pencil marks.
>
> All crews were told not to transport papers and other extraneous documents, but the men persisted in doing so for a variety of reasons. The most serious violations involved dairies. One dairy revealed the number of crews undergoing training in the US, as well as how many heavy bombers were available for that purpose. It also divulged highly secret data about the heavy bombardment programme.
>
> The photographs furnished to airmen to facilitate their escape through the underground sometimes served to identify their unit also. Photographs from the 91st. Bomb Group, for instance, had a particular brown colour. Everyone from the 95th. Bomb Group wore the same checkered coat when he had his picture taken.

Numerous other sections plied their trade in the interrogation centre, and they all added pieces to the puzzle. The Yellow File Section collected biographical information on Allied personnel, using newspapers, awards lists, magazines, radio broadcasts and censored mail, and carefully catalogued it for quick reference.

The Squadron History Section gathered data on every Allied squadron and its historical development - facts on past and present location, postal addresses, names of its leading personalities, and the special equipment it was known to operate.

The Attack Section prepared a map each day displaying the Allied air operations of the preceeding twenty-four hours. Based chiefly on German radar tracking and Observer Corps reports. The map showed targets, courses, results of Missions, numbers of aircraft, numbers of aircraft involved, and even cancelled actions.

Information obtained from interrogations in progress was incorporated into the display so that each interrogator has access to the work of the others.

Two Situation Rooms also contributed to the interrogator's arsenal of knowledge. One attended to British activities and the other to American actions. Maps showed the location of recent raids, the progress of raids still taking place, and the front lines of the opposing armies. They even gave the fullest possible details of ferry flights and transport movements.

A staff of translators in the Press Evaluation Section went through copies of all Allied newspapers and magazines, looking for pertinent movements.

The photograph Section developed and printed all film found on a prisoner, as well as any that was recovered from the gun cameras of downed aircraft.

The Technical Section maintained a library and a museum of Allied equipment. Files were kept for every known crash site in Germany or German-occupied territory. Each crash received a number, and the file contained the type of aircraft, location of crash, and such details about the personnel on board and the home unit as emerged in later interrogations.

And finally, a group of linguists listened to the airman's wireless communications around the clock seven days a week - plane to plane, plane to base, and base to plane - recording and transcribing conversations and the radio frequencies along with the place of origin.

Armed with such information, the interrogators confronted each prisoner. The object was not to learn any great secrets about grand strategy or similar matters. It was commonly understood that the average airman was not privy to such information. Rather, the interrogator sought tactical and operational information that would help the anti-aircraft gunners place their weapons, assist in the evaluation of the latest technical equipment used on the missions, determine important targets, and gather small talk that would assist them in breaking down the resistance of future prisoners. "

In the face of such thoroughness, organisation and intelligence-gathering ability it's a wonder that more men did not respond to their interrogators in the way the Germans hoped they would. Hans Joachim Scharff, one of the interrogators at Dulag Luft, gave it as his view that the prisoners who did talk did so because the Germans' methods were, "almost irresistible." I for one would not differ with him on that assertion.

The next day I was taken from the 'cooler' to the transit camp there to await transport to a permanent POW camp somewhere in Germany. Before leaving the 'cooler' I was told I could be referred to as *Kriegsgefangener* Number 4460. I was given a POW identity 'disk' that took the form of a small soft metal rectangular plate made up of two separate pieces joined together by a strip of metal. It was worn round my neck at all times.

Although our lives in the transit camp remained restricted there was a more relaxed atmosphere in this part of Dulag Luft. What is more, the food provided by the Germans was augmented by the contents of red Cross food parcels and this alone made the condition that much more bearable. It was refreshing to be able, once more, to talk to people who were in the same predicament as oneself and to do so without wondering whether they were in fact the genuine article. But above all else it was wonderful to be able to stand under a hot shower, there to soak away the grime of past weeks and in doing so regain the pride in self that had been mine before I had fallen into German hands.

Three or four days later I became one of a group, or a 'purge' as it was known to we prisoners, of some fifty RAF 'kriegies' who were moved by train from Frankfurt to Sagan in Upper Silesia there to become inmates of Stalag Luft 3.

The journey of some three hundred miles was made under guard and lasted for a little longer than two days. Ours was by no means a speedy process. There were repeated delays, some because of damage to the lines caused by Allied air raids and others when we were shunted into railway sidings to allow trains with a higher priority to proceed. These were in the main, troop trains heading eastwards to the Russian front where the human carnage had reached terrifying proportions. We could see the pale, expressionless faces of the young German soldiers pressed to the windows of their carriages as though they sought a final glimpse of their homeland before meeting what many of them, in the depths of their despair, held to be the fate awaiting them on the frozen wastes of the Russian steppes.

The food given us on the train was meagre in amount and very basic, consisting largely of black bread and some of the most nauseating cheese I have ever been offered. Drinking water was almost non-existent, now and again tin mugs of erzatz coffee were collected from railway stations where a military canteen was in situ. As there were no on-board lavatory facilities it was a question of holding on until the train stopped, which fortunately was often enough, when we were allowed to clamber down to relieve ourselves by the side of the track in full view of the curious local inhabitants.

Eventually we arrived in Sagan where a posse of armed guards from the camp awaited us on the platform. From them came the usual Germanic shouting and waving of weapons to be met with studied and resentful silence from us.

The camp was within easy walking distance and as we turned a bend in the road we were confronted with the mass of barbed wire fences, "Goon Boxes,' overhead floodlights and squat, grey, wooden buildings surrounded by dank and forbidding pine forests which, when taken all together, formed a prison for thousands of British, American and other Allied airmen. It was an utterly depressing sight that readily brought to mind Captain Scott's despairing comment as recorded in his journal during the course of his last expedition to the South Pole. "Great God ! This is an awful place."

Group Captain Charles Hobgen died in 2005 from prostate cancer. He was two weeks younger than John Grimer. His *obit* in the Daily Telegraph dated Thursday July 28th. reads as follows :-

> "Hobgen - Charles. Grp Capt RAF (ret'd) passed away peacefully at Bradford-On-Avon Hospital on July 26th after a long illness courageously borne. Dearly loved husband of Joyce. . . Funeral at Semington Crematorium, West Wiltshire at 2p.m. on Thursday 4th. August. . ."

End.

Appendix Eight

Prince of Wales Own Civil Service Rifles

2/15TH BATTN COUNTY OF LONDON REGIMENT

Prince of Wales Own Civil Service Rifles

Longbridge Deverell, Warminster, May 1916

2/15th BATTALION COUNTY OF LONDON REGIMENT
(P.W.O.) Civil Service Rifles.

OFFICERS.

Lieut-Col. C. de PUTRON.
Major A. A. OLIVER.
Captain A. W. GAZE.
Lieut. W. S. H. SMITH.
Lieut. A. A. JOSLIN.
Lieut. F. J. W. LEECH.

Major H. F. M. WARNE.
Capt. C. A. BAILY.
" F. J. TARVER.
" F. R. RADICE.
" A. C. H. BENKE.
" K. W. M. PICKTHORN.
" K. A. WILLS.
Lieut. C. H. RIMINGTON.
" H. F. RUST.
" P. W. THOROGOOD.
" J. H. RANDOLPH.
" B. PEATFIELD.

2nd-Lieut. F. W. LEWIS.
" " C. M. KILNER.
" " A. V. JAMES.
" " F. J. SMITH.
" " E. E. ANDREWS.
" " S. G. BENNETT.
" " H. J. SPENCER.
" " G. E. THOMPSON.
" " F. T. BAILEY.
" " F. E. GEARING.
" " L. H. HART.
" " F. W. WESTMORE.
" " K. A. HIGGS.

142

2/15th BATTALION COUNTY OF LONDON REGIMENT.
(P.W.O.) Civil Service Rifles.

REGIMENTAL STAFF.

Commanding Officer	Lieut.-Colonel C. de PUTRON.
Second-in-Command	Major A. A. OLIVER.
Adjutant	Capt. A. W. GAZE.
Medical Officer	Lieut. F. J. W. LEECH (R.A.M.C.).
Quartermaster	Lieut. A. A. JOSLIN.
Transport Officer	2nd-Lieut. F. T. BAILEY.
Machine Gun Officer	Lieut. W. S. H. SMITH.
Signalling Officer	Lieut. P. W. THOROGOOD.
Scout Officer	Lieut. B. PEATFIELD
Bombing Officer	Lieut. J. H. RANDOLPH.
Sergeant-Major	No. 3259 (S. Gds.) A. H. FREEMANTLE.
Quartermaster-Sergeant	No. 98 A. C. GIBSON.
Armourer Sergeant	W. FORDHAM (A.O.C., attached).
Orderly Room Sergeant	No. 2743 C. J. NEWMAN.
Orderly Room Clerk	No. 2498 P. POSTLE.
Pioneer Sergeant	No. 2122 C. W. FRYER.
Transport Sergeant	No. 2948 F. D. WOODWARD.
Sergeant Master Cook	No. 2351 C. B. HART.
Shoemaker Sergeant	No. 3443 G. F. DENTON.
Sergeant Tailor	No. 2921 A. SILVERSTONE.
Chaplain	Capt. The Revd. J. G. L. ANDERSON (C.E.).

2/15th BATTALION COUNTY OF LONDON REGIMENT.
(P.W.O.) Civil Service Rifles.

WARRANT OFFICERS AND SERGEANTS.

R.S.M. 3259 (S. Gds.) A. H. FREEMANTLE.   R.QM.S. 98 A. C. GIBSON.

A	B	C	D
1415 C.S.M. H. A. SYRAD.	415 C.S.M. H. F. BASSETT.	1458 C.S.M. OLDCORN.	530 C.S.M. H.W. LOVELOCK
1305 C.QM.S. J. C. SALE.	1260 C.QM.S. W. D. SHANAHAN.	257 C.QM.S. RODD.	1573 C.QM.S. F. KING.
2351 Sgt. Master Cook C. B. HART.	1900 Sgt. W. BAILEY.	2638 Sgt. BOUTCHER.	3440 Sgt. B. C. DYER.
1447 Sgt. F. LORD.	1461 ,, J. E. BOWSTEAD.	59 ,, CARR.	2621 ,, J. E. CHALKE.
890 ,, H. L. PEARCE.	868 ,, H. COOK.	2540 ,, FROST.	3283 ,, J. STEPHENSON.
2085 ,, R. R. RICH.	1578 ,, D. A. MURRAY.	2122 ,, FRYER.	1257 ,, H. BARRETT.
961 ,, H. D. SETTLE.	1465 ,, J. S. PEARCE.	2718 ,, GROSVENOR.	1993 ,, J. C. McNEILL.
1422 ,, J. WIGNEY.	2115 ,, A. E. M. PRATT.	1958 ,, GULLY.	1428 ,, J. T. HARRIS.
1453 ,, H. G. ROWLES.	2080 ,, J. H. PREVOST.	3155 ,, MOUNT.	4441 ,, J. VINCENT.
1698 L.-Sgt. W. S. PITKIN.	2921 ,, A. S. SILVERSTONE.	3056 ,, NEALL.	2145 ,, F. H. WAGSTAFF.
1568 ,, C. J. QUINTON.	1880 ,, S. STAINES.	2745 ,, NEWMAN.	2849 ,, C. G. O. CROSS.
3253 ,, F. TICKLE.	2948 ,, F. D. WOODWARD.	5219 L.-Sgt. EDWARDS.	3443 ,, DENTON.
	2961 L.-Sgt. A. J. CRAUFORD.	3048 ,, ETHERIDGE.	
	2963 ,, W. B. CHARLTON.	313 ,, TUBB.	
	3133 ,, D. LEVY.		

2/15th BATTALION COUNTY OF LONDON REGIMENT.

(P.W.O.) Civil Service Rifles.

SIGNALLING SECTION.

LIEUT. P. W. THOROGOOD.

868	Sgt. H. Cook.		3169	Pte. W. Wilson.		2929	Pte. C. F. Stafford.
874	Cpl. E. A. C. Ward.		3162	,, S. V. Parker.		1383	,, S. W. Green.
2920	L/Cpl. E. W. Short.		3074	,, L. G. Gray.		2181	,, C. H. Jones.
1482	L/Cpl. J. Galloway.		2817	,, A. H. Allen.		3306	,, R. A. Williams.
2429	L/Cpl. R. H. Elkington.		3179	,, J. R. Dickinson.		2940	,, P. H. Vernon.
3077	L/Cpl. C. F. Hammer.		3211	,, B. L. Waters.		2229	,, P. W. Martin
2795	L/Cpl. H. Moore.		2637	,, G. W. Bazley.		3166	,, M. A. Scott.
2895	Pte. A. F. May.		3298	,, W. Flood.		3342	,, J. R. Bayley.
2448	,, L. P. Hall.		2299	,, P. R. Dyer.			

End.